Postal culture in Europe, 1500-1800

OXFORD UNIVERSITY STUDIES IN THE ENLIGHTENMENT – formerly *Studies on Voltaire and the Eighteenth Century* (*SVEC*), is dedicated to eighteenth-century research.

The Voltaire Foundation is a department of the University of Oxford. It furthers the University's objective of excellence in research, scholarship and education by publishing worldwide.

Postal culture in Europe, 1500-1800

JAY CAPLAN

VOLTAIRE FOUNDATION
OXFORD

www.voltaire.ox.ac.uk

ISBN 978 0 7294 1175 2
Oxford University Studies in the Enlightenment 2016:04
ISSN 0435-2866

Voltaire Foundation
99 Banbury Road
Oxford OX2 6JX, UK
www.voltaire.ox.ac.uk

A catalogue record for this book is available from the British Library

The correct style for citing this book is
J. Caplan, *Postal culture in Europe, 1500-1800*, Oxford University Studies in the Enlightenment (Oxford, Voltaire Foundation, 2016)

Cover illustration: *Bureau de poste* 1760 / A French post office in 1760. Photo © L'Adresse Musée de La Poste, Paris / La Poste.

FSC® (the Forest Stewardship Council) is an independent organization established to promote responsible management of the world's forests.

This book is printed on acid-free paper

Printed in the UK by TJ International Ltd, Padstow, Cornwall

Oxford University Studies in the Enlightenment

Postal culture in Europe, 1500-1800

During the early modern period the public postal systems became central pillars of the emerging public sphere. Despite the importance of the post in the transformation of communication, commerce and culture, little has been known about the functioning of the post or how it affected the lives of its users and their societies. In *Postal culture in Europe, 1500-1800*, Jay Caplan provides the first historical and cultural analysis of the practical conditions of letter-exchange at the dawn of the modern age.

Caplan opens his analysis by exploring the economic, political, social and existential interests that were invested in the postal service, and traces the history of the three main European postal systems of the era, the Thurn and Taxis, the French Royal Post and the British Post Office. He then explores how the post worked, from the folding and sealing of letters to their collection, sorting, and transportation. Beyond providing service to the general public, these systems also furnished early modern states with substantial revenue and effective surveillance tools in the form of the Black Cabinets or Black Chambers. Caplan explains how postal services highlighted the tension between state power and the emerging concept of the free individual, with rights to private communication outside the public sphere. Postal systems therefore affected how letter writers and readers conceived and expressed themselves as individuals, which the author demonstrates through an examination of the correspondence of Voltaire and Rousseau, not merely as texts but as communicative acts.

Eighteenth-century literature / eighteenth-century history / cultural and social history

Littérature du dix-huitième siècle / histoire du dix-huitième siècle / histoire culturelle et sociale

Table of contents

List of illustrations and tables ix
List of abbreviations xi
Acknowledgments xiii

Introduction 1
1. A brief history of Western European postal services in the early modern period 23
2. Signed, sealed and delivered 53
3. Surveillance and secrecy: the Black Cabinets 95
4. Voltaire's post: 1760-1770 125
5. Rousseau: *vox clamantis* 141
6. A postal world 167

Bibliography 195
Index 207

List of illustrations and tables

Figure 1: *Facteur petite poste* 1760 / A *petite poste* mailman 1760. Photo © L'Adresse Musée de La Poste, Paris / La Poste. 45

Figure 2: *Bureau de poste* 1760 / A French post office in 1760. Photo © L'Adresse Musée de La Poste, Paris / La Poste. 74

Figure 3: *1ère expérience de petite poste* / The first *petite poste* experiment was a failure. Photo © L'Adresse Musée de La Poste, Paris / La Poste. 76

Figure 4: La petite poste / Sending a *poulet.* Photo © L'Adresse Musée de La Poste, Paris / La Poste. 77

Figure 5: *Carte des Postes de France* 1748 / Post offices in France 1748. Photo © L'Adresse Musée de La Poste, Paris / La Poste. 78

Figure 6: *Turgotine* 1775 / A *turgotine* stagecoach. Photo © L'Adresse Musée de La Poste, Paris / La Poste 80

Figure 7: *Malle aux lettres* / A speedy *malle-poste.* Photo © L'Adresse Musée de La Poste, Paris / La Poste. 88

Figure 8: *Claquoir de facteur* XVIIIe / A clapper announced the arrival of *petite poste* mail carriers. Photo © L'Adresse Musée de La Poste, Paris / La Poste. 172

Table 1: Examples of the rates for letters in France by type / distance (as established by the Royal Decree of 1703). 67

Table 2: Reduction in postal delivery times, mid-seventeenth to late eighteenth centuries. 86

List of abbreviations

CC	*Correspondance complète de Jean-Jacques Rousseau*, ed. R. A. Leigh, 52 vols (Geneva; Madison, WI; Banbury, Oxford, 1965-1998).
D	Voltaire, *Correspondence and related documents*, ed. Th. Besterman, in *Œuvres complètes de Voltaire* 85-135 (Oxford, 1968-1977).
M	Voltaire, *Œuvres complètes*, ed. Louis Moland, 52 vols (Paris, 1877-1885).
OCV	*Œuvres complètes de Voltaire* (Oxford, 1968-).
Petit Robert	*Le Petit Robert de la langue française 2010* (Paris, 2010), ed. Josette Rey-Debove and Alain Rey.
QE	*Questions sur l'Encyclopédie, par des amateurs*, ed. Nicholas Cronk and Christiane Mervaux, in *Œuvres complètes de Voltaire*, vol.42B (Oxford, 2012).

Acknowledgments

The publication of this book has been supported, in part, by the Office of the Dean of Faculty of Amberst College. I also wish to thank the Office of the Dean of Amherst College for its generous support of travel necessary to complete this project through successive grants from the Faculty Research Award Program and Faculty Research Grants.

I am also grateful to Mme Laure Faure for guiding me to the remarkable resources of the library of the Musée de la Poste in Paris, and to M. Jean-Philippe Sartout of the library's *photothèque* for generously assisting me in identifying suitable illustrations for this book. At various stages in the long development of this interdisciplinary project I have greatly benefited from the knowledge and support of many colleagues, among whom: Wilda Anderson, Ute Brandes, Rosalina de la Carrera, Malcolm and Odile Cook, Antonio Feros, Beatrice Fink, Pierre Frantz, Dena Goodman, Alden Gordon, Margaret Groesbeck, Maria Heim, Marcel Hénaff, Marie-Hélène Huet, Margaret Hunt, Richard John, James Maraniss, Lyle McGeogh, Uday Mehta, Ourida Mostefaï, Jacques Neefs, Ronald C. Rosbottom, David Schneider, English Showalter, Natasha Staller, Edward Tarr, Christopher van den Berg, Donald O. White and Susan Whyman.

Introduction

This book is a study of the nature and history of the European post in the early modern period (roughly 1500-1800), its everyday reality and its culture. New postal systems that first became available to the general public during the Renaissance made possible the letter culture of the Age of Enlightenment.[1] The book focuses on the reasons why these systems were developed and how they functioned on a practical level, as well as how new postal institutions and practices affected their users and changed the world. It aims to update our knowledge of a broad range of issues related to the early modern post, while placing that knowledge within a conceptual framework. Within this period it places special emphasis on the eighteenth century, which was the high point of personal letter-writing in Europe, and on France in particular.[2] I focus on France because the 'communications revolution' in the Holy Roman Empire and Prussia has been comprehensively treated elsewhere.[3] Although the Introduction and last chapter of this work contain references to postmodern theorists, the book is primarily concerned with the practical reality of early modern postal relations and its impact upon its users.

It has often been noted that email and other forms of electronic communication are not only much faster than paper mail, but that they also affect its content and its users in specific ways. The conditions in which paper mail was written and delivered in the early modern period also exerted a specific influence upon its users and the nature of their communications.[4] However until very recently little was known about

1. Gerhard Dohrn-van Rossum makes this point in *The History of the hour: clocks and modern temporal orders* (Chicago, IL, and London, 1996; orig. pubd in German as *Die Geschichte der Stunde: Uhren und Moderne Zeitordnungen*, Munich and Vienna, 1992), p.344.
2. Clare Brant makes this point in *Eighteenth-century letters and British culture* (London, 2006), p.2., as do Amanda Vickery ('Do not scribble', *London review of books*, 32:21 (4 November 2010), p.34), Georg Steinhausen (*Geschichte des deutschen Briefes* (Zurich, 1968), II, p.245ff)), and Wolfgang Behringer (*Thurn und Taxis: die Geschichte ihrer Post und ihrer Unternehmen* (Munich and Zurich, 1990), p.114).
3. Wolfgang Behringer's *Im Zeichen des Merkur: Reichspost und Kommunikationsrevolution in der Frühen Neuzeit* (Göttingen, 2003) offers a magisterial treatment of these matters.
4. For the relationship between electronic mail and social relations see: Sherry Turkle, *Alone together: why we expect more from technology and less from each other* (New York, 2011), as well as Robert Kraut, Michael Patterson, Vicki Lundmark, Sara Kiesler, Tridas Mukophadhyay and William Scherlis, 'Internet paradox: a social technology that reduces social involvement and psychological well-being?', *American psychologist* 53:9 (1998), p.1017. On email and identity: David L. Chaum, 'Untraceable electronic mail, return addresses, and digital

the practical conditions in which letters were exchanged at the time. The main reason for this gap in our knowledge probably lies in the methods that had long been used by historians and literary scholars to study the post and the epistolary. In literary studies, scholars had until recently tended either to take a formalist approach to the epistolary, by focusing upon the poetics and rhetorical aspects of letters, or to prepare critical editions of correspondence in a perspective derived from textual criticism.[5] These methods have not required them to concern themselves with such practical questions as how letters were written, posted and paid for. Such matters have no relevance either to the study of the epistolary as a form or to the establishment of critical editions.[6] Critical editions of correspondence are invaluable works of scholarship in many ways, but since their primary objective is to produce a text that is as close as possible to the original, they have not traditionally been concerned with determining whether the letters they contain were conveyed to their destinations by organized postal systems or by messenger, by what routes they traveled and the difficulties correspondents encountered in sending and receiving letters; nor have they sought to explain the numerous allusions that correspondents make to these and other practical questions, or to consider the ways in which such practical matters affected the nature of the letters themselves. The present book is concerned with all of these matters, which it situates in a broad European context, with special emphasis on the situation in France.[7] Historians,

pseudonyms', *Communications of the ACM* 24:2 (1981), p.84-90. Benoît Melançon reflects on the differences between email and paper mail in *Sévigné@internet: remarques sur le courrier électronique et la lettre* (Montreal, 1996).

5. Janet Altman's *Epistolarity: approaches to a form* (Columbus, OH, 1982) and Benoît Melançon's *Diderot épistolier* (Montreal, 1996) are two excellent works in the formalist tradition, while the textual-critical approach to French-language correspondence is perhaps best exemplified by Theodore Besterman's critical edition of Voltaire's correspondence [*D*] and R. A. Leigh's superb critical edition of the correspondence of Jean-Jacques Rousseau [*CC*].
6. In *Special delivery* (Chicago, IL, 1992) Linda S. Kauffman approaches the twentieth-century epistolary 'mode' from a perspective informed by feminist and postmodern theory. In more recent years a number of works by literary historians have been devoted to the social and rhetorical dimensions of the epistolary in the early modern period. See Eve Tavor Bannet, *Empire of letters: letter manuals and transatlantic correspondence, 1688-1820* (Cambridge, 2005); Brant, *Eighteenth-century letters*; James How, *Epistolary spaces: English letter writing from the foundation of the Post Office to Richardson's Clarissa* (Aldershot, 2003). See also Susan Whyman, *The Pen and the people: English letter writers 1660-1800* (Oxford and New York, 2009).
7. Two recent books make significant contributions to our understanding of the practical dimension of postal history. Michèle Chauvet's two-volume *Introduction à l'histoire postale des origines à 1849* (Paris, 2000) provides a lucid and thoroughly-researched account of the organization and functioning of the French post; Whyman's *The Pen and the people* devotes an entire chapter to the practical aspects of 'Sending the letter' in the United Kingdom

for their part, had primarily focused upon the emergence and development of various urban, national and private postal institutions; but since the 1990s social historians of the post and the epistolary have begun to investigate the rhetorical dimension of letter-writing.[8] In addition, while institutional histories of the post provide some indications of how early modern postal systems worked internally, they have almost nothing to say about how letters were exchanged between one system and another: for example how a letter entrusted to the British Post Office in London made its way to Paris or Vienna, not to mention how the cost of postage was determined. As David M. Henkin has put it in his study of the emergence of modern communication in nineteenth-century America, these latter questions 'inevitably lead us beyond the confines of an institutional history of the Post Office Department into the world of everyday experience and belief – to a diffuse *culture* of the post'.[9] This book is a guidebook to that culture. Building upon the recent work of Michèle Chauvet (2000), James How (2003), Patrick Marchand (2006) and Susan Whyman (2009),[10] it offers a fuller account of how the practical conditions of early modern epistolary exchange disposed users of the post to write and to see themselves, their interlocutors and their world.

The early modern post was qualitatively different from the postal arrangements that preceded it, a point that previous authors have not brought out. In this Introduction I seek to define the historical specificity of the early modern post and describe the range of economic, political, social and existential interests that were invested in it: that is, both what the early modern post was and who wanted it. In addition, since the history of European postal institutions has not been updated since Ludwig Kalmus published his *Weltgeschichte der Post* in 1937, I have devoted a chapter to the history of early modern European postal services – the most important of which were the Thurn and Taxis post,

during the eighteenth century and sheds new light on the ways in which the Post Office altered the rhythms of daily life. I have not been able to find any studies of the material conditions of epistolary exchange in Germany, the Habsburg Empire or Russia (since I do not read Russian I was limited here).

8. See Dena Goodman, *The Republic of Letters: a cultural history of the French Enlightenment* (Ithaca, NY, and London, 1994); Dena Goodman, 'Epistolary property: Michel de Servan and the plight of letters on the eve of the French Revolution', in *Early modern conceptions of property*, ed. John Brewer and Susan Staves (London and New York, 1995), p.339-64; Tiziana Plebani, 'La correspondenza nell'antico regime: lettere di donne negli archivi di famiglia', in Gabriella Zarri (ed.), *Per lettera: la scrittura epistolare femminile tra archivio e tipografia, secoli XV-XVIII* (Rome, 1999), p.43-78.

9. David M. Henkin, *The Postal age: the emergence of modern communications in nineteenth-century America* (Chicago, IL, and London, 2006), p.5. Original emphasis.

10. Chauvet, *Introduction à l'histoire postale*; How, *Epistolary spaces*; Patrick Marchand, *Le Maître de poste et le messager: une histoire du transport public en France au temps du cheval 1700-1850* (Paris, 2006); Whyman, *The Pen and the people.*

the French Royal Post and the British Post Office – from their emergence in the Renaissance to the end of the eighteenth century. This chapter also contains an account of the complex state of international postal relations during this period, a topic to which little attention has been given. In the early modern era the post was the primary public means of both communication and transportation. For the most part, these systems were private but state-controlled, and their development was linked to the emergence of the State.

Chapter 2 describes the workings of the post at the most practical level, covering such matters as: paper and ink, folding, sealing and envelopes; addresses, postage and posting; collection, sorting, transportation and delivery. It also discusses the relationship between this everyday reality and the problematic but essential practice of publishing what were originally autograph manuscripts.

The institution of public mail systems provided a much-needed service to the general public, while at the same time furnishing rulers with a source of substantial revenue and a terrifyingly effective surveillance mechanism, in the form of the so-called Black Cabinets or Black Chambers, which flourished in eighteenth-century Europe. Chapter 3 considers the paradoxical logic of these institutions, how they functioned and the ways in which they exemplified the tension between state control and public service, between state secrecy and the emerging belief in the right of individuals to keep the contents of their letters secret.

The next two chapters examine how the practical conditions of epistolary exchange – such as the frequent delays in delivery, the occasional loss of mail, prohibitions on sending books by post, the high cost of postage (which was usually paid by the recipient), not to mention surveillance – affected two of the eighteenth century's greatest writers, Voltaire and Rousseau. In the process, they provide insights into the attitudes of these authors toward the public, the state and life in general. Previous studies of Voltaire's correspondence have not underlined the extent to which his letters are devoted to practical considerations about the post, such as how to exploit the constraints of the system. Nor has much attention been paid to how Jean-Jacques Rousseau's relationship to the post mirrors his vexed relationship to all forms of communication at a distance and to communication in general.

The last chapter is devoted to a discussion of some of the ways in which the institution of publicly available postal systems transformed the early modern world, from its 'sonic environment'[11] to the perception, experience and control of time and space. It concludes with a discussion of Thomas Pynchon's novella *The Crying of lot 49* (1966), in which a California

11. I borrow this term from R. Murray Schafer, *The Soundscape: our sonic environment and the tuning of the world* (Rochester, VT, 1977).

housewife investigates the apparently centuries-old conflict between the Thurn and Taxis post and Trystero, an underground post invented by Pynchon. Although much has been written about this classic postmodern text, little has been said about its specifically postal dimension.

What the post was (definitions)

The early modern post was *an impersonal and continuously available system for the collection and delivery of mail and the transport of passengers along fixed routes.* Until the middle of the fifteenth century, the word 'post' (from the Latin, *statio posita*)[12] designated a relay,[13] an established stopping place on a route, where horses and riders were kept ready for couriers. Communication systems that relied on posts, in this sense, existed throughout the ancient world (China, Egypt, Persia, Rome), where they were established to facilitate the delivery of messages for a few powerful individuals. In the travel narrative attributed to Marco Polo, the author reported that on main roads in China *poestes* had been set up for the sovereign's couriers at twenty-five mile intervals.[14] However during the two centuries of rapid economic and demographic expansion in Europe that began around 1450, the word 'post' came to designate not just relays, but the men stationed at relays, those who traveled with letters or messages, the vehicles in which they traveled and, finally, the official agency that organized the collection, transmission and distribution of letters and related matter (that is, 'what everyone believes they understand' by the word post).[15]

During those two centuries what changed most dramatically about the post was not the meaning of the word, but the scale and nature of the

12. 'Post': Vulgar Latin *postum*, Latin *statio posita*. According to the *Oxford English dictionary* (henceforward *OED*), the earliest known use of 'post' in the modern sense is found in Marco Polo (1298). By metonymic extension, 'post' also designated the couriers (and later the coaches) who made use these of these relays. In Chapter 6, p.176-80, I discuss the connotation of 'speed' that the term quickly acquired.
13. The word 'relay' (from the Old French, *relais*) originally referred to 'a set of fresh hounds (and horses) posted to take up the chase of a deer in place of those already tired out' (*OED*). Throughout its subsequent history (during which it has come to mean, among other things: a crew of workers relieving others at a shift, any of the legs or laps of a relay race, a stage or intermediary between two points or persons, and a device that serves to retransmit a signal by amplifying it), the 'relay' has remained an agency of retransmission, that which receives energy and or information, and dispatches it to a further destination.
14. Martin Dallmeier, *Quellen zur Geschichte des europäischen Postwesens 1501-1806* (Kallmünz, 1977), vol.I, p.47.
15. Jacques Derrida, *La Carte postale: de Socrate à Freud et au-delà* (Paris, 1980), p.72; in English *The Post card: from Socrates to Freud and beyond*, translated, and with an introduction and additional notes, by Alan Bass (Chicago, IL, and London, 1987), p.64. Because there is no English equivalent of the French word *courrier*, which means both 'courier' and 'mail', Bass leaves it in French.

enterprise itself. For one thing, during the Middle Ages posts had provided message delivery services for powerful people and for institutions, such as monastic orders, guilds and universities. But starting in the Renaissance, as demand from merchants for mail-delivery services grew apace, European sovereigns began to make them available to the general public.[16] Messengers carry letters for private individuals, whereas the post, in the modern sense, is available to anyone who can afford the service. As Sombart puts it: '[O]ne could speak of "mail" only when the regular opportunity of letter dispatch became accessible to the general public.'[17] Consequently, not only did the volume of mail increase enormously, but the post (in the singular) became a *business*, open to a vast and impersonal market. In the second place, while a messenger carries communications for specific persons, following whatever route is convenient or required by the sender, for the past 500 years the post has been an institution that sends mail to its destination along previously-existing routes. Moreover, in the early modern period this business entailed carrying not just messages or letters, but also packages, newspapers, books, as well as passengers. Furthermore, it was not just the impersonal character of the early modern post that distinguished it from private messenger services, which were only available on an ad hoc basis, but the fact that the post was now continuously available. For millennia posts had met the occasional demands of important persons, allowing messengers to travel whenever and wherever they were needed. In order for there to be a post, in what has become the usual sense, it is necessary that 'a sender have the permanent possibility of letter delivery, without himself having to engage a courier'.[18] Thus it was that by the middle of the eighteenth century, in the article 'Postes' in Diderot and d'Alembert's *Encyclopédie*, the chevalier de Jaucourt could take it for granted that posts were continuously accessible to the general public, for both the delivery of mail and the transport of passengers:

> [L]es postes sont des *relais* de chevaux établis de distance en distance, à l'usage des courriers chargés de porter les missives, *tant du souverain que des*

16. Wolfgang Behringer stresses the importance of this point in his seminal article, 'Communications revolutions: a historiographical concept', *German history* 24:3 (2006), p.333-74. See especially p.340ff. Behringer's 2006 article touches on many of the points that he had developed at much greater length in *Im Zeichen des Merkur*. Chapter 1 (below) provides a brief account of the history of postal services in early modern Europe.
17. This in Werner Sombart's *magnum opus*, *Der moderne Kapitalismus*, 3rd edn (Munich and Leipzig, 1919), vol.2, p.369), cited by Jürgen Habermas in *The Structural transformation of the public sphere: an inquiry into a category of bourgeois society* (Cambridge, 1991), p.16.
18. Brigitte Schnaitl, *La Poste française: ihre Entwicklung und Erbreiterung sowie die Aufbau des französischen Wegenetzes im 18. Jahrhundert im Konnex politischer und gesellschaftlicher Ereignisse* (Salzburg, 1995), p.5.

> *particuliers*; ces *relais* servent aussi à tous les voyageurs qui veulent en user, en payant toutefois le prix réglé par le gouvernement.[19]
>
> [[P]osts are horse relays established at regular distances, for the use of the couriers charged with carrying the missives *of both the sovereign and private citizens*; these *relays* also serve all the travelers who wish to use them, by nonetheless paying the price set by the government.]

The advent of this continuously available system had the effect of bringing forth the institutionalized spaces of connection that James How calls 'epistolary spaces'.[20] Finally, because this new kind of post served an extensive market rather than the needs of relatively few persons, it was not just a system of relays for conveyance of mail and passengers, but also a collection agency. This is why Schnaitl defines the post as 'a *collection institution* for letters, packages or (in the time of postal coaches) for travelers' (emphasis added).[21] In other words, a modern postal system requires not just 'posts' (relays), but 'post offices'.[22]

To recapitulate, the early modern post was a business that collected and delivered mail and transported passengers along fixed routes; it was continuously available to the public, and it was a system, composed of post offices, relays and workers. The object of this book is to provide a detailed account of that system ('the early modern post') and the culture that arose around it between the Renaissance and the early nineteenth century in Europe, with special emphasis on the eighteenth century (the 'Century of Letters') and France. In the 1840s, when steam-driven trains began to replace the post as a means of passenger transport and prepaid postage stamps came into general use, the early modern postal era came to an end.

19. *Encyclopédie ou, Dictionnaire raisonné des sciences, des arts et des métiers par une société de gens de lettres/mis en ordre et publié par M. Diderot; et quant à la partie mathématique, par M. d'Alembert (Paris, Briasson et al., 1751-1765). Emphasis added.*
20. 'Epistolary spaces do not become apparent when sending a piece of correspondence by a private messenger precisely because such spaces need to be immutably already there before you even begin to write a letter. A Post Office, as its primary function, sets up and then advertises the existence of impersonal spaces, which are continually there, and into which you can send your letters once they are written.' *Epistolary spaces*, p.4. See Chapter 6, p.173-76.
21. *Epistolary spaces*, p.4.
22. According to the *OED*, the term 'Post Office' made its first appearance in a 1657 Act of Parliament. The first example cited by the *Dictionnaire Littré* of *poste* in the sense of 'maison [...] bureau où l'on porte les lettres' is taken from the correspondence of Mme de Sévigné (1626-1696). The postal historian Ludwig Kalmus (1937) situates the post in the context of modern industrial processes: *Weltgeschichte der Post* (Vienna, 1937), p.4. Eugène Vaillé emphasizes the economic requirements of the institution in its early modern form in *Histoire des postes jusqu'à la Révolution* (Paris, 1946), p.45 (henceforward *Histoire des postes*). In the first volume of *Histoire générale des postes françaises* (Paris, 1947-1953) (henceforward *Histoire générale*), Vaillé offers a different and, in many ways, less satisfactory definition. (vol.1, p.1). Geoffrey Bennington points to the inconsistencies of Vaillé's efforts to define the post in *Legislations: the politics of deconstruction* (London and New York, 1994), p.244. Unless otherwise indicated, all translations into English are mine.

Who wanted the post? (interests)

> [L]a poste est le lien de toutes les affaires, de toutes les négociations; les absents deviennent par elle présents; elle est la consolation de la vie/ [T]he post is what binds all transactions, all negotiations; through it the absent become present; it is the consolation of life.
>
> Voltaire, 'Poste' in *Questions sur l'Encyclopédie*[23]

Publicly available and fairly reliable postal service was brought into existence by the convergence of a diverse set of economic, political, social and psychological interests. In the context of the expanding European economy, posts enabled merchants to manage their widespread business concerns; they also provided considerable revenue to the rulers of emerging states and to the tenants or 'farmers' who were employed to manage them. From a political perspective, all postal systems are what Bernhard Siegert has called *instrumenta regni.*[24] As Siegert recalls, the Egyptian and Achaemenid (Persian) empires provided Rome with the model for the *cursus publicus*, the post road used exclusively for the transmission of imperial decrees, military communications and the transport of high-level functionaries. Under such conditions, which in some parts of Europe prevailed well into the sixteenth century, members of the public who attempted to avail themselves of postal services were severely punished and could even be put to death.[25] The Republic of Venice, where messenger and mail services were never limited to official communications, constituted a significant exception to this norm.[26] In the sixteenth and seventeenth centuries, when many

23. 'Poste', in *Questions sur l'Encyclopédie, par des amateurs* [henceforward *QE*] ed. Nicholas Cronk and Christiane Mervaux, in *Œuvres complètes de Voltaire* [henceforward *OCV*], (Oxford, 1968-), vol.42B (2012), p.471. This article was ultimately incorporated into the *Dictionnaire philosophique* in the posthumous Kehl edition of 1789. On the consolations of the post Voltaire had also written: 'Est-il possible que la plus grande consolation de ma vie, celle d'envoyer des contes par la poste, soit interdite aux pauvres humains? Cela fait saigner le cœur.' ('Is it possible that sending tales by post, the greatest consolation of my life, can be forbidden to poor humans? It makes the heart bleed.'), Voltaire to Charles Augustin Feriol, comte d'Argental and Jeanne Grâce Bosc Du Bouchet, comtesse d'Argental, 18 January 1764, D10812.
24. Bernhard Siegert, *Relays: literature as an epoch of the postal system* (Stanford, CA, 1999), p.7. Summarizing the remarks of Innis, Kieblowicz and Behringer on this subject, Susan Whyman notes that 'the Post Office in every age and place has been linked to culture and power', *The Pen and the people*, p.48. In ch.13 (p.240ff) of *Legislations*, Bennington also reflects on the relationship between the postal and the political.
25. Siegert, *Relays*, p.5-8.
26. Doubtless because there was no difference between the political and mercantile leadership of the Republic. See Adriano Cattani, *Storia dei servizi postali nella Repubblica di Venezia et catalogo dei timbri postali* (Venice, 1969).

European sovereigns were in the process of centralizing their power, they began to make postal services available to members of the public and discovered in the post not only a source of revenue, but a very effective means of ensuring security by eliciting and controlling the speech of their subjects.[27] To that end the rulers of nascent states instituted the so-called Black Cabinets (discussed in Chapter 3, p.95-123), nominally secret agencies where mail was opened, read, translated if necessary, copied and passed on to the sovereign or his representatives. It has been argued that the 'tension between state control and public service was at the very heart of the postal system, just as it was at the heart of the state itself'.[28] Indeed the post facilitated both the creation of a cosmopolitan intellectual community and surveillance of that community's members by the state.

In addition to these economic and political interests (both of which will be discussed at greater length in the following chapters), social and psychological forces were invested in modern postal systems. As early as the mid-sixteenth century, writing and receiving letters became a sort of status symbol, upon which one's career – and perhaps even one's reputation – could depend. In 1535, for example, the papal nuncio in Regensburg asked a friend to send him a blank letter, simply in order to display himself as someone who was privileged to receive correspondence.[29] By the time of the Enlightenment, for many people the rhythm of daily life had become attuned to the arrivals and departures of the

27. 'Absolutism made words available to the people, and a medium available to the words, in order to make the people speak about themselves, to control their speech, and to finance the state's expenditures for such control with the postage charged for that speech.' Siegert, *Relays*, p.9. As Patrick Marchand puts it: 'Even if the Posts ultimately linked their development to commerce and social relations, they would always be invested by the State with a security mission.' *Le Maître de poste et le messager*, p.183. In her discussion of the development of the French postal service, Schnaitl (*La Poste française*, p.6-7, 83-92) emphasizes the political role that was played by a combination of royal centralization and the accession of the *noblesse de robe* to key state administrative positions, including the postal administration.
28. 'Because this tension not only persisted but intensified as the state and its institutions grew stronger, the public increasingly demanded both better service and less control. In the case of the post, the public wanted faster and more dependable service, on the one hand, and, on the other, absolute privacy of the letters that passed through the mails and freedom of movement for printed goods – journals in particular.' Goodman, *The Republic of letters*, p.19. See also Goodman's 'Epistolary property'. These matters are discussed in Chapter 3, p.95-104.
29. Fedele, *Le Antiche poste: Nascita e crescita di un servizio (secoli SIV-XVIII)*, in Clemente Fedele, M. Gallenga, *'Per servizio di Nostro Signore': strade, corrieri e poste dei Pai dal Medioevo al 1870*, preface by G. Andreotto (Prato, 1988), p.74. Cited in Plebani, 'La correspondenza nell'antico regime', p.74. n.22. On p.48 Plebani uses the English expression 'status symbol'. Jean-Jacques Rousseau imagined another way of using blank letters. Rousseau to Sophie d'Houdetot, 15 January 1758, Jean-Jacques Rousseau, *Correspondance complète de Jean-Jacques Rousseau*, ed. R. A. Leigh, 52 vols (Geneva; Madison, WI; Banbury, Oxford, 1965-1998) (henceforward *CC*), vol.5, p.21 (609); I briefly discuss this letter in Chapter 5, p.156-57.

post, and letter-writing had become a 'cult,' a 'mania'.[30] This was especially the case in Germany where, in contrast to France, there was no central and unified high society.[31] As Behringer remarks in his history of the Thurn and Taxis post, it was no coincidence that Goethe's father's house was in the immediate vicinity of the Taxis palace in Frankfurt.[32] In England, as Susan Whyman has noted, receiving or not receiving mail had a great emotional impact on persons in all classes of society. A letter could now be perceived as a 'document of friendship'.[33] Psychological dependence upon letters is a topic to which I shall return in the last chapter of this book.

As a publicly available telecommunications system,[34] the post created and responded to the desire to transmit and receive 'news' (a notion that, like the institution of newspapers, was made possible by the post) of distant people and places.[35] Epistolary networks played an essential role in the lives of merchants, voyagers, academicians and intellectuals of all kinds.[36] It was thanks to the post that Voltaire, who spent much of his peripatetic life in places far removed from the great European capitals, could maintain the voluminous correspondence that put him at an important nexus of the international Republic of Letters.[37] Voltaire

30. Behringer, *Thurn und Taxis*, p.114.
31. Norbert Elias, *The Civilizing process*, trans. Edmund Jephcott (New York, 1978), p.28; cited in Thomas O. Beebe, *Epistolary fiction in Europe: 1500-1800* (Cambridge, 1999), p.16-17.
32. Behringer, *Thurn und Taxis*, p.115-16.
33. Anne Vincent-Buffault, *L'Exercice de l'amitié: pour une histoire des pratiques amicales aux XVIIIe et XIXe siècles* (Paris, 1995), p.19-34. Cited by Pierre-Yves Beaurepaire in the Introduction to *La Plume et la toile: pouvoirs et réseaux de correspondance dans l'Europe des Lumières: études réunies par Pierre-Yves Beaurepaire* (Artois, 2002), p.26, n.4.
34. 'From the perspective of everyday life (as opposed to scientific experimentation), it is difficult to establish a trans-historical criterion by which to distinguish modern telecommunication from long-distance communication more generally. Although there may be a clear difference between modes of contact that appear instantaneous to users (smoke signals, telegraphs, telephones, electronic mail) and those that involve a perceptible time lag (carrier pigeon, bike messenger, DHL air courier), any other dividing line runs the risk of being arbitrary. The ability of locomotive trains or optical telegraph relays to carry information faster than the "speed of a galloping horse or the fastest sailing ship" [...] did not produce instantaneous communication, nor did the invention of jet airplanes.' Henkin, *The Postal age*, p.15-16.
35. See Chapter 6, p.178-81.
36. On the relationship between correspondences and voyages in the Enlightenment, see Daniel Roche's discussion of the epistolary network of Jean-François Séguier, in *Les Républicains des lettres: gens de culture et Lumières au XVIIIe siècle* (Paris, 1988), p.263-85.
37. Data compiled by the 'Mapping the Republic of Letters' project suggests that while Voltaire's correspondence network had a cosmopolitan reach, it was significantly regional and mostly French: https://republicofletters.stanford.edu/ (last accessed 30 July 2015). Insofar as conversation with visitors (as well as the letters and conversations of visitors within their own social networks) made Voltaire's thought available beyond his network of correspondents, estimations of the impact of Voltaire's (or any other correspondent's) thought based solely upon the tracing of epistolary networks should be subject to caution.

occupies an important place in our study of the early modern post, not just because of the pivotal role that he played in the Republic of Letters or the sheer volume of his letters (estimated at over 40,000) and correspondents (nearly 1,500 of them), but because so many of his letters concern themselves with the practical workings of the post and its meaning to him. To him the post was an essential medium, and not just a medium in the utilitarian sense of a means or instrument (or as Derrida puts it, 'un même type de service, une technologie' – 'a same type of service, a technology'),[38] but also implicitly a medium in the spiritual sense, an entity 'through [which] the absent become [...] present'.[39] Even when his friends were thousands of miles away, it could make him feel that he was conversing with them:

> Autrefois, si vous aviez eu un ami à Constantinople et un autre à Moscou, vous auriez été obligé d'attendre leur retour pour apprendre de leurs nouvelles. Aujourd'hui, sans qu'ils sortent de leur chambre ni vous de la vôtre, vous conversez familièrement avec eux par le moyen d'une feuille de papier. Vous pouvez même leur envoyer par la poste un sachet de l'apothicaire Arnoult contre l'apoplexie, et il est reçu plus infailliblement qu'il ne les guérit.
>
> Si l'un de vos amis a besoin de faire toucher de l'argent à Pétersbourg et l'autre à Smyrne, la poste fait votre affaire.
>
> Votre maîtresse est-elle à Bordeaux, et vous devant Prague avec votre régiment, elle vous assure régulièrement de sa tendresse; vous savez par elle toutes les nouvelles de la ville, excepté les infidélités qu'elle vous fait.[40]

> In the past, if you had had a friend in Constantinople and another in Moscow, you would have been obliged to await their return to hear news of them. Today, without their having to step out of their bedroom or you out of yours, you converse with them familiarly by means of a sheet of paper. You can even send them a packet of the apothecary Arnoult's remedy for apoplexy by the post, and it is received more infallibly than it cures them.
>
> If one of your friends needs to have access to money in Petersburg and the other in Smyrna, the post is just what you need.
>
> Should your mistress be in Bordeaux and you before Prague with your regiment, she regularly assures you of her tender feelings; through her you get all the news of the city, excepting the infidelities she commits.

By means of the post, Voltaire believed, the people whose conversation one misses can magically come alive. Likewise, in the past, when the post

38. *La Carte postale*, p.72; *The Post card*, p.64. Beebe rehearses a Derridean theme, when he remarks (*Epistolary fiction*, p.12-13) that '[T]he English word "letter" points back, through French *lettre* and the Latin *littera* (both meaning a letter of the alphabet and the mark of writing in general) to the origin of writing as such. This idea of the letter as signifying and supplementing absence was standard from the Middle Ages to the modern period'.
39. '[L]a poste est le lien de toutes les affaires, de toutes les négociations; les absents deviennent par elle présents; elle est la consolation de la vie.' 'Poste', in *QE*, *OCV*, vol.42B, p.470.
40. 'Poste', in *QE*, *OCV*, vol.42B, p.470-71.

served a powerful elite, one would not have been able to conduct one's business as efficiently, and one would also have had to suffer the absence of those one holds dear. But he notes that – thanks to fairly recent improvements in the postal service (which he situates in 'nos temps barbares,' meaning the late Middle Ages)[41] – suffering is no longer an inevitable part of the human condition. In this enlightened age, he affirms, the wonders of telecommunications shrink time and space: while one is sitting in a comfortable armchair, the postal medium enables us to 'converse' (have intercourse with, talk with) absent friends through a mere sheet of folded paper. In a letter to Mme Fontaines, Voltaire exclaims, 'C'est une grande consolation d'écrire aux gens qu'on aime: c'est une belle invention que de se parler de 150 lieues pour vingt sous!' (It is a great consolation to write to the people of whom one is fond: it is a fine invention to converse at 150 leagues for 20 sous!).[42] So even if, like Voltaire, one does not believe in what are ordinarily called miracles (that is, violations of physical laws), one can appreciate that the post is a miracle in the etymological sense (*miraculum*: marvel, wonder).[43] If one is wealthy (as Voltaire was when he wrote the *Philosophical dictionary*), one can use the post to send one's needy friends in St Petersburg or Izmir a sheet of paper called a bill of exchange (*lettre de change*), which postal alchemy can then turn into money.[44] Never one to belittle material comforts,[45] Voltaire also appreciates the fact that one can do all of these things without leaving one's bedroom!

41. Voltaire is alluding here to the centralisation of postal relays under Louis XI, which he evokes in the *Essai sur les mœurs*: 'De [Louis XI] vient l'établissement des postes, non tel qu'il est aujourd'hui en Europe; il ne fit que rétablir les *veredarii* de Charlemagne et de l'ancien empire romain. Deux cent trente courriers à ses gages portaient ses ordres incessamment. Les particuliers pouvaient courir avec les chevaux destinés à ces courriers, en payant dix sous par cheval pour chaque traite de quatre lieues. Les lettres étaient rendues de ville en ville par les courriers du roi. Cette police ne fut longtemps connue qu'en France.' *OCV*, vol.24 (Oxford, 2011), p.462 (ch.94). See also Chapter 1, p.35, below. In Voltaire's historiography, the Middle Ages is a period of obscurantism caused by the fusion of temporal and spiritual power.
42. Voltaire to Marie Elisabeth de Dompierre de Fontaine, Marquise de Fontaine, 27 February 1761, D9655.
43. As Voltaire puts it in the *Dictionnaire philosophique*: 'Un miracle, selon l'énergie du mot, est une chose admirable.' 'Miracles', *OCV*, vol.36 (Oxford, 1994). As I explain in Chapter 6, p.183, the notion of the post as a *belle invention* seems to have become a commonplace by the late seventeenth century.
44. As Cronk and Mervaux point out, Voltaire had complained in the 'Usure' article of the *Encyclopédie* about the fees that the post imposed for carrying money orders from one place to another. *OCV*, vol.42B, p.470, n.2.
45. 'Miracles'.

Consolation

Consolation is a leitmotif of Voltaire's remarks on the post. He spent most of his life at a considerable distance from his interlocutors: not just because of his incessant travels or his status as a dissident, with the attendant exiles from Paris and France; but also because his correspondents lived in so many different places, from Naples to Stockholm, from London to St Petersburg. During the Renaissance, at the formative stage of the Republic of Letters, Erasmus had (like Voltaire) also changed residences frequently, exchanged a vast correspondence across the European continent and also taken refuge in Switzerland. But subsequent developments in postal infrastructure, especially in the eighteenth century, made it easier for people to travel and thus more likely that they would find themselves far apart. Which is another way of saying that the post offered Voltaire consolation for a situation to which it had itself contributed. Publicly available postal systems came into existence in response to economic and political forces (most notably: the spread of merchant capitalism, with its need for adequate infrastructure; the emergence of the state, with its need for revenue and surveillance of its subjects) that also increased the distance between persons and fostered in them an ardent desire to communicate at a distance.

Bitter experience had taught Voltaire that although, in principle, his letter or bill of exchange was 'received [...] infallibly', it could also fail to reach its destination, but he did not think that such failures happened for any reason intrinsic to the medium itself. Still, like all the pleasures in life (luxury, for example), it could be corrupted and abused; and he and his correspondents knew perfectly well that employees of the Black Cabinets (see Chapter 3) regularly opened and even confiscated suspicious letters and packages. His correspondence, especially in the 1760s, is filled with complaints about seizures of letters and books (especially those bound for Paris), and with attempts to devise schemes for eluding interference with the free circulation of ideas by agents of the state. In the summer of 1763, when Voltaire was having a particularly hard time sending and receiving books, he repeatedly grumbled about suffering from a kind of spiritual blockade. For example, in a letter dated 9 June 1763, he writes: 'Il y a depuis peu une petite inquisition sur les livres, on coupe les vivres à nos pauvres âmes.' (There has recently been a little inquisition on books, our poor souls are being deprived of their means of subsistence.)[46] For Voltaire, books and letters were food for the soul. Six months later, upon learning that the Post Office was seizing all copies of

46. Voltaire to Louis René de Caradeuc de La Chalotais, 9 June 1763, D11257. Voltaire uses the same figure ('On coupe les vivres à l'âme, comme on coupe les bourses.') in a letter of 29 July 1763 (D10506) to the count and countess d'Argental.

a tale in verse called *Les Trois Manières*, Voltaire asked his friends the count and countess d'Argental: 'Est-il possible que *la plus grande consolation de ma vie, celle d'envoyer des contes par la poste*, soit interdite aux pauvres humains? Cela fait saigner le cœur.' (Is it possible that *the greatest consolation of my life, that of sending tales by post*, can be forbidden to poor humans? It makes the heart bleed.)[47]

In the 'Post' article of *Questions sur l'Encyclopédie* (posthumously incorporated into the *Dictionnaire philosophique*), Voltaire calls the post *la consolation de la vie*: 'the consolation of [and for] life', without qualification. It is the consolation not only for 'the evils that ambition and politics spread across the earth', but *for* life (for the suffering that is part of life) and *of* life (provided by life itself: the preposition *de* means 'for', 'of' and 'from') in general. Voltaire may seem to be contradicting himself when, in the article entitled 'War', he refers to *love* as 'the only consolation of human kind [*le genre humain*] and the only way to make up for it [*le réparer*]'. But although Voltaire was hardly a passionate man, it may well have been through the post that he was best able to give and receive, if not passionate love (like Diderot), at least consoling affection, devotion and friendship.[48] According to received opinion, it is religion that offers us consolation for life – that is, consolation for the suffering that is life or at least part of it; whereas the elite are supposed to take solace in 'the consolation of philosophy'. Yet while Voltaire shared some of the concerns of Boethius (480-524 CE) and his followers – how evil can exist in a world governed by God, how happiness can be achieved amidst inconstant fortune – he was too skeptical, too pragmatic and above all too sociable a thinker to believe that one could find consolation by looking inside oneself. Whether 'live' or by postal proxy, it was conversation, life with people that provided him with solace. It is thus no accident that 'the age of conversation' has also been called the 'Century of Letters', for the

47. Voltaire to the count and countess d'Argental, 18 January 1764, D11649. Emphasis added. In a letter to Damilaville, he complains about what happens when the post refuses to offer this consolation: '[...] Je vous ai prié de parler à Mr Jeannel, d'offrir le payement du paquet et de redemander la lettre à vous adressée qui était sous votre enveloppe. [...] Il est bien douloureux que la poste soit infidèle, et que le commerce de l'amitié, la consolation de l'absense soient empoisonez par un brigandage digne des houzards. C'est répandre trop d'amertume sur la vie. Je me sers cette fois cy de la voye de M. Dargental sous l'enveloppe de monsieur de Courteilles.' 11 May 1763, D11204.

48. In *Le Siècle de Louis XIV* (1st edn 1752), Voltaire had referred to the bonds that correspondence in the Republic of Letters creates beyond (and despite) national boundaries as '*consolations* pour les maux que l'ambition et la politique répandent à travers la terre', *Œuvres complètes*, ed. Louis Moland, 52 vols (Paris, 1877-1885) (henceforward *M*), vol.14, p.563-64, emphasis added. See 'Vos Lettres, mon cher frère, sont une grande *consolation* pour le quinze vingt des alpes'. Voltaire to Etienne Noël Damilaville, 22 January 1764, D17724. Emphasis added in both cases.

post gave Voltaire and his contemporaries the impression of prolonging conversation beyond the physical presence of an interlocutor.[49] Despite great distances and sometimes irreconcilable differences of opinion, they could, like optimistic Candide and pessimistic Martin, find consolation in the simple act of exchanging ideas:

> Cependant le vaisseau français et l'espagnol continuèrent leur route, et Candide continua ses *conversations* avec Martin. Ils disputèrent quinze jours de suite, et au bout de quinze jours ils étaient aussi avancés que le premier. Mais enfin *ils se parlaient, ils se communiquaient des idées, ils se consolaient.*[50]

> Meanwhile the French and Spanish vessels continued on their journey, and Candide continued his *conversations* with Martin. They argued for a fortnight, and at the end of that time they had got no further than at the beginning. But at least *they were talking, they were exchanging ideas, they consoled each other.*

To a man who wrote at least 21,221 letters (and probably closer to 40,000 of them: in a letter to Mme Du Deffand, Voltaire claims that he has stopped writing letters, in order to avoid 'tiring' the post[51]), the postal medium made 'the absent become... present' in simulated conversation, and in so doing afforded consolation for life and the consolation of life.[52]

The limits of postal communication

In the 'Post' article, Voltaire remarks that what a letter or package contains may not be worthy of faith: 'you' may doubt the efficacy of Arnoult's miracle remedy for apoplexy, but you can be sure that the post will 'infallibly' carry it to its receiver. If you are off in Bohemia with your regiment, you can rely on the post for faithful delivery of news from home, even more surely than you can count on the unfaithfulness of the mistress who sends the news to you. Despite Voltaire's pointed remarks about miracle cures and the fidelity of women (and later in the article, about the secrecy of correspondence), there is nothing ironic about his eulogy of the post;[53] although he knows that the authorities may intercept and read his letters or even confiscate his books, he does not doubt

49. Benedetta Craveri, *The Age of conversation*, translated by Teresa Waugh (New York, 2006, orig. pubd Milan, 2001 as *La Civiltà della conversazione*); Behringer, *Thurn und Taxis*, p.114.

50. *Candide ou L'Optimisme*, ch.20, l.64-68, *OCV*, vol.48 (Oxford, 1980), p.204. Emphasis added.

51. 'Au reste je n'écris à personne, et je ne fatigue la poste qu'à porter les montres que ma colonie fabrique.' Voltaire to Mme Du Deffand, 5 May 1772, D17724.

52. One notes the recurrence in this passage of the prefix 'con-' [with]: *con*verse [literally, 'turn with'], *Con*stant(inople) ['standing with'], *con*solation ['with relief']); it is a marker of Voltaire's passion for acting and being *with* others. The trope of epistolary exchange as conversation is discussed below, Chapter 6, p.175-76, 185.

53. '[J]amais le ministère qui a eu le département des postes n'a ouvert les lettres d'aucun particulier, excepté quand il a[vait] un besoin de savoir ce qu'elles contenaient.' *QE*, *OCV*, vol.42B, p.470.

the ability of the post to deliver a letter to its destination.[54] And behind the wry smile that he directs at human credulity – not just at the belief in miracle cures or the faithfulness of a mistress, but also at the belief in a better world beyond this one – Voltaire has faith in the ability of epistolary conversation to feed the soul. He truly believes in communication by post, in the capacity of a letter to carry the ideas and feelings of one soul and deliver them to another without loss. That belief, which is part of a more general belief in human communication (along with the related notions of reciprocity, exchange of ideas, and so on) underlies the ideology of the Enlightenment Republic of Letters.

As a man of the Enlightenment, Voltaire harbored no doubts about the possibility of rational communication or about the post as a medium for delivering it.[55] In contrast, Jean-Jacques Rousseau, who first came to public attention by denouncing the ravages of Enlightenment, had a much more ambivalent and characteristically paradoxical attitude toward rational communication, and postal communication in particular.[56] In the next century Rousseau's lonely skepticism about the post turned into a full-fledged crisis of confidence in epistolary communication. The early modern postal era was drawing to a close. What has become a characteristically modern attitude toward postal communication found its most eloquent expression in a letter that Franz Kafka wrote to his Czech translator, Milena Jesenská, in March 1922. To explain why he has not written to her sooner, he begins by reminding her, 'Well, you know how I hate letters'. And after reflecting on the various mishaps that have befallen him because of letters (including his own), Kafka writes the following:

> Die leichte Möglichkeit des Briefschreibens muß – bloß theoretisch angesehn – eine schreckliche Zerrüttung der Seelen in die Welt gebracht haben. Es ist ja ein Verkehr mit Gespenstern und zwar nicht nur mit dem Gespenst des Adressaten, sondern auch mit dem eigenen Gespenst, das sich einem unter der Hand in dem Brief, den man schreibt, entwickelt oder gar in einer Folge von Briefen, wo ein Brief den andern erhärtet und sich auf ihn also Zeugen berufen kann. Wie kam man nur auf den Gedanken, daß Menschen durch Briefe miteinander verkehren können! Man kann an einen fernen Menschen denken und man kann einen nahen Menschen fassen, alles

54. See Lacan, 'Le séminaire sur *La Lettre volée*', in *Ecrits* (Paris, 1966) and Derrida, 'Le facteur de la vérité' in *La Carte postale*.

55. The possibility of rational communication is at the heart of the so-called Foucault-Habermas debate. See Bent Flyvbjerg, 'Habermas and Foucault: thinkers for civil society?', *British journal of sociology* 49:2 (June 1998), p.208-33; David Ingram, 'Foucault and Habermas on the subject of reason', in Gary Gutting (ed.), *The Cambridge companion to Foucault* (Cambridge, 1994), p.215-61; and Michael Kelly (ed.), *Critique and power: recasting the Foucault/Habermas debate* (Cambridge, MA, 1994).

56. I return to Rousseau in Chapter 5, p.141-66.

andere geht über Menschenkraft. Briefe schreiben aber heißt, sich vor den Gespenstern entblößen, worauf sie gierig warten. Geschriebene Küsse kommen nicht an ihren Ort, sondern werden von den Gespenstern auf dem Wege ausgetrunken.[57]

The easy possibility of letter writing must – from a simply theoretical point of view – have brought into the world a terrible derangement of souls. It is truly a communication with specters, and not only with the specter of the addressee but also with one's own specter, which develops underneath one's own hand in the very letter one is writing or even in a series of letters, where one letter corroborates the other and can refer to it as a witness. How has one come to believe that people can communicate with each other by letter? One can think about a man who is far away and one can grasp a man who is near, but all else exceeds human power. Writing letters is like exposing oneself in the presence of the thirstily waiting specters. Written kisses do not reach their destination, rather they are drunk up on the way by specters.

Nothing could be easier than simply to think about a person who is far away (or even dead), but *to communicate* with a distant person, this is something else entirely.[58] What troubles Kafka is his sense that when the person with whom one tries to communicate is not physically present, an imaginary being, a specter, is conjured up and maintained in her place, while another imaginary being, the specter of oneself (of one's self) appears to address it. To sustain the illusion of communicating with a distant person, one conjures up not just the specter of one's addressee, but also a simulacrum or specter of oneself. And it is 'with' these specters, to them and through them, that one communicates by letter. This is why, even though Kafka wrote hundreds of letters, including many to Milena Jesenská, he does not see letter-writing as 'natural communication' (*natürlicher Verkehr*): like all forms of telecommunication (he puts the telephone, the telegraph and the radio telegraph in the same enemy camp), letter-writing conjures up *Gespenster*, spectral creatures who surreptitiously take the place of both sender and receiver, alienating them from each other and from themselves. Kafka (or his specter) implicitly compares these creatures to vampires: '[W]riting letters is like exposing oneself in the presence of the thirstily waiting specters. Written kisses do not reach their destination, rather they are drunk up on the way by specters.' When one tries to communicate with someone

57. Kafka to Milena Jesenská, end of March 1922(?), in *Briefe an Milena* (New York, 1952), p.259-60.

58. Thinking about someone does not entail anticipating his or her thoughts or responses, but thinking about *communicating* with someone or actually communicating with that person does. For as Bakhtin put it, '[E]very word [*slovo*] is directed towards an *answer* and cannot escape the profound influence of the answering word that it anticipates'. Mikhaïl Bakhtin, *The Dialogic imagination* (Austin, TX, 1981), p.280. There is nothing inherently dialogic about focusing one's attention on an object, because as an object it cannot speak; but all human communication, real or imaginary, is dialogic, since it implies addressing oneself (one's self) to a (speaking) subject.

by letter, one offers up one's most intimate thoughts and feelings to the specters, who greedily suck them up before they can reach their destination. One can try to dismiss this argument by pointing out that the supposed impossibility of communicating by letter is exactly what Kafka so admirably succeeds in communicating, in this very letter. But this kind of objection assumes precisely what remains to be proved: namely, that the letter we are reading is really a communication between Franz Kafka and Milena Jesenská, and not a communication between and with their alien doubles, their specters.

Kafka's reflections on the impossibility of communication by letter draw attention to several features that are inherent to all discourse, but which letter-writing brings to the fore.[59] All discourse is dialogic, in the sense that it addresses itself to an interlocutor and anticipates the interlocutor's reactions: but the letter *explicitly* addresses itself to a specific but absent interlocutor. Second, though all discourse has an Imaginary (in Lacanian terms) dimension, because one cannot address oneself to another person without conjuring up mental images of oneself and one's interlocutor(s), letter-writing draws one's attention to this process.[60] In discourse these interdependent images or 'selves', the images of oneself and the receiver, are always being generated and modified; but one is usually not so conscious of these mediating images when engaged in 'live' conversation as one is when writing a letter. Hence Kafka's sense that when writing letters one communicates with both 'the specter of the addressee [and] with one's own specter'.

In stark contrast to Voltaire, for whom the post was a good communications medium, which could – at least in principle – always be relied upon to make 'the absent become [...] present' and carry one's letter to its destination, Kafka sees it as an alienating medium. Instead of nourishing the soul, letter-writing empties it of its vital substance; rather than making the soul of the writer present to that of the addressee, it conjures up specters who feed on them, thereby bringing into the world a *Zerrüttung der Seelen*, a derangement or unhinging of souls. For him, the post, like all telecommunications media, belongs to the ghostly 'opposing side' [*Gegenseite*]. For both writers, letter-writing conjures a presence (or 'present-ness'). In Voltaire's eyes, a letter conjures the real presence of sender and receiver, writer and reader, present to themselves and to each other, as self-identical as the message itself. While for Kafka, writing a

59. In *L'Equivoque littéraire* (Paris, 1990) Vincent Kaufmann reflects on what he sees as the paradoxical status of the modern letter-writer.

60. On the Imaginary, see Anthony Wilden's introduction to his translation of Lacan's so-called 'Rapport de Rome' (originally 'Fonction et champ de la parole et du langage en psychanalyse', in *Ecrits*), *Speech and language in psychoanalysis* (Baltimore, MD, 1981).

letter conjures specters who suck the life out of the sender and the receiver, deranging their souls, and who find themselves alienated from each other and from themselves: so that long before a letter leaves its sender it has been transformed into an affectless machine, like a replicant in Ridley Scott's *Blade runner*.[61] For Voltaire, at the high point of the early modern postal era, the letter was a consoling presence; while for Kafka, writing at the dawn of the age of modern telecommunications, it was a profoundly disturbing one.[62] Roland Barthes once disparagingly referred to Voltaire as 'The last of the happy writers', that is, the last writer for whom neither history nor writing itself posed a (moral, political or existential) problem.[63] In none of these respects could the same be said about Kafka. Indeed it would seem that there could not be a starker contrast between the attitudes of these two men toward the writing of letters, and toward writing in general. All the same, for both writers what was at stake was a thirst for epistolary communication, a spiritual investment in the post that was at least as substantial as the economic and political interests that brought publicly available postal services into existence.

Postmodern

In *The Post card,* Jacques Derrida offers a structural explanation of Kafka's sense that, whenever one writes, a spectral third party is always alienating one's meaning and frustrating one's desire for intimate communication by letter. 'Already within each sign', Derrida writes, 'in every mark or every stroke, there is distancing, *post,* what is necessary for it to be legible to another, another than you and me'.[64] I have just translated *l'éloignement,* the word that he places in apposition to *la poste,* as

61. In their discussion of Kafka's 'literary machine', Deleuze and Guattari claim that 'Il y a un vampirisme des lettres, un vampirisme proprement épistolaire' (There is a vampirism of letters, a vampirism that is specifically epistolary), *Kafka: pour une littérature mineure* (Paris, 1975), p.53. Siegert (*Relays,* p.4ff) places this letter in the historical and philosophical context of a media theory on which he will base the claim that: 'Once social life itself came to depend on systems for the transmission of information – systems that claimed a monopoly on long-distance discourses, both written and oral – love did not dream of interpreting the soul of the man or woman who had written the text of the letter it was reading, but dreamed instead of calculating postal modalities. "Written kisses don't reach their destination", Kafka declared, 'simply because the postal detour no longer led them to literature, but to the power of the media themselves.' (p.16-17).
62. In Janet Altman's formulation: 'Haunted by the interlocutor's absence, letter-writers conjure a presence through writing. [...] Letters... are the product of temporal absence, yet they are preoccupied with the compensatory creation of present-ness.' '"The triple register": introduction to temporal complexity in the letter novel', *L'Esprit créateur* 1:4 (Winter 1977), p.310.
63. Roland Barthes, 'Le dernier des écrivains heureux', in *Essais critiques* (Paris, 1964), p.94ff.
64. Derrida, *La Carte postale,* p.34. Translation modified. Emphasis added.

'distancing'; but it also means (among other things) 'taking away, removal' (of persons or things) and 'putting off' or 'postponement'. All these meanings are crucial to the points that Derrida is trying to make here.

First, he maintains that everything that is said or written (not just letters and other forms of so-called telecommunication) is necessarily inscribed at a certain temporal and spatial *distance* from both the agent who appears to say or write it and its nominal addressee. In all of these senses, he argues, inscriptions are postal, they are 'always already' relays and relayed. From the earliest formulations of the deconstructive project (for example, in *De la grammatologie* and *L'Ecriture et la différence* [both 1967]), Derrida had questioned the classic opposition between presence and absence, speech and writing, and in *The Post card* (1980) he makes no distinction between 'natural' (or live) communication and technologically-assisted (or tele)communication.

Second, in principle, the inscription can therefore always be read, lost or even *taken away* by a third party. It follows that the post is a name for that which, within each mark or sign, posts it, places it at a distance and removes it from 'you' and 'me', terms that have to be bracketed once the original distance has been noted. Derrida ostensibly wrote all the words in his book on post cards, personal messages that could be read by anyone. But if a sign is (in Umberto Eco's definition) 'everything that, on the grounds of a previously existing social convention, can be taken as something standing for something else',[65] then the signs that compose *any* message can always be read, removed or even stolen by someone (perhaps a specter) other than 'you' and 'I', its nominal receiver and sender.

Once Voltaire's traditional notion of communication – which posits the self-presence of the sender, the message and the receiver – has been called into question, there is no tenable difference between 'live' or 'natural' communication and telecommunication: '[A]s soon as there is, there is *différance* [difference, deferment] [...], there is postal maneuvering, relays, delay, anticipation, destination, telecommunicating network, the possibility and therefore the fatal necessity of going astray, etc.'[66] Derrida makes these points affirmatively, without nostalgia for self-presence or 'natural communication', as befits a 'postmodern' philosopher: all 'communication' is postal (communication at a distance, telecommunication), and all (tele)communication entails delay,

65. Umberto Eco, *A Theory of semiotics* (Bloomington, IN, 1975), p.194, n.53.

66. *La Carte postale*, p.66. It is for this reason that Derrida takes issue (in 'Le Facteur de la vérité') with Lacan's claim (in the 'Seminar on "The purloined letter"') that 'a letter always arrives at its destination'. On the notion of *différance*, see 'La différance', in Jacques Derrida, *Marges de la philosophie* (Paris, 1972).

postponement. Since it would be prohibitively expensive for a postal system to relay letters and packages immediately upon reception, it must collect, postmark and sort mail (at 'Post Offices') before sending it off in packages at regular intervals. But here, too, the postal service merely makes the postality of all communication more visible: to the *original* difference or deferment that is inherent to all being, the post adds another, systematic delay.

1. A brief history of Western European postal services in the early modern period

The establishment of efficient postal services, and of the avenues of communication upon which postal services rely, has been a constant feature of empires, from the ancient world (for example, China, the Aztec empire, Egypt, Persia and Rome) to the present.[1] As Lucien Febvre has observed, '[R]oads and communication routes are elements that generate or conserve States and empires'.[2] But by the end of the twelfth century little remained in Europe of the Roman *cursus publicus*, the exclusive post road system that had enabled reliable and speedy imperial communications with the governors of distant provinces, and without which Rome could not have become a vast empire.[3] Postal routes had become so unsafe that royal horse messengers carried swords. Moreover the absence of postal relays severely limited the distance that a messenger could cover in a given period of time, making delivery times slow: in the spring of 1215 it took a rider 30 days to travel from Liège to Rome.[4]

Throughout the Middle Ages, European postal arrangements were purely local in scope and restricted to official messages. As there was not yet any notion of state sovereignty over postal routes, various private message-delivery services were created to serve the needs of the powerful. On foot, on horseback and (in the case of Venice) by boat, messengers traveled from place to place on behalf of princes, monastic orders (the Benedictines of Cluny, the Cistercians of Cîteaux), courts of justice, guilds, the Hanseatic League, universities, municipalities and within

1. See Whyman, *The Pen and the people*, p.48; Harold Innis, *Empire and communications* (Toronto, 1951); Richard Kieblowicz, *News in the mail: the press, post office, and public information 1700-1860* (New York, 1989), p.5-6; Behringer, *Thurn und Taxis*, p.22-23; Behringer, 'Communications revolutions'; Siegert, *Relays*, p.3, 5ff; Anthony C. Wilson, 'A thousand years of postal and telecommunications services in Russia', *New Zealand Slavonic journal* (1989-1990), p.137-38. In *Empire of letters*, Eve Tavor Bannet remarks that 'The extension of letter-writing to all manner and ranks of people in late seventeenth- and eighteenth-century Britain and British-America by means of manuals such as Hill's coincided with the expansion of empire, which was its *sine qua non*'. However she also notes that epistolary networks permitted only 'putative' government control of the empire. Bannet, *Empire of letters*, p.4.
2. Lucien Febvre, *Studi su Riforma e Rinascimento e altri scritti su problemi di metodo e di geografia storica*, Preface D. Canimori, trad. Di C. Vitanti (Turin, 1966) [orig. edn Paris, 1957], p.690. Cited in Plebani, 'La correspondenza nell'antico regime', p.47, n.18. See Whyman, *The Pen and the people*, p.47-48.
3. Behringer, *Thurn und Taxis*, p.2-4. The English word 'travel' is derived from the French *travail* (work).
4. Behringer, *Thurn und Taxis*, p.5.

cities.[5] In Flanders and southern Germany, the *Metzgerpost* (run by the butchers' guild) was required to deliver mail for the authorities and, occasionally, for merchants.[6] Likewise various municipal guilds created messenger services for interurban correspondence. To a limited extent, most of these systems (with the exception of the Teutonic Knights and the courts of justice) would eventually also carry private letters.[7] In late fourteenth-century France, even royal couriers began carrying messages for other institutions.

Due to its early rise to commercial and military ascendancy, the Republic of Venice was probably the first European power whose courier system was used for unofficial correspondence.[8] It would soon become a general practice for these theoretically closed systems to carry letters for private individuals.[9] For during what Braudel has called the 'long sixteenth century' (1450-1650) Europe underwent radical economic and demographic growth that resulted in the creation of the first 'world economy'.[10] Messengers, whether on foot or on horseback, were no longer sufficient to enable European merchants to manage their wide-spread business interests. In fifteenth-century Italy, economic centers such as Rome, Venice and Milan, established an extensive network of messengers, first on foot and then on horseback, that connected them with Holland and other economic centers of Northern Europe. In addition to these couriers, a limited number of 'posts' – stations where fresh horses and riders could be supplied – were set up between some of these cities, eliminating the need for rest stops. Due to the politically fragmented state of the Italian peninsula, there was no real network of posts before the late fifteenth century. Only a much larger political

5. On *messageries* in France, see Marchand, *Le Maître de poste et le messager*, p.21ff. It is unfortunate that this otherwise excellent work contains no footnotes.
6. Gottfried North, *Die Post: Ihre Geschichte in Wort und Bild* (Heidelberg, 1995), p.30. In principle, if not in practice, these were all closed systems, circulating only the messages of their respective institutions. Siegert, *Relays*, p.7-8.
7. Laurin Zilliacus, *From pillar to post: the troubled history of the post* (London, 1956), p.43.
8. Cattani, *Storia dei servizi postali nella repubblica di Venezia et catalogo dei timbri Postali*, p.5ff. Cattani notes that as early as 959 the doge sought to achieve exclusive control over the mails, by forbidding private contractors to carry letters. However that effort does not seem to have succeeded, since on 6 January 1305, the Senate decreed that all couriers would thenceforth be under control of the Republic and officially recognized the profession of Procaccia [carrier]. *Storia dei servizi postali*, p.9.
9. Kalmus, *Weltgeschichte der Post*, p.51ff; Paul Charbon, *Quelle belle invention que la poste!* (Paris, 1991), p.13-29.
10. Fernand Braudel, *Civilization and capitalism, 15th-18th century* vol.3, *The Perspective of the world* (New York, 1984). What Braudel calls an '*économie-monde*' (his translation of *Weltwirtschaft*) was a much more limited, fragmentary system than what Wallerstein calls the 'European world economy'. Immanuel Wallerstein, *The Modern world system: capitalist agriculture and the origins of the European world economy in the sixteenth century* (New York, 1974). See also Kalmus, *Weltgeschichte*, p.357.

entity, such as the Habsburg Empire that took shape at the end of the sixteenth century, would be capable of organizing such a system.[11] Although Venetian mail traveled primarily by sea, its post was also the first to establish overland relays, for couriers traveling between Venice, Bologna, and Rome.[12] Even so, in the second half of the fifteenth century it took four days for a letter from Venice to reach Rome in the warm months, and seven days in the cold and rainy months.[13]

In the early sixteenth century, European sovereigns began to realize that an efficient postal system could provide them with substantial economic and political benefits. As the demand for service grew among merchants and others, rulers authorized use of the post for the dispatch of private letters, and discovered in this service both a source of revenue – which they sought to monopolize – and a means of controlling what their subjects wrote to each other.[14] They sought to bring postal activities under their control and suppress rival postal organizations.[15] During the early modern period, the emerging modern states did not yet operate their postal systems, but instead employed private contractors for this purpose. This chapter focuses on the emergence of state-sponsored postal services in the three great powers of early modern Europe: the Habsburg Empire, the United Kingdom and France; it also considers the salient features of smaller European postal systems of the period. The chapter concludes with a discussion of the arrangements for transmission of mail between these systems.[16]

Thurn and Taxis: a family business

In the late fifteenth century, the growth of private demand for letter-carrying brought a number of profitable businesses into existence, the

11. Kalmus, *Weltgeschichte*, p.53.
12. Cattani, *Storia dei servizi postali*, p.6.
13. *Storia dei servizi postali*, p.13-14. In Venice an official registry, the *Mariegola*, was kept, starting in 1489; the Mariegola (interrupted only once in the 1760s) has become a treasure of information about the Venetian postal services.
14. In the early modern world letters exchanged between merchants served as the model for the earliest private correspondence. Plebani, 'La correspondenza nell'antico regime', p.51. As Plebani remarks, the 'letter copy', with the same format (composition, folding, indication of addressee) as the original, also derives from business correspondence.
15. '[I]n the sixteenth century, the organization and control of postal routes became a privileged field for the exercise of power.' Plebani, 'La correspondenza nell'antico regime', p.47. See discussion of the relationship between state-controlled postal systems and the violation of postal secrecy in Chapter 3, p.95-104.
16. '[T]his history of the posts [...] cannot be a history of the posts; primarily because it concerns the very possibility of history, of all the concepts, too, of history, of tradition, of the transmission or interruptions, goings astray, etc. And then because such a "history of the posts" would be but a minuscule *envoi* in the network that it allegedly would analyze.' Derrida, *The Post card*, p.66.

most famous of which was operated by the family that would eventually be known as Thurn and Taxis. Since the late thirteenth century, the Tassis (or Tassi) had been operating a courier system in the Italian city-states. From their roots in the Bergamo area of Lombardy, they eventually developed an extensive network of dedicated post roads with relays that radiated throughout the vast Habsburg Empire (Spain, Naples, the Low Countries and Austria) from their seat in Brussels.[17] The first Tassis to be involved with postal services was a certain Janetto Tassis (*c.*1450-*c.*1517), whose family name was soon changed to the German *Dachs* and later to the Germanized *Taxis*, which also had an aristocratic connotation. The badger (*tasso* in Italian) ultimately became part of the family's coat of arms.[18] In Germany, the post was imported from Italy as a technical innovation, as a way of ensuring more rapid delivery of official messages, rather than (as in Italy) in response to the requirements of international trade. Since the main residence of Maximilian I, the German king (and later Holy Roman Emperor [1493-1519]) and husband of Maria of Burgundy, was in Innsbruck, while his son Philip dwelled in the Burgundian Low Countries, and his daughter Margaret at the French court, Maximilian required a means of ensuring secure communications over this entire region.[19] The Tassis had become known to Maximilian in their capacity as couriers for the pope and the Republic of Venice. In 1490, he engaged Janetto Tassis, the latter's brother Francesco (or Franz) and nephew Johann Baptista, to set up an express courier system between these areas, with changes of horses and an additional connection to Rome. Since the Taxis postmasters and couriers were not imperial subjects, Maximilian and his successors could not simply com-

17. On the history of the Thurn and Taxis family and its postal system see Behringer, *Thurn und Taxis*; Martin Dallmeier and Martha Schad, *Das fürstliche Haus Thurn und Taxis: 300 Jahre Geschichte in Bildern* (Regensburg, 1996); Werner Muenzberg, *500 Jahre Post: Thurn und Taxis* (Regensburg, 1990); Dallmeier, *Quellen zur Geschichte*; and Siegfried Grillmeyer, *Habsburgs Diener in Post und Politik: das 'Haus' Thurn und Taxis zwischen 1745 und 1867* (Mainz, 2005). For the history of the Taxis post in a European context, see Kalmus's *Weltgeschichte*. Tassis postal routes traversed France to Spain and the Italian city-states, beyond which private messengers took over. Moreover from 1474 to 1539 the Tassis directed the papal Post Office in Rome. Behringer, *Thurn und Taxis*, p.24, 36. Since the Habsburgs had no interests to pursue in northern and eastern Germany, the Tassis post did not extend into those regions. *Thurn und Taxis*, p.30.
18. According to one version of the Tassis story (cited in Zilliacus, *From pillar to post*, p.47), the family name came from the custom, among families of couriers from the Bergamo area, 'of tying a badger skin over the foreheads of their horses, presumably for protection against insects, low branches or falling stones in the mountain passes, or possibly against the evil eye of those that possessed such magic'. The first Tasso to become famous for his achievements outside of the family business was the poet Torquato Tasso, author of *La Gerusalemme liberata* (1580). Rainer Maria Rilke composed his *Duino elegies* at the castle of Princess Maria von Thurn und Taxis-Hohenlohe and dedicated them to her.
19. Kalmus, *Weltgeschichte*, p.58.

pel them to serve, but had to pay them in cash.[20] Habsburg rulers could also seek to enlist the support of the Taxis by offering them prestigious titles. In 1501 Maximilian and Philip had Franz Taxis named 'capitaine et maistre de nos postes' in the Burgundian Netherlands. In 1512 Maximilian rewarded the Taxis brothers and their sons with a grant of patent nobility (or *Briefadel*), and the family name became *von* Taxis; soon thereafter (1518), Queen Juana (Johanna) of Spain and her son Charles V 'naturalized' Johann Baptista von Taxis and two of his brothers, thus conferring upon them a status legally equivalent to that of the native-born Spanish nobility.[21] When the Brussels branch of the family was granted hereditary nobility in 1624, it became necessary to legitimize that nobility by identifying noble ancestors whose title could be added to the family name. These ancestors were duly discovered in the Torriani or della Torre [tower] (which became *von Thurn* in German; *de la Tour* in French) family, who had ruled in Milan and Lombardy until 1311; in 1650 Habsburg Emperor Ferdinand III gave the Taxis permission to call themselves *Thurn* and Taxis and to add the image of a tower to the family coat of arms.[22]

With Philip of Burgundy's ascension to the throne of Spain in 1504, the Habsburgs became a great European power. In 1505, drawing on the enormous profits from his silver mines in the Tyrol, Emperor Maximilian signed a contract with Franz Taxis, whereby Taxis would establish and manage a network of relays and riders – the first in modern Europe – that linked Maximilian's court with the Netherlands, the Tyrol and the Spanish court, in exchange for an annual lump sum payment.[23] Since Maximilian's foreign wars made demands on his purse such that he could not pay his bills in a timely fashion, the Taxis quickly started carrying

20. Behringer, 'Communications revolutions', p.341.
21. A few dates in the social rise of the Taxis family: in 1608 they were raised to the rank of *Freiherr* (baron), in 1615 their title of Postmasters General became hereditary, and in 1624 they were raised to the rank of *Graf* (count); in 1681 the Taxis were granted princely rank in the Spanish court, and finally, in 1695 they acquired the rank of *Gefürsteter Graf* (princely count).
22. Behringer, *Thurn und Taxis*, p.205. On the Thurn and Taxis coat of arms, see Bernhard Peter, 'Wappen der Grafen und Fürsten von Thurn und Taxis' at http://www.dr-bernhard-peter.de/Heraldik/thurntaxis.htm (last accessed 29 September 2015). The family's website (http://www.thurnundtaxis.de/en/family/in-regensburg-for-250-years/history.html, last accessed 29 September 2015) tells the story this way: 'Emperor Ferdinand III recognized the Taxis as successors of the Torriani, and granted them permission to incorporate the Torre arms, and name, with their own. The tower (torre) became Thurn.'
23. Behringer, *Thurn und Taxis*, p.21. Because Maximilian's court was always traveling, at the beginning there were no fixed postal routes, except between Innsbruck and Mecheln; when postal couriers were not needed, they were 'on leave'. Kalmus, *Weltgeschichte*, p.59. Behringer (*Thurn und Taxis*, p.35) has shown that, despite some of the feudal terminology, the 1505 postal accord set a new precedent, since it defined Franz Tassis as an independent contractor.

private correspondence, but only for those individuals who could afford very high fees.[24] Fortunately for the Taxis, Maximilian's son Phillip, by then king of Castile, was much wealthier and paid his bills on time and in full. The Taxis post would soon become a vast network, linking the Burgundian (later Spanish) Lowlands, Burgundy, the Germanic Empire, the hereditary states of Austria, northern Italy, Naples and Spain. The Thurn and Taxis post in the Habsburg territories was the first European postal system to become open to the public, a century before this would happen in England and France.[25] Contemporaries viewed the emergence of this trans-European postal service as tantamount to the discovery of a new world.[26] The Taxis established offices in Austria (where the rival Paar family already ran its own postal system), Spain, Germany, the Low Countries, Scandinavia, Eastern Europe and in parts of Italy (Rome, Venice, Trent) that were not part of the Habsburg dominions; all of these were run by members of the Taxis family.[27] Beyond its political importance, the Taxis post began to play a crucial economic role, ensuring rapid delivery of information between Antwerp and Naples (via Innsbruck and Rome), thus allowing for the integration of the northern and southern poles of Wallerstein's 'European world economy'. Following the practice in the duchy of Milan, the Taxis sought to increase the speed and efficiency of their couriers by having time sheets (dockets with the so-called *Cito* mark) attached to their mail.[28]

In 1516, the Habsburgs were at war with France. Emperor Charles (Karl) V nonetheless made an agreement with Francis I of France that would enable Taxis couriers to travel across France on their way to Spain. This would not be the last time that these warring empires sought to maintain their postal relations.[29] It was in the same year that, follow-

24. Behringer, *Thurn und Taxis*, p.30-33; Kalmus, *Weltgeschichte*, p.57.
25. Behringer, 'Communications revolutions', p.341-42, 347. 'One result was the fixing of communications routes and the establishment of permanent "offices": this was the origin of "post offices"'. 'Communications revolutions', p.342.
26. 'In the literature of the early modern period the discovery of America was compared to a contemporary invention: the "invention" of the postal system by Franz von Taxis.' Behringer, *Thurn und Taxis*, p.13.
27. Although the Habsburgs allowed the Paar family to run the Austrian postal system, in direct competition with the Thurn and Taxis, they entrusted the Taxis with the operation of the secretive Black Cabinet there. Emil König, *Schwarze Cabinette: eine Geschichte der Briefgeheimniss Entheiligungen, Perlustrationen und Brieflogen, des postalischen Secretdienstes, des 'kleinen Cabinets', der 'Briefrevisionsbureaus' und sonstiger Briefgeheimnisverletzungen* (Berlin and Leipzig, 1899), p.70-71. I discuss the European Black Cabinets in Chapter 3, p.95-123.
28. Behringer, 'Communications revolutions', p.339.
29. Vaillé, *Histoire générale*, vol.5, p.452-53. This multivolume work remains the most thorough and reliable source of information on the history of postal administration in France through the end of the old régime. Siegert (*Relays*, p.14ff) posits a link between the postal ideal of communication by letter and the project of world peace. Although states sought to ensure that postal relations continued normally in times of war, they could not keep

ing the signing of a new contract with Franz von Taxis, Charles V transformed the Taxis post into a franchise system, open to the public, that would endure within the realm of the imperial (*kaiserliche*) post (after 1597 the *Reichspost*) until the Napoleonic wars: the Taxis managed the system, but transferred the financial risk to innkeeper franchisees. During the regency (1643-1661) of Anne of Austria in France, an agreement prohibited the secret letter-opening office (or Black Cabinet) from opening mail carried between Flanders and Spain.[30] Nevertheless such an agreement must have been quite exceptional. For war concerned relations between states, whereas mail involved relations between private individuals; in times of war (that is, most of the time) states had a vital interest in intercepting the military and diplomatic communications of their enemies.[31] Although its ideals carried no political weight, the Republic of Letters posited a relationship between its cosmopolitan vision and the postal service. Moreover, as Siegert has pointed out, there is a conceptual link between the postal ideal of universal epistolary communication between individuals and the project of world peace.[32] In any case, when the international postal service was interrupted, the managers of the various state-sponsored postal services sought and obtained indemnities.[33]

In times of war and peace, it also became necessary to find means of ensuring the security of international communications, which is why the Taxis perfected an encrypted writing system. The post horn, to which Franz von Taxis obtained exclusive rights in Habsburg territory, became the symbol of the imperial post, and hence of the post in general.[34] Moreover, as Behringer has pointed out, the creation in 1530 of the *ordinari* post (riders, and later coaches, that circulated on a regular basis) produced a qualitative transformation in the communications system: its periodicity influenced all kinds of correspondence (government, com-

---

'irregular' troops from interfering with the post. Lucien Bély, *Espions et ambassadeurs au temps de Louis XIV* (Paris, 1990), p.138.

30. Eugène Vaillé, *Le Cabinet noir* (Paris, 1950), p.65.
31. Bély, *Espions et ambassadeurs*, p.138.
32. Goodman, *The Republic of letters*, p.20-21; Siegert, *Relays*, p.14ff.
33. Vaillé, *Histoire générale*, vol.5, p.301ff and Christian Nodé-Langlois, 'La poste internationale de 1669-1815' (Doctoral dissertation, Paris, Faculté de droit et de sciences économiques, 1960), p.153. On the aspiration to 'eternal postal peace', see Siegert, *Relays*, p.2-3.
34. Behringer, *Thurn und Taxis*, p.364. Behringer also discusses the use of the Roman god Mercury as a symbol of postal speed in *Im Zeichen des Merkur*, p.650ff. See also Albert Hiller, *Das große Buch vom Posthorn* (Wilhelmshaven, 1985). Even today, in many European countries the post horn remains the symbol of the state postal system. In Chapter 6, p.167-71, I discuss the role of the post horn in the 'soundscape' of early modern Europe. Thomas Pynchon makes brilliant use of the post horn symbol in *The Crying of lot 49* (New York, 1986; orig. pub 1965).

mercial, individual) and gave rise to periodic newspapers as well.[35] Soon the 20,000 couriers of the Taxis postal system covered most of Europe (including the Italian city-states, France and Spain) with a speedy, regular and efficient relay system. On occasion, the Taxis post also provided delivery of mail from countries, such as England, that were beyond the geographical limits of its own system.[36] These improved possibilities for communication brought Europeans closer together: in the sixteenth century, Taxis relays were between four and five miles apart, and the average speed of transport was slightly less than one mile per hour.[37] This meant that letters posted in Brussels or Mecheln took five and a half days to reach Innsbruck in summer, six and a half days in winter; to arrive at Paris, 44 (54) hours; and they got to Granada or Naples in 15 (18) days.[38] The breadth, depth and efficiency of the imperial post under Charles V (Emperor of Spain starting in 1516, Holy Roman Emperor from 1519 to 1556) were such that this period has rightly been termed 'a golden age for communications'.[39]

After the defeat of François I by the imperial forces at Pavia in 1525 and well into the seventeenth century, a significant portion of northern France (the Artois, Flanders) fell under Habsburg control. However at the beginning of this period, various communal postal services delivered mail within the provinces, while the Royal Taxis post dealt with mail from areas outside the provinces or destined to those areas; the Taxis couriers quickly encroached upon the privileges of the communal services of the Low Countries. In the sixteenth century, the stability of the Taxis post (based, at this time, in Brussels) was threatened by its reliance upon Spanish financing. After the voluntary abdication of Charles V (1556), both the Empire and the Taxis postal entity split into several branches, precipitating a financial crisis and near collapse of the business.[40] It did not fully recover until after the last few years of the century,

35. Behringer, 'Communications revolutions', p.349-50. I shall return to this question in Chapter 6, p.180-81.

36. '[W]e find the English Exchequer showing large payments to "Master of the Posts Francis de Taxis" for conveying the correspondence of Henry VIII to and from Italy and France.' Zilliacus, *From pillar to post*, p.50.

37. Dohrn-van Rossum, *History of the hour*, p.338.

38. North, *Die Post*, p.32.

39. Behringer, 'Communications revolutions', p.348. He adds that 'There had not been such efficient infrastructure since the days of the *Imperium romanum* – a fact that has gone curiously unmentioned in Anglo- and Francophone historiography and has therefore also escaped the attention of theorists of communication from Albion to Innis and McLuhan and all later authors.'

40. The business's financial crisis was aggravated by the revolt of the Netherlands, confessional conflicts within empire, the 1557 bankruptcy of the Spanish state and, later, by William of Orange's coup d'état in 1577. It recovered thanks to the 'postal reformation' of 1577-1595. See Dohrn-van Rossum, *History of the hour*, p.340; Behringer, *Thurn und Taxis*, p.54ff, 73-74.

when, following the stabilization of conditions in the Catholic provinces of the Netherlands, Habsburg Kaiser Rudolph II appointed Leonard von Taxis Postmaster General of the Empire (1595), and declared (1597) that what he called the *Reichspost* was an imperial prerogative (*droit régalien*), and made its unauthorized exercise punishable.[41] The idea that operation of the postal system was an imperial prerogative became almost universal in the seventeenth century, and was linked to the modern notion of sovereignty.[42]

For over a century, postal service in the Habsburg Empire had not actually belonged to the Taxis family, but to the Kaiser and the King of Spain, whom the Taxis served on a contractual basis. However in 1615 Lamoral von Taxis succeeded in transforming the business into an extremely prosperous hereditary fief, which it would remain for 190 years, until the abdication of Kaiser Franz II in 1806.[43] Although the Taxis post would long retain its importance as a long-distance and 'international' mail service (see below), it now had to compete with various emergent regional (in the German *Länder*) and national mail services for the delivery of local mail.[44] For example, the Brandenburg State Post was founded after the Thirty Years War under Elector Friedrich Wilhelm, providing service from Memel to Berlin to Kleve.[45] In the hereditary states even the Austrian Habsburgs eventually created postal services that were separate from the imperial post.[46] Since these new postal systems were exclusively devoted to specific regions or nations, they covered their territory more densely than did the imperial post, while linking together the transport of letters, passengers and small goods.[47] Following the War of Spanish Succession (1701-1714), the

41. Behringer, *Thurn und Taxis*, p.204; Dohrn-van Rossum, *History of the hour*, p.340.
42. Nodé-Langlois, 'La poste internationale', p.103ff. Siegert frames this development in terms of the transition from imperial postal systems to absolutist or territorial postal systems. 'The interpretation of *principium rationis* as *principium reddendae rationis* thus described precisely the transition from the old imperial postal systems – in which the delivery of being constantly transcended the people – to the new absolutist postal systems and their new vassals, or subjects' (*Relays*, p.9).
43. Behringer calls the seventeenth century 'the century in which the [Taxis] post became a gold mine'. (*Thurn und Taxis*, p.204). He also notes (p.149, 191ff) that not only did the Thurn and Taxis post outlive the empire by 60 years, albeit in new form, but a diversified family business has continued to thrive. The family's brewery was sold in 1996 but the family still produces beer under the Thurn and Taxis brand.
44. Dallmeier, *Quellen zur Geschichte*, p.141ff; Kalmus, *Weltgeschichte*, p.357ff.
45. The Prussian State Post emerged directly from the Brandenburger post. North, *Die Post*, p.35. After the Seven Years War, Frederick II appointed 1500 French officials to the Prussian Post, in order to improve the administration and income of the system. The officials of the 'französische Postregie' were hated by the people, so much so that (according to North, *Die Post*, p.37) the spying and denunciations were reciprocal.
46. Nodé-Langlois, 'La poste internationale', p.36-40.
47. Dohrn-van Rossum, *History of the hour*, p.342.

Thurn and Taxis temporarily lost control of the post in the Lowlands and moved their main office to Frankfurt-am-Main, which became the new hub of the system. Thanks to the diligence of its administrators, the frequency of mail deliveries improved dramatically: by 1750 the company was able to provide daily service from Regensburg (the residence of the Thurn and Taxis family) to Vienna and from Strasbourg to Paris and Munich.

The influence of the Thurn and Taxis family reached its apex in the middle of the eighteenth century, when it acquired a seat and voice on the Imperial Council. Set off by a yellow background, the black eagle of the Habsburg empire had become the symbol of the Thurn and Taxis post, which itself was synonymous with speed: 'By day and by night', writes Behringer, 'the resounding sound of the post horn became the embodiment of speed, the symbol of an entire epoch.'[48] The yellow color of the post horn derived from the imperial coat of arms (black eagle on yellow background), and is still the color of the post in Denmark, Germany, Sweden and parts of Central Europe.[49] The Thurn and Taxis postal monopoly was finally nationalized in 1867.

Postal service in the British Isles

Early in his reign Henry VIII appointed Brian Tuke England's first Master of the Posts, but for nearly two centuries Henry and his successors were too fearful of sedition to actually encourage the delivery of private correspondence.[50] Although post boys were allowed to include private letters in their packets, the post primarily served the interests of the royal court. Despite the poor condition of the roads, the expressions 'post' and 'post haste' became synonymous with speedy delivery.[51] Postal couriers conveyed mail packets on horseback along four regular routes (to Scotland, Ireland and Plymouth, as well as to Dover and the Conti-

48. Behringer, *Thurn und Taxis*, p.364, and *Im Zeichen des Merkur*, p.644ff, 653-57, 665ff, 684ff. See my discussion of speed in Chapter 6, p.176-80.

49. *Thurn und Taxis*, p.364.

50. Howard Robinson, *The British Post Office: a history* (Princeton, NJ, 1948), p.7. See also Philip Beale, *History of the post in England from the Romans to the Stuarts* (Aldershot, 1998); and Kenneth Ellis, *The Post Office in the eighteenth century: a study in administrative history* (London, New York and Toronto, 1958). For a broader social and cultural perspective on the period from 1600 to 1800, see Whyman, *The Pen and the people.* Richelieu believed that letter-writing among the king's subjects would cause economic and political disaster: '[L]e commerce des lettres bannirait absolument celui de la marchandise, ruinerait l'agriculture et déserterait en peu de temps la pépinière des soldats qui s'élève plutôt dans la rudesse et l'ignorance que dans la politesse des sciences.' Armand Jacques du Plessis, duc de Richelieu, *Testament politique*, ed. Louis André (Paris, 1947). Cited by Janet Altman, 'La politique de l'art épistolaire au XVIIIe siècle', in *Art de la lettre, art de la conversation à l'époque classique en France* (Paris, 1995), p.143.

51. Robinson, *The British Post Office*, p.8.

nent).[52] Later than had been the case on the Continent (especially in the Habsburg empire), the crown eventually recognized the advantages, in terms of security and revenue, of a state-controlled system for delivery of private correspondence between cities, and it contracted or farmed the right to operate that system.[53] Even though there was some movement in the 1630s toward the establishment of a public postal service,[54] it was not until 1655, after the execution of Charles I, that Cromwell placed the Post Office directly under the control of his Secretary of State, John Thurloe. After the Restoration the Post Office was finally placed on a strong foundation by passage of the Act of 1660, which became known as the Post Office Charter.[55] Even so, the growing profits from the royal monopoly were mostly used to establish various pensions, rather than to improve the system's service to the public. Moreover despite such modest innovations as the construction of new byroads that connected the main post roads (of which there were six in 1660, all radiating from London), and the invention of date-stamps and post labels ('to be signed by the postmasters stating the hour of arrival and dispatch of each mail'), overall rates of travel did not greatly improve, as roads were still maintained in a rather primitive fashion.[56]

At the time of the Restoration, London had become a burgeoning metropolis of over a half-million inhabitants (one-tenth of the population of England), a situation that created a pressing need for better local mail service. There was but one General Letter Office in the city, where persons (or their servants) could call for their mail: it was easier to send a letter from Westminster in the western part of London to Edinburgh than from that same district to Blackwall in the eastern part of town. Finally, despite considerable opposition, William Dockwra was allowed to create a Penny Post (so called because it delivered letters for a penny) in 1680, for delivery of mail within London. With the support of his associates (a group of Whig 'undertakers', the most important of whom was Lord Shaftesbury), Dockwra devised an ingenious system in which all letters weighing less than a pound were prepaid at the same rate rather than charged to the receiver according to the number of sheets in the letter, a change that reduced the time needed to process letters. Dockwra also ensured the safe and timely delivery of

52. *The British Post Office*, p.21-22.

53. Whyman, *The Pen and the people*, p.48.

54. '[I]n 1635, Thomas Witherings offered a proposal to reorganize the "Letter Office" for public use. A central London office coordinated mails on six main post roads and charged 2d per letter.' Whyman, *The Pen and the people*, p.48. See also 'Postal system', *Encyclopaedia Britannica* (2006). Encyclopaedia Britannica Online (http://search.eb.com/eb/article-15425, last accessed 19 September 2015).

55. *The Pen and the people*, p.48.

56. Robinson, *The British Post Office*, p.58ff, 64ff.

letters by requiring the use of postmarks to indicate time and place of reception (a practice that the Thurn and Taxis post had inaugurated at the beginning of the sixteenth century).[57] Moreover the Penny Post furnished the Whigs with a cheap and expeditious way of distributing anti-papist propaganda. Meanwhile the Duke of York (the future James II) had been granted the profits of the Post Office by an Act of Parliament. He successfully brought suit against Dockwra, arguing that the Penny Post infringed on his postal monopoly. When Shaftesbury was forced to flee the country in 1682, the Penny Post was taken over by York and his Postmaster General, Lord Arlington.[58] It was only in 1685 that 'the post office became a single, integrated, government-run service'.[59] After the Glorious Revolution of 1688, Dockwra briefly regained control of his 'invention', whose 'very commodious' service won enthusiastic admiration throughout the next century.[60] Even so it was not until 1765 that the authorities were permitted to establish Penny Posts outside of London.[61]

Postal service in Ireland and Scotland suffered from habitual neglect throughout the seventeenth century. Finally, due to the heavy financial burden imposed by the War of Spanish Succession, the Act of 1711 created a unified Post Office for the British Isles. The Act increased postal rates, established a weekly packet boat service to Ireland, and thoroughly revised the 1660 postal regulations; it would remain the fundamental postal law until Victoria became queen in 1837.[62] Under the stewardship of Ralph Allen (the model for Fielding's Squire Allworthy in *Tom Jones*), postal service and revenues increased significantly during the first half of the eighteenth century.[63] Nevertheless the Post Office remained rife with corruption and inefficiencies. What finally did improve after 1760, and in dramatic fashion, was the quality of the roads, as English road builders began to make the first hard-surfaced highways. These new highways made it possible for the Post Office to use mail coaches throughout the entire land, so that, for example, by 1786 a coach could travel from London to Edinburgh in sixty hours. Like passengers on today's high-speed trains, some travelers complained that the speed of the mail coach prevented them from viewing the scenery.[64]

57. *The British Post Office*, p.71ff. See also Whyman, *The Pen and the people*, p.52-53.
58. How, *Epistolary spaces*, p.58.
59. Bannet. *Empire of letters*, p.9.
60. *Empire of letters*, p.85-86.
61. *Empire of letters*, p.111.
62. *Empire of letters*, p.90ff.
63. *Empire of letters*, p.99ff. See also Ellis, *The Post Office in the eighteenth century*, p.38ff; Whyman, *The Pen and the people*, p.55-57.
64. Robinson, *The British Post Office*, p.140.

The French post

> 'Metzger', it occurred to her, 'what is a post-master'?
> 'Guy in the scullery', replied Metzger authoritatively from the bathroom, 'in charge of all the heavy stuff, canner kettles, gunboats, Dutch ovens...'.
>
> *The Crying of lot 49*[65]

In the late 1470s, King Louis XI of France (1461-1483) instituted a set of relays (or *postes assises*) at which his couriers could mount fresh horses, in order to shorten the delivery time of his messages and as part of an overall strategy of consolidating the power of the French state.[66] Shortly thereafter, the Comptroller General of the king's riders, Robert Paon, began the construction of the 'post roads' (roads equipped with *postes*, or relays) on which the riders were required to travel, and which were made available to private travelers early in the next century.[67] In the sixteenth century, these relays enabled a courier to cover 90 kilometers in a single day.[68] They were originally placed at intervals of approximately seven leagues (30 km, 18.6 miles), an improvement that is recorded in Perrault's classic fairy tale (1697) about an ogre with 'seven-league boots'.[69] At the end of *Le Petit Poucet* [*Hop-O'-My Thumb* or *Little Tom Thumb*, in English] the tiny hero becomes a royal courier and uses the magic boots to make a fortune delivering express messages for amorous young maidens: '[U]ne infinité de dames lui donnaient tout ce qu'il voulait, pour avoir des nouvelles de leurs Amants et ce fut là son plus grand gain.' (An infinite number of ladies gave him all he wanted in order to have news of their lovers, and that was how he made his greatest

65. Pynchon, *The Crying of lot 49*, p.46.
66. Vaillé, *Histoire des postes*, p.28-30.
67. Chauvet, *Introduction à l'histoire postale*, p.32; Vaillé, *Histoire des postes*, p.28-31.
68. Antoine Graziani, *La Grande Aventure de la poste* (Paris, 1965), p.44, tells an amusing story about one of these riders: 'L'usage voulait que le messager baise le pli qu'il avait porté avant de le remettre à son destinataire. Un de ces messagers, un débutant sans doute, avait été chargé de porter une lettre à la reine de Navarre. "N'oublie pas de la baiser avant de la lui remettre", lui avait-on recommandé. Le brave garçon ne se le fit pas dire deux fois. Arrivé à destination, il se jeta au cou de la reine éberluée, l'embrassa fougueusement, puis lui remit son pli.'
69. Charbon, *Quelle belle invention que la poste!*, p.32. Under the *ancien régime* units of measurement varied considerably over time and from place to place, so that this definition of the *lieue* is necessarily approximate. For example, the *old* Paris league (used until 1674) measured 10,000 feet or 3.248 km, the *new* Paris league (1674-1793) was 2000 *toises* or 3.898 km in length, and the so-called Postal league (*lieue des Postes*) (1737-1793) equaled 2200 *toises* or 4.288 km. To further complicate matters, the *poste aux chevaux* continued to measure distances in leagues, rather than kilometers, until 1840. See Chauvet, *Introduction à l'histoire postale*, p.32.

gain.).[70] On post roads, the standard distance between relays would eventually be shortened to two leagues (7-10 km), which corresponded to the units (also called *postes*) used by postal guide books to indicate the distance between one town and another.[71] The proprietors of these relays would soon bear the title of 'postmasters' (*maîtres des postes* or *maîtres de postes*). Because he created a state-sponsored postal relay system – even though it was reserved for court correspondence – Louis XI has become known as the 'Father of the French post'. By the end of the sixteenth century, the demand for transportation of unofficial (and therefore unauthorized) correspondence increased to the point that the state began to see the financial advantage of legalizing this practice. Francis I had granted the postmasters the exclusive privilege of renting horses on the Paris-Lyon route, a situation that Henry IV extended in 1602 to the entire postal system.[72] The letter post, founded by Henry IV in 1603, was the first state postal system for private letters in France. It connected Paris with Dijon, Lyon, Bordeaux and Toulouse and for a time it co-existed peacefully with the more important message services of the universities and municipalities.[73]

Two distinct mail services (the word 'mail' is metonymically derived from the *malle*, or bag, in which letters and packages were carried) would co-exist until the horse post was abolished in 1672 by François Michel Le Tellier, Marquis de Louvois (1641-1691): the privately-owned *horse post* [*poste aux chevaux*] (for the operation of post roads and provision of means of transportation) and the state-controlled *letter post* [*poste aux lettres*] (for collection, transport and distribution of correspondence). Postmasters owned their relays and horses; they also recruited and paid the postilions (guards). Mounted on a horse in his blue uniform with its red lining, the postilion led the postal coach, accompanied a courier of the letter post to the next relay and then brought the horses back to their point of departure.[74] In practice, however, it was not uncommon for a haughty noble to insist upon having one of his servants take the postilion's place, beat the horses and take other liberties with the privileges and property of the *maître des postes*.[75]

70. Charles Perrault, *Contes*, textes établis et présentés par Marc Soriano (Paris, 1989), p.293. My translation.
71. Like the length of the league, the distance between relays varied considerably during this period. Moreover guidebooks would round off the distance between two places by up to several leagues. Chauvet, *Introduction à l'histoire postale*, p.32.
72. Charbon, *Quelle belle invention que la poste!*, p.33.
73. Marchand, *Le Maître de poste et le messager*, p.97.
74. Chauvet, *Introduction à l'histoire postale*, p.31. See also Yvette Mience, *Histoire des postes du Rhône* (Lyon, 1997), vol.1, p.32.
75. See *Ordonnance du Roy portant deffenses à tous courriers de faire conduire des chaises et des berlines par d'autres postillons que ceux des postes; de faire précéder les domestiques de ceux qui coureront que*

For the period prior to 1672 a clear distinction must be made between the postmaster (*maître des postes*), who was the proprietor of a horse post relay, and the letter postmaster (*maître des courriers*: after 1672, *directeur des postes*) or manager of a letter post office: both users of the post and members of the royal administration often confused the two.[76] The *poste aux chevaux* provided horses for the couriers of the *poste aux lettres* for a minimal charge. A royal decree of 26 April 1728 reminds the *maîtres des postes* of their duty and extends it to roads not mentioned in the decree of 1630:

> [L]es maîtres des postes desdites routes seront tenus... sur les ordres qui leur en seront donnés par le grand Maître et Surintendant général des postes, de fournir deux fois la semaine, en allant et autant pour le retour, faisant quatre voyages, le nombre de chevaux qu'il sera nécessaire pour le passage dudit courrier, en payant seulement par ledit courrier, cinq sols par poste les guides des postillons, sans que les maîtres des postes puissent exiger pour lesdits deux ordinaires, aucune autre rétribution.[77]

> [T]he postmasters of these routes will be required... on the orders that will be given them by the grand Master and Superintendent of the posts, to supply twice weekly the number of horses needed for the passage of the courier, on the inward and outward journeys, at five *sols* per post for the postilion's guides, without the postmasters being able to require any further retribution for these ordinaries.

The *poste aux chevaux* also rented horses to travelers or to rapid transport services, both public and private. Postmasters operated a rather profitable public transportation business, whose efficiency depended largely upon the state of the roads.[78] Until 1672, like other functions in the royal

---

d'une poste à l'autre et aux courriers de fouetter ou frapper, ni souffrir qu'aucun de leurs domestiques fouettent et frappent aucun des chevaux attelés auxdites voitures, et qui ordonne que la poste sera payée d'avance avant chaque départ, selon le règlement (Paris, Chez Louis-Denis Delatour, Imprimeur de la Cour des Aydes en la maison de feuë la veuve Muguet, rue de la Harpe, aux trois Rois, 1 October 1726).

76. The change in name corresponded to a change in status. In the system of *offices* the *maître des courriers* was the titular owner of his position, whereas in the farm system (adopted in 1672) the *directeur des postes* was simply the subordinate of his hierarchical superior. Marchand's *Le Maître de poste et le messager* contains the most thorough account of the *maîtres de poste* and their role in the provision of transport services. See also Louis Lenain, *La Poste de l'ancienne France: La Poste dans la Drôme et l'Ardèche des origines à 1920* (Arles, 1972), p.12.

77. *Ordonnance concernant le service que les maîtres des postes seront obligéz de faire* (Paris, Imprimerie Royale, 1734). In the *Bibliographie critique de l'histoire postale française* (Montpellier, 1970), n°1248, Pierre Nougaret incorrectly states that this service was to be provided free of charge. Patrick Marchand offers a detailed account of the *maquis* of public transport institutions available to travelers during this period: *Le Maître de poste et le messager*, p.19.

78. See Vaillé, *Histoire générale*, vol.3, p.212ff, as well as Georges Livet, 'La route royale et la civilisation française de la fin du XVe au milieu du XVIIIe siècle', in Louis Trénard *et al.*, *Les Routes de France depuis les origines jusqu'à nos jours* (Paris, 1959), p.110-13. According to Martine Biard, roads tended to be better maintained in the wealthy province of

administration, the charge (*office*) of postmaster was venal (General Superintendents of the Post – as successors to the Comptroller General were called – derived most of their income from selling charges to the postmasters) and hereditary. Under Louis XIV *maîtres des postes* were required to be Roman Catholics, doubtless for security reasons.[79] Available only to the richest persons in a parish (usually wealthy farmers), the position of postmaster was so prestigious that members of the nobility did not lose their rank and title by occupying it.[80] The privileges of a *maître des postes* (exemptions from taxes – most importantly, the *taille* – and from the duty to house soldiers) were much more important to the office-holder than the associated expenses, a fact that did not prevent these relatively wealthy persons from regularly petitioning the government for increases in rental fees for horses.[81] The inequity of exempting relatively wealthy citizens from a tax whose weight then fell upon the poorer members of the society was so flagrant that in 1688 Louis XIV issued an ordinance limiting this exemption to the sum of 30 livres. However this reduced incentive proved inadequate to guarantee acceptable service, and the king was soon forced to rescind the restriction.[82] The *maître des courriers* derived some of his income from the tax on letters and correspondence and enjoyed the same privileges as the *maître des postes*; but since *maîtres des courriers* were poorly paid, they derived most of their income from other kinds of mercantile activity.[83]

Languedoc than in other regions of the kingdom. *Postes et messageries en Languedoc de Louis XIV à la Révolution: communiquer dans l'Ancien régime, essai* (Paris, 2011). This 'essay' does not provide sources for much of its information.

79. Vaillé, *Histoire générale*, vol.3, p.7-8; Marchand, *Le Maître de poste*, p.223. In England '[t]he political value of controlling postmasters far surpassed its monetary worth, and their ousting and resettling affected local politics. Postmasters were... forced to take oaths not to use their position to "meddle in ye elections"'. Whyman, *The Pen and the people*, p.54.
80. Marchand, *Le Maître de poste*, p.223ff.
81. The ordinance of 2 February 1728, in which Louis XV's chief minister Cardinal Fleury takes to task the *maîtres de poste* of the Grenoble-Lyon route for their careless handling of packages, provides one illustration of the chronic tensions between the *maîtres de poste* and the state. *Ordonnance de son Eminence Monseigneur le cardinal de Fleury grand maître et surintendant général des Courriers, postes et relais de France portant règlement pour la diligence et la seureté des malles ordinaires de la route de Lyon à Grenoble* (Paris, L.D. Delatour, 2 February 1728). The magistrate Nicolas de La Mare (1639-1723) provides a history of these tensions in the *Continuation du Traité de la police, contenant l'histoire de son établissement, les fonctions, les prérogatives de ses magistrats; toutes les loix, les réglemens qui la concernent... tome quatrième. De la voirie, de tout ce qui en dépend ou qui y a quelque rapport* [....] (Paris, Michel Brunet and J.-F. Hérissant, 1738), bk VI, title XIV, ch.IV. Between the first edition of 1705-1710 and 1750 the four-volume *Traité de la police*, the first ever published on this topic, underwent several editions.
82. De La Mare, *Continuation du traité de la police*, p.566ff. See *Pétition à l'Assemblée Nationale par les maîtres des postes à chevaux, des routes de Paris à Marseille, et à Montpellier* (Paris, Didot le jeune, 1792).
83. See Jean Kipper, 'La lettre et son acheminement postal', in Jean Lerat (ed.), *La Lettre dans*

As demand for postal services continued to increase, it became obvious that treating these positions as venal *offices* was much more profitable for the postmasters (and General Superintendents) than for the crown.[84] Starting in 1662, under the impetus of Colbert, the postmasters (*maîtres des postes*) were therefore divested of their charges. In 1672, Louvois was named General Superintendent of the Post and transformed the system of *offices* into a farm system, the *Ferme générale des postes*, which was the first state postal monopoly in France. The way the postal farm worked was quite simple: in exchange for a (usually nine-year) lease paid to the crown, the farmers-general retained all the profits from the sale of letters and organized the practical details of postal service.[85] An exception to this monopoly was made for letters and packages delivered by private messenger or *exprès* (the mail service that today is called *courrier express* was then referred to as *courrier extraordinaire*).[86] The farm lease [*bail à ferme*] arrangement enabled the state to derive considerable profit from activities that previously had primarily benefited the office-holder. In this scheme, there were basically two sources of authority. As liaison to the king, the General Superintendent regulated tariffs and oversaw the general policy lines of the business; the *Fermier-général* officially controlled the day-to-day operation of the system, hired the postmasters, and so on.[87] In practice, because the fee required to pay for a lease (*ferme*) was extremely large and was increased at each renewal, *Fermiers-généraux* could not afford it without outside support. Consequently two successive 'dynasties' of guarantors or *cautions* (the Pajot and Rouillé families from 1672 to 1738; the Grimod[88] and Thiroux families from 1738 until the Revolution) wielded the real power; they made even larger profits than a long succession of *Fermiers-généraux*, although the secretive accounting

---

tous ses états (Barcelona, 1991), p.169; Vaillé, *Histoire générale*, vol.5, p.233ff. Nodé-Langlois, 'La poste internationale', p.23; Marchand, *Le Maître de poste*, p.112.

84. Since the sale of charges in the royal administration had become the most famous expedient of the royal treasury, postal *offices* thus constituted a significant exception to the general rule. Of course, the possession of offices did not normally generate much (if any) revenue. See Roland Mousnier, *La Vénalité des offices sous Henri IV et Louis XIII* (Paris, 1970).

85. For an example of this process, see *Lettres patentes... concernant les nouvelles conditions du bail de la ferme générale et des postes et messageries de France... Registrées en la Chambre des Comptes* [17 octobre 1759] (Paris, Imprimerie Royale, 1759).

86. Chauvet, *Introduction à l'histoire postale*, p.59, 112. 'Les courriers extraordinaires, comme les courriers de cabinet, font le trajet de bout en bout. Ils utilisent les relais de la Poste aux Chevaux sur le territoire français et ceux de la poste locale lorsqu'ils sont en terre étrangère.' Chauvet, *Introduction à l'histoire postale*, p.112. Foreign couriers enjoyed the same privileges as ordinary and extraordinary royal couriers. De La Mare, *Continuation du traité de la police*, p.580.

87. Vaillé, *Histoire des postes*, p.69.

88. The famous gastronomer Grimod de la Reynière (1758-1838) belonged to this same family.

practices of the Pajot-Rouillé family (they were alleged to have burned their books every fortnight) have made it impossible to determine exactly how much they made.[89] The certainty of profits from the postal farm system also enabled the state to issue postal bonds (*rentes*), which it used to finance pensions for groups (such as stockholders of the Hôtel de Ville lottery) and individuals (such as the great scientist Réaumur).[90]

The postal farmer managed his territory so as to make as much profit as possible, beyond the cost of the lease. After 1700 the farmer would hire a director to oversee the day-to-day operations of each post office.[91] The *Ferme* also carried French newspapers for the same price as letters; and it had a monopoly on the introduction and sale of foreign newspapers, an arrangement that facilitated censorship and increased profits. This system had the advantage, fully intended by Louvois, of increasing centralized state control over the delivery of mail. At a time when most political, social and economic life in France remained fragmented (by provinces, *parlements*, etc.), the Royal Post may indeed have been the most important centralized institution in the kingdom.[92] By the time of the 1789 Revolution the farm had lost its independence, and delivery of mail between cities had been taken over almost entirely by the state, with the exception (especially on secondary roads) of various municipal mail

89. This allegation, according to Vaillé, was made by the memorialist Charles-Philippe Albert de Luynes (1695-1758). *Histoire des postes*, p.84. The original Pajot and Rouillé were brothers-in-law. The questionable accounting practices of the Pajot-Rouillé group led to its replacement in 1738 by the Grimod and Thiroux families, who were then required to keep transparent books. At the same time, Louis XV transformed the position of Surintendant Général des Postes into that of a simple intendant (later Intendant Général), who was directly dependent upon the king. The first of these intendants, Grimod-Dufort, quickly acquired the king's confidence, and became an important personage at court. Vaillé, *Histoire générale*, vol.6, p.i-ii; Marchand, *Le Maître de poste*, p.80.

90. See *Edit du Roy, Portant Création de Cent mille livres de Rentes viagères assignées sur la Ferme des Postes, pour les Actionnaires de la Loterie, Establie en conséquence de la Déclaration de Sa Majesté du 21 août 1717* (Paris, Imprimerie Royale, 1717); *Edit du Roy, Portant création de six cens mille livres de Rentes sur la Ferme Générale des Postes, novembre 1735* (Paris, Imprimerie Royale, November 1735); *Edit du Roy, Portant création de six cens mille livres de Rentes sur la Ferme générale des Postes, juin 1742* (Paris, Imprimerie Royale, June 1742); *Edit du Roy, Portant création de cinq cens mille livres de rentes héréditaires au denier vingt, sur la ferme générale des Postes, décembre 1746* (Paris, Imprimerie Royale, December 1746); *Edit du Roy, Portant création de deux millions de livres de rentes viagères sur l'Hôtel de ville de Paris; et de neuf cens mille livres de rentes héréditaires sur la Ferme générale des Postes* (Paris, Imprimerie Royale, May 1751). It is worth noting that the headpieces of the last three of these royal edicts contain Masonic symbolism. Both the statesman Marc-Pierre de Voyer de Paulmy, comte d'Argenson (1696-1764), who was Superintendent of the Posts from 1744 to 1757, and his brother René Louis de Voyer de Paulmy, 2e marquis d'Argenson, secretary of state for foreign affairs from 1744 to 1747, were affiliated with Freemasonry. See also Marchand, *Le Maître de poste*, p.98.

91. *Le Maître de poste*, p.111.

92. On Louvois's centralizing strategy, see Vaillé, *Histoire des postes*, p.68ff.

services (such as that of the 'free city' of Mulhouse), and of principalities within French borders (such as Montbéliard) that belonged to foreign powers.

Last in the hierarchy of postal profiteers were the superintendents (later simply called intendants), whose job it was, in collaboration with the guarantors, to make sure that the terms of the lease were respected.[93] Louvois was the only superintendent who benefited more from the post than the farmers and guarantors. For during his tenure as Surintendant Général des Postes, he was also granted the privilege of reaping all the profits from foreign mail.[94] The approximately 200,000 livres net generated annually by foreign mail, plus his salary as General Superintendent, was said to have made Louvois one of the richest private individuals in Europe.[95] None of his successors enjoyed this additional privilege. Upon the death of Louvois in 1692, Louis XIV transformed the position of General Superintendent from a charge to a simple commission, Louvois having 'established such good order and exact discipline in all the posts of our kingdom that we may hope that order can henceforth be maintained solely through inspection by the commissionaires we have assigned to the provinces'.[96] Immediately after the death of the Sun King that decision was reversed. A royal edict of September 1715 reestablished the charge (arguing that commissionaires 'lacked the necessary authority to remedy abuses') along with a number of lower-level positions, and set the annual salary of the Grand Master and Superintendent of the Post at 40,000 livres, plus a base compensation of 10,000 livres and an annual bonus of 12,000 livres drawn from postal revenue; within a year parliamentary remonstrances led the Regent to reduce the salary by half (by virtue of an 'interpretation') to 20,000 livres. Upon the deaths of the Regent and his prime minister Cardinal Dubois in 1723, Louis IV Henri de Bourbon-Condé ('M. le Duc') became Prime Minister and Superintendent of the Posts. After his disgrace and fall in 1726, he was replaced in both positions by his enemy Cardinal Fleury, and the charge was once again turned into a commission. Further attempts at cost reductions followed, with the elimination of the charges

93. Vaillé, *Histoire générale*, vol.4, p.11.

94. Louvois was later granted the right to treat all lands conquered by the crown as if they were still foreign territory. Vaillé, *Histoire générale*, p.78-79.

95. On this point Vaillé (*Histoire générale*, vol.4, p.12) cites Louvois's contemporary Ezéchiel Spanheim, *Relation de la Cour de France en 1690* (Paris, 1882), p.200.

96. *Edit du Roy, Portant création de la Charge de grand Maistre & Sur-Intendant général des Postes, Courriers & Relais de France, & d'autres Charges subalternes pour le service des Postes* (Chez la Veuve de François Muguet, Hubert Muguet, Premier Imprimeur du Roy, et Louis Denis de Latour Libraire, rue de la Harpe, aux trois Rois, September 1715).

of provincial controllers of the post (1728) and of a whole set of lower-level administrative charges (1738).[97]

Until the second half of the eighteenth century, official correspondence was carried from one branch of government to another either by regular messenger service (paid for by the community) or express service, but there was no intraurban postal system in France. To send a letter from one neighborhood of Paris, those who had servants could entrust them with the letter and have them wait for reply; those who could not afford this luxury had to carry their own letters. Perhaps because provision of such service was considered a waste of time and money, it was actively discouraged.[98] In 1653, Jean-Jacques Renouard, Comte de Villayer (or Vélayer) obtained royal authorization to provide mail service within Paris. For the price of an inexpensive prepayment ticket (an ancestor of the postage stamp), one could simply drop a letter in one of several mail boxes and expect it to be delivered to the addressee on the same day.[99] Villayer's business failed, but his mail boxes continued to be used by the *poste aux lettres* (see fig.3, p.76). However it was not until 1760 that, after traveling to London to observe the functioning of the Penny Post, Claude-Humbert Piarron de Chamousset (1717-1773) was allowed to open a *petite poste* (as municipal mail services would be called) for the delivery of mail within Paris (see fig.1, p.45).[100] Other French cities soon established their own *petites postes* until all of these services were finally absorbed by the state in 1795.[101] In towns where a post office was lacking,

97. See *Déclaration du Roy en interprétation de l'Edit de Création de la Charge de Grand Maistre et Sur-Intendant des Postes* (Chez la Veuve de François Muguet, Hubert Muguet, Premier Imprimeur du Roy, et Louis Denis de Latour Libraire, rue de la Harpe, aux trois Rois, 28 August 1716); *Edit du Roy, Portant suppression de la Charge de Grand-Maître et Surintendant général des Postes et Relais de France* (Paris, Pierre Simon, August 1726). *Edit du Roy, Portant suppression des Offices de Controlleurs Provinciaux des Postes & Relais de France* (Paris, Pierre Simon, March 1728). *Edit du Roy, Portant suppression de plusieurs Charges & Offices sur les Postes* (Paris, Imprimerie Royale, May 1738).

98. See Chapter 2, p.72ff.

99. Chauvet, *Introduction à l'histoire postale*, p.261. Joan DeJean discusses Renouard de Villayer's short-lived *petite poste* of 1653 in *How Paris became Paris: the invention of the modern city* (New York, 2014), p.123-25.

100. The privilege was taken away from Chamousset in 1763. For at least half a century postal farm regulations had made it illegal for mail to circulate within Paris. Voltaire's earliest reference to the *petite poste* is in a letter to Damilaville of 16 January 1761, D8784. The *Correspondance littéraire* of 1767 contains a reference to *La Petite Poste dévalisée* (Paris and Amsterdam, J. B. Artaud, 1767), a collection of letters supposedly stolen from the *petite poste*. Melchior Grimm, *Correspondance littéraire*, critical edn Ulla Kolving with Jean de Booy and Christoph Frank; preface Roland Mortier (Ferney-Voltaire, 2006-2013), p.311. In Chapter 2, p.72-73, I discuss Louis-Sébastien Mercier's fantasies about this book: Louis-Sébastien Mercier, *Le Tableau de Paris* (Paris, 1994), 2 vols, ch.296, 'La Petite Poste'.

101. Nougaret, *Bibliographie critique*, p.957. After Paris, *petites postes* were founded in Bordeaux (1766), Lyons (1777), Marseille (1777), Nantes (1777), Rouen (1778), Nancy (1779),

one could pay a distribution assistant (*commis-distributeur*) or a private individual to post a letter or have it fetched. In 1791 the centrally-administered *poste aux lettres* covered the entire kingdom of France with 1321 offices, supplemented on secondary roads by private citizens. Unlike *maîtres des courriers* (later, 'directors'), postmasters (who derived their income from the rental of horses to travelers and transport service) did not receive salaries until 1798.

'International' postal service

As we have seen, once the princes of Europe had recognized the advantages they could gain from allowing the general public to have access to the post, they contracted with private parties for the operation of postal systems in their name and sought to achieve monopolies over the domestic post. At the same time, they aggressively competed with each other for a share of the profitable market for mail that passed from one system to another.[102] Since it was not until the nineteenth century that there were 'nations' in the sense that the word has today, it is somewhat of an anachronism to call this market 'international'; perhaps a more accurate term would be 'intersystemic'. Be that as it may, the imperial (Taxis) post contended with the French postal farm for control of the connection between the north and the south, and with postal services in the German Länder for both the north-south route and the route that connected Poland and Russia in the east with Western Europe. Due to the growing importance of trade with the Levant, postal traffic along that route also became the object of fierce competition.[103] Regardless of the outcomes of these struggles for intersystemic mail business, the mercantilist and statist policies that were adopted during this period worked to the advantage of the post as an institution.[104] A complex and inefficient legal framework governed postal relations among all of these postal territories until 1874, when the General Postal Union (which in 1878 became the Universal Postal Union) was created in Bern.[105] For

Strasbourg (1779) and Lille (1784). See also Chauvet, *Introduction à l'histoire postale*, p.262. Chapter 2, p.72ff, contains an account of how the *petites postes* worked.

102. Nodé-Langlois, 'La poste internationale', p.2, p.103. In the United Provinces, Amsterdam held sway in the foreign mail market; in Portugal, from 1606-1792 all foreign mail was in the hands of the Gomès da Matta family. 'La poste internationale', p.46-47.

103. Kalmus, *Weltgeschichte*, p.360.

104. *Weltgeschichte*, p.358.

105. For example, prior to 1874 it was necessary to affix the stamps of any country through which one's letter or package would pass. On international postal relations in the sixteenth and seventeenth centuries, see Joseph Rübßam, 'Zur Geschichte des internationalen Postwesens im 16. und 17. Jahrhunderte nebst einem Rückblick auf die neuerere historisch-postalische Literatur', in *Historisches Jahrbuch* 13 (1892), p.15-79.

centuries many countries maintained offices on foreign soil; these offices met diplomatic needs and played an important role in political and commercial relations.[106] The individuals who ran early modern postal systems, by contract or by 'farm', were businessmen, who everywhere treated letters as negotiable commodities. It was common to speak of the *letter trade* and *le commerce des lettres*, expressions in which 'trade' ('Intercourse in the affairs of life; dealings' [*OED*] and *commerce* ('*Relations que l'on entretient dans la société*' [*Petit Robert*]) still retained some of their now archaic social meaning. Like wheat and spices, letters were viewed as commodities bought and sold on a market. Each system aimed to obtain a letter at the lowest possible price, pass on expenses and sell it to the addressee as profitably as possible.[107] Rates for postage between systems (unpaid by the addressee, except in France) were determined according to a rather complex calculus that rarely worked to the advantage of the consumer. Nodé-Langlois cites the example of the postage paid by a businessman in Lyons for a letter from Amsterdam: the bill included the price of purchasing the letter from the Amsterdam office, the transit fee, the normal cost of transport from the point of entry to Paris, and the tax for forwarding the letter from Paris to Lyons.[108] Although the competition sometimes yielded lower prices and speedier delivery, it usually meant higher prices and less direct routes.[109] For much of the early modern period, the various state-sponsored postal systems also had to compete with private 'day messenger' services.[110]

The importance that rulers attached to the speed, punctuality and

---

The latter half of the early modern period is covered in Nodé-Langlois, 'La poste internationale'. For a discussion, from the standpoint of France, of the administrative aspects of international postal relations, see Vaillé's *Histoire générale*, vol.3, part 2; vol.4, part 3; vol.5, parts 3, 4; vol.6, part 2.

106. The Piedmont, the Kingdom of Naples, Milan and France kept offices in Rome; the Ottoman Empire established them in Austria, Russia and German Hanseatic cities. There were three foreign post offices in Geneva, belonging to the French *Ferme*, the Piedmont and the Fischers of Bern. Along with offices in independent municipalities, Germany and the Ottoman Empire, France established post offices in Venice, Turin (abandoned in 1740 under political pressure), Genoa (closed in 1750) and Rome. Vaillé, *Histoire générale*, vol.5, p.iii-iv; Nodé-Langlois, 'La poste internationale', p.27, 131ff. Although it became increasingly impractical and expensive, the nominally domestic service between Paris and Rome was maintained until the Revolution for reasons of politics and prestige: 'La poste internationale', p.123ff.

107. 'La poste internationale', p.148.

108. 'La poste internationale', p.152.

109. When several postal companies co-existed on the same border (for example between France and Switzerland), competition was especially intense for transit fees. In France, there was also domestic competition between the farm and various illegal forms of mail delivery. Nodé-Langlois, 'La poste internationale', p.285.

110. Vaillé, *Histoire générale*, vol.3, p.303-308.

Figure 1: *Facteur petite poste* 1760 / A *petite poste* mailman 1760.

security of trans-European communications was matched by the interest of merchants in their reliability. Numerous agreements were made in order to ensure the intermeshing and coordination of postal routes.[111] At the beginning of the seventeenth century, the only two solidly established postal systems in Europe were based in the Habsburg Empire (the Taxis post) and in France. Due to the instability of the general political situation at the time, postal treaties between systems were mainly concerned with stipulating every conceivable practical detail, whether financial (taxes, duties, reimbursement, postage, etc.) or administrative (responsibilities, scheduling, personnel, etc.).[112] In January 1601 Don Juan von Taxis, the *correo mayor* of Habsburg Spain, and the French *contrôleur général des postes*, Guillaume Fouquet de la Varane (or Varenne) signed one of the earliest international postal treaties. According to Joseph Rübßam (who discovered this document in the archives of Simancas), the treaty contained the following stipulations: the Spanish Postal Superintendent, Don Juan I von Taxis, had to dispatch ordinary mail intended for Italy by way of Bordeaux through Lyons. In Lyons the Spanish rider gave the Italian mail to the local postal employee of M. de la Varenne, who in turn took charge of having the mail carried from Lyons to Rome and other cities after delays of no more than one day. The trip from Lyons to Rome was to take eleven days in summer and twelve in winter. At the last relay immediately before Rome, the French courier sent from Lyons had to hand his correspondence over to two postilions, one of whom conveyed the post from Spain to the Spanish post office in Rome, while the other carried the French post to the French post office there.

Don Juan von Taxis ordered that M. de la Varenne be paid either three sueldos per ounce of letters or 200 gold scudi per shipment for mail thus carried to Rome by ordinary post. Varenne was to make up his mind within the next three months as to which mode of payment he preferred. Don Juan von Taxis was meant to send the amounts due, in cash, with each ordinary post.[113]

To deliver mail to Paris and along the stretch of the routes to Italy and Spain that crossed French territory, the Taxis had to obtain the consent of the French king. In the seventeenth century, the French *Ferme* dealt exclusively with the imperial Taxis post, despite the emergence of rival postal services at the local and 'national' levels.[114]

A travel guide published at the beginning of the seventeenth century

111. Dorhn-van Rossum, *History of the hour*, p.340.
112. Kalmus, *Weltgeschichte*, p.361.
113. Rübßam, 'Zur Geschichte', p.59-60.
114. Dorhn-van Rossum, *History of the hour*, p.40.

also supplies precious information about this early stage of intersystemic postal relations.[115] The *Nuovo itinerario delle poste per tutto il mondo* (1608) of the Milanese postal administrator Ottavio Codogno is divided into three parts:

1) A history of the postal services from their origins to Codogno's day, with an annex that explains the obligations and powers of the *correo mayor* and other employees of the postal service
2) A description of the major postal routes, with a list of relays, the distance between them, the obstacles (such as streams) to be encountered along the way, as well as indications of maritime connections
3) A schedule of the arrival and departure times of ordinary posts in each state, with explanations of how connections were arranged

In this last part, the routes to and from Prague – at that time the Kaiser's residence – receive the most emphasis. Among the most significant of the routes described are those from Madrid through France via Lyons to the Spanish Lowlands and Rome. Madrid was also connected with, among other places, Valencia, Seville, Cartagena and Lisbon; the mail for East India left from Lisbon, and the West Indian mail from Seville. It was Antwerp merchants who arranged for carriage of letters to Holland, England and the Hansa cities in the north. The post left the imperial court in Prague for Rome, the Lowlands and Vienna, from which connections could be made with Steiermark, Carinthia, Bosnia, Hungary and Transylvania. Correspondence addressed to Poland was carried by foot messengers and carters.

In addition, most of the most important traffic arteries converged at Brussels, the seat of the von Taxis family. The line that connected Brussels, Augsburg, Trent, Milan and Rome was particularly well served. From Brussels a line branched off via Namur toward Cologne, and correspondence was forwarded from there for northwest Germany. The correspondence for the imperial court, Bavaria and Switzerland was sorted at Augsburg. Letters for Venice and the Orient were separated in Trent. In Venice there were monthly opportunities for dispatching of correspondence by sea for Dalmatia, Albania, Morea and Constantinople. The traffic between Brussels and Antwerp was so lively that hourly service between them was available. A post connected

115. The contents of this treaty are summarized in Rübßam, 'Zur Geschichte', p.64-72. The earliest edition of this book (whose complete title is *Nuovo itinerario delle poste per tutto il mondo, aggiuntovi il modo di scriver à tutte le partì: Utilissimo non solo à 'Secretarij de' prencipi, ma à Religiosi e à Mercanti ancora*) that Rübßam could locate was published in Milan by Girolamo Bordoni in 1608, and is 430 pages long; he also consulted two editions published in Venice, in 1611 and 1646.

Brussels and Madrid every four weeks, and was dispatched from Brussels on Saturday or Sunday.

Between Paris and Rome there were 122 postal stations. Paris was linked to Prague and Vienna by the line that passed through Ligny, Toul, Nancy, Rheinhausen, Augsburg and Pilsen. At the head of Codogno's painstakingly synthesized overview of the European postal network were two of the most famous and most visited pilgrimage destinations of Christianity, Loreto and Santiago de Compostela.[116]

Directly after the Treaty of the Pyrenees (1659) brought an end to a nearly twenty-five-year conflict between France and Spain, an international postal conference was convened in Paris, for the purpose of regularizing intersystemic postal service. The participants were: the French postmaster; the Antwerp postmaster (Lamoral C. F. von Thurn und Taxis), who represented the general postmasters of Germany, the Lowlands and Burgundy; and the postmaster of Madrid, as representative of the Spanish postmaster (and heir to the Spanish branch of the Thurn and Taxis business). As private individuals, rather than representatives of states, these parties signed a treaty in December 1660, restoring the mail service that had been disturbed by the wars.[117] Between Paris and the Pyrenees, conveyance of Spanish and Flemish ordinary mail was entrusted to the French couriers, at fixed rates and delivery times.[118] The delivery of Italian mail was organized in a similar manner, with a route leading from Milan to Lyons, and then branching north and south. The treaty also restored regular postal relations with England. Shortly thereafter the Taxis post took charge of delivering letters from England to Germany, Scandinavia, Eastern Europe and Italy (where Venice still served as 'the gateway to the East').[119]

Political obstacles also prevented mail delivery between systems from achieving a high level of service. It was particularly difficult to negotiate the transit of correspondence through the Netherlands, where the post offices of the largest cities competed for a share of the international mail business.[120] Customs security made it necessary to inspect parcels at international borders, and foreign newspapers could not enter a country

116. Rübßam, 'Zur Geschichte', p.69-70.

117. Vaillé, *Histoire générale*, vol.3, p.333.

118. From Paris to the Pyrenees: 5.5 days in summer, 6.5 days in winter; Paris to Brussels, 2 days (in 1516 Franz von Taxis had set 1.5 days as a limit!). Behringer, *Thurn und Taxis*, p.106-107. In a strange exception to international postal conventions of the time, the postal treaty of 1660 stipulated that letters between France and Spain (or Spain and France) would be delivered at no cost, a principle that was maintained throughout the *ancien régime* and First Empire. As Vaillé points out (*Histoire générale*, vol.3, p.336), this reciprocity was actually fictive, since most of the transit expenses were paid by France.

119. Behringer, *Thurn und Taxis*, p.106.

120. Kalmus, *Weltgeschichte*, p.362.

without being subjected to state censorship.[121] Until the end of the *ancien régime* in France, only the chief administrator of the postal service could issue the passports that authorized selected foreigners to pass through war zones. The fact that the most powerful of these officials, Louvois, was also the Minister of War of Louis XIV, and that his successor as General Superintendent of the Posts, Torcy, was Minister of Foreign Affairs, underscores the close relation between state security and the postal service that existed at this time. Above all, reasons of state made the inviolability of correspondence, both domestic and international, somewhat of a joke. In the 'Poste' article of the *Dictionnaire philosophique*, Voltaire ironized that: '[J]amais le ministère qui a eu le département des postes n'a ouvert les lettres d'aucun particulier, excepté quand il a un besoin de savoir ce qu'elles contenaient.' ([N]ever has the ministry responsible for the postal department had to open the letters of any private individual, except when it needed to know what they contained.)[122] In England, the original purpose of the state monopoly on the transmission of letters 'was not so much to stamp out competition as to give the government of the time access to the correspondence of persons suspected of plots'.[123] Letters from abroad were especially subject to this practice, which I shall discuss more fully in Chapter 3. Despite systematic violation of the secrecy of correspondence, European states did their best, during the numerous wars that raged throughout Europe during the seventeenth and eighteenth centuries, to maintain postal relations whenever possible. Given the existence of so many obstacles to speedy and reliable international mail service, it is all the more understandable that news of the Lisbon earthquake on 1 November 1755 took so long to reach the outside world.[124]

121. The proliferation of contraband led to frequent customs inspections, which in turn led to frequent delays in delivery of mail. For this reason there was a conflict in France between customs regulations and the interests of the *Ferme générale* (the tax farm), on the one hand, and the interest of the *Ferme des Postes* in the safekeeping of dispatches. The *Ferme* had a monopoly on transport and distribution of 'foreign' newspapers, a category that included the many French newspapers that were printed abroad (especially in the United Provinces). All subscription requests had to go through the *Ferme*. In 1779, nine foreign papers were distributed in France, providing the *Ferme* with large profits. Nodé-Langlois, 'La poste internationale', p.309-18.

122. 'Postes', in *QE*, *OCV*, vol 42B, p.470.

123. Evelyn Murray, *The Post Office* (London, 1927), cited by How, *Epistolary spaces*, p.12. In France, the postal administration had the exclusive privilege of delivering passports, even though other ministries could sign them.

124. Anne Saada and Jean Sgard discuss the process by which news of the earthquake filtered through to the Francophone press in Europe. 'Tremblements dans la presse', Theodore E. D. Braun and John B. Radner (eds), *The Lisbon earthquake of 1755: representations and reactions*, *SVEC* 2005:02, p.208-24.

I have mentioned that the Spanish post had an office in Rome. France considered its offices in Venice and Rome as part of the domestic postal system, since employees of the French postal farm had complete responsiblity for the operation of that service. After 1669 France also maintained a post office in Geneva. In 1630 a royal edict had created two offices of Foreign Postmaster (*Maîtres des Courriers pour les Postes étrangères*) – one in Paris, one in Lyons – each with three incumbents.[125] France also provided postal service for foreign territories (the Comtat Venaissin, the Principality of Monaco) enclosed within its borders.[126] The foreign postmaster in Paris administered postal relations with Spain, Flanders, England, Holland and Germany; while the *Maître des courriers étrangers* in Lyons concerned himself with ordinary letters that transited from Spain to Italy, from Italy to Spain, as well as letters from Lyons to Italy and back.[127] Starting in 1672, when the system of postal charges (*offices*) was abolished, Louvois took over the position of Foreign Postmaster, negotiated postal agreements and (as we have seen) personally appropriated all the income from the country's foreign post offices.[128] For foreign mail properly speaking – that is, mail that was carried to and from France by foreign postal services – the arrangements varied from country to country. Occasionally one postal service would gain a minor advantage over another. The 1698 postal treaty between England and France entitled the English Post Office to collect part of the postage for conveyance of mail from Calais to Paris, while no other foreign post offices acquired such a right. Between 1720 and 1740 the advantage went to the French, when their postal farm managed to impose fees for letters addressed to France that passed through Amsterdam from several other Dutch cities.[129] For service to Switzerland, the French had treaties with the rival post offices of Basel and Bern, and attempted to play them off against each other.[130]

In England, after a brief period of control by continental merchants of the so-called 'Strangers' Post', postal service to the continent was placed in the hands of English subjects (1633). Thomas Witherings (who in 1635 had proposed to reorganize the Letter Office for public use) became England's sole 'Postmaster-General for Foreign Parts'. He improved what had been a very inefficient service, instituted regular 'packet boat' service

125. Vaillé, *Histoire générale*, vol.3, p.298.
126. Chauvet, *Introduction à l'histoire postale*, p.40.
127. Vaillé, *Histoire générale*, vol.3, p.298, 309-21.
128. *Histoire générale*, vol.3, p.12. Upon Louvois's death in 1691, the income from carriage of foreign letters reverted back to the king's privy purse. Vaillé, *Histoire générale*, vol.3, p.79 and p.113-14.
129. Vaillé, *Histoire générale*, vol.3, p.401ff.
130. *Histoire générale*, vol.3, p.488ff.

between England and France and the Netherlands and made connections with the imperial post system of the Taxis family. Toward the end of the century (1689) an additional packet station was founded in Cornwall at Falmouth (in order to avoid 'the exactions of France') for mail to the Iberian Peninsula and the Mediterranean, as well as America and the Caribbean. Under the auspices of the Foreign Post Office mail service was irregular and insufficient throughout most of the eighteenth century, so that many foreign letters were carried unofficially by vessels other than packet boats.[131] Even after the Act of 1660 placed domestic and foreign mail service under the control of a single Postmaster-General, the two were run as separate operations, as in France.[132] Until 1784, the British Post Office possessed a monopoly on postal transport across the English Channel to France and the Lowlands.[133]

The postal convention of December 1660 regularized mail service from Spain and the Spanish Lowlands across France.[134] To ensure rapid service, couriers were required to travel the route from Irun to Paris in five or six and a half days in spring and summer, and six and seven and a half days in autumn and winter. In marked exception to the rule of international postal relations, the convention specified that letters between Spain and France were to be delivered free of cost. This principle would remain in force throughout the *ancien régime*. After 1660, the imperial Taxis post played a dual role in postal relations with France. At the common border it provided a direct exchange for letters to 'Upper' (southern) Germany, and for 'Lower' (northern) Germany it received items transported through the intermediary of the Spanish Taxis post, as well as all mail for the northern countries (Scandinavia, Poland, Russia).[135] In France various municipal mail-coach services also maintained postal relations abroad at this time: Reims with the Spanish Lowlands, the principality of Orange with Holland. The mail-coach between France and the territory of Liège was the most extraordinary of these services: for as it was under the authority of the prince-archbishop of Cologne, it undermined the sovereign rights of the French king.[136]

131. Robinson, *The British Post Office*, p.31ff, 159 ff; Vaillé, *Histoire générale*, vol.3, p.322 ff.
132. Robinson, *The British Post Office*, p.25. See also Robinson's *Carrying British mail overseas* (London, 1964), p.24-25.
133. Robinson, *Carrying British mail*, p.32. Mail across the Channel was carried in 'packet boats' (*paquebots*). In March 1777, the entrepreneurial Caron de Beaumarchais submitted a project for instituting packet boat service between Calais and Dover. Vaillé, *Histoire générale*, vol.6, p.460, n.2.
134. Vaillé notes (*Histoire générale*, vol.3, p.333) that the 1660 postal convention was an agreement between individuals, not between states.
135. Vaillé, *Histoire générale*, vol.4, p.459.
136. *Histoire générale*, vol.3, p.345-46.

Prior to the last quarter of the seventeenth century, private (and costly) mail services (*messageries*) were responsible for international service from Switzerland to France. Soon after the creation in 1669 of a postal route between Geneva and Lyons, a new French post office was established in Geneva. Until invading French armies established the Helvetic Republic (1798-1803), each Swiss canton had its own postmaster and postal administration. In the aristocratic cantons, the post was organized as a farm, as in France. In 1675 Beat (von Reichenbach) Fischer founded a postal dynasty, centered in Bern, which eventually extended to more than half of the Swiss cantons. From the end of the seventeenth century to the French Revolution the Fischer post was a serious rival to the Thurn and Taxis family and the French farm in the market for international mail delivery.[137]

We have seen that as centralized nation-states gradually emerged from more fragmented, 'feudal' arrangements between 1500 and 1800, postal relations in Western Europe changed accordingly. The princes of Europe recognized the economic and political advantages that could be gained by centralizing postal relations and asserted the 'kingly right' to control operation of the post. The post became available to the general public – for transport as well as for mail – and was no longer restricted to official communications. By the time of the French Revolution, European states did not yet operate their postal systems directly, but they had nevertheless achieved near monopolies over the delivery of mail. Between the Renaissance and the end of the eighteenth century, a patchwork of private messenger services, available only to powerful individuals, had evolved into an interlocking, public system of state-controlled mail and transport services. A slow and unreliable method of communication had become a speedy and efficacious system that was both a source of considerable profit and a powerful means of state surveillance and control.

137. Nodé-Langlois, 'La poste internationale', p.43.

2. Signed, sealed and delivered

Matter and meaning

In the published edition of Diderot's correspondence, there is a letter to Sophie Volland dated 31 August 1760 that concludes with the following lines:

> Je baise tes deux dernières lettres. Ce sont les caractères que tu as tracés; et à mesure que tu les traçois, ta main touchait l'espace que les lignes devoient remplir, et les intervalles qui devoient les séparer.
>
> Adieu, mon amie. Vous baiserez au bout de cette ligne, car j'y aurai baisé aussi là, là. Adieu.[1]

> I kiss your last two letters. These are the characters that you traced; and as you traced them, your hand touched the space that the lines would fill, and the intervals that would separate them.
>
> Adieu, my dear friend. You will press a kiss at the end of this line, for I shall have pressed a kiss there too, there. Adieu.

It is well known that all of Sophie's letters have been lost. Yet even if the two that Diderot kissed were someday discovered and published, one would not see the physical reality of the handwriting, 'the characters that [they] traced', without which one has even less chance of imagining the traces of their kisses. Likewise the printed page on which we read Diderot's response to those letters prosaically discourages us from trying to imagine the places where Diderot and Sophie pressed their kisses.[2] Or to take a well-known example from epistolary fiction, consider what the libertine protagonist of Laclos's *Dangerous liaisons* calls his 'Dijon letter'. This is the love letter that the Vicomte de Valmont sends to Mme de Tourvel with a postmark from Dijon, so that this virtuous lady, who has been refusing to accept any letters from him, will open it in the belief that it was sent by her husband. Valmont eventually discovers that after having shredded it into pieces, Tourvel has painstakingly reassembled the letter, and moreover that it bears traces of her tears. There can obviously be no printed version of such a letter.[3] When manuscript

1. Diderot to Louise-Henriette (Sophie) Volland, 21 August 1760, in Diderot, *Correspondance* (Paris, 1955-1970), vol.3, p.47.
2. In *Diderot ou Le Matérialisme enchanté* (Paris, 1984) Elisabeth de Fontenay stresses the 'réflexion sur l'écriture et sa matérialité' that is characteristic of Diderot's correspondence. Melançon develops this theme in *Diderot épistolier*, p.128ff.
3. P. A. Choderlos de Laclos, *Les Liaisons dangereuses*, preface, notes and dossier by Michel Delon (Paris, 2002). The 'Dijon letter' is I, xxxvi, le vicomte de Valmont à la Présidente de Tourvel; Valmont gives it this name in I, xl, le vicomte de Valmont à la marquise de Merteuil, p.134.

letters are printed and published, material elements (such as color and scent of the seal, calligraphy and ink, quality and fragrance of the paper, how the paper was cut and folded) and circumstances of their posting and delivery (whether or not the letter was prepaid, the route and distance it had traveled, how much time it had taken to reach its destination, and so on) are no longer perceptible, even though they contributed to the meaning of the original text.[4] The physical reality of manuscript letters does not lend itself to publication, and the circumstances in which they were posted, delivered and subsequently handled are largely unknowable. In sum, the constituent substance and material context of a hand-written letter contribute to its meaning, even though this materiality does not lend itself to publication. In this chapter I shall attempt to restore some of this significant but imperceptible reality – this 'dark matter,' so to speak – by describing and reflecting upon the practical conditions in which letters were exchanged in the early modern era, with special attention to the case in France.

Paper

Throughout the millennia of premodern postal history, during the period that lasted roughly until the Renaissance, documents and letters were written (usually by scribes), first on clay tablets, and then on parchment. Since it is impossible to fold a clay tablet and nearly impossible to fold parchment, one could not assure the privacy or secrecy of messages written on these materials. In Siegert's words, '[A]ll sending was a dispatch of postcards, and therefore fundamentally public'.[5] However toward the end of the fifteenth century, at the same time that postal services started to become available to the public, demand for paper in Europe increased dramatically, responding to the introduction of movable type printing and the mechanical printing press.[6] Letters could then be folded and their contents held private, at least in principle.[7] In early modern France a letter consisted of one or more folded sheets of paper

4. As Clare Brant notes, 'Certainly there were manuscript features that mattered to eighteenth-century writers of familiar letters which do not all survive the transition into print: the quality and size of paper chosen, spacing between greeting and text, closing flourishes, whether the letter was franked and the choice of seal were all expressive'. *Eighteenth-century letters*, p.9.
5. Siegert, *Relays*, p.30. This claim only holds true for the European continent. In the ancient Middle East, hollow, clay spheres were wrapped around small tablets and financial tokens and used in private transactions. In China, where paper was invented by the second century BCE, paper envelopes were used to story money or distribute monetary gifts to officials.
6. 'Papermaking', in *Encyclopaedia Britannica. Encyclopaedia Britannica online*, http://search.eb.com/eb/article-82429 (last accessed 29 September 2015).
7. See Chapter 3, p.95-123.

(*lettre simple* or *lettre double*)[8] whose dimensions were determined by the size of the wooden frames (or *formes*) that were used to make the sheets. According to a 1691 *Traité de la civilité*, decorum required that one use at least two sheets of in-quarto (32.1cm x 45cm) paper when addressing oneself to a superior (letter manuals intended for polite society throughout the following century concur on this and nearly all the other points discussed below).[9] This was called 'large' letter paper; 'small' letter paper could be used for *billets* (short notes).[10] Unlike today, at that time a letter was defined by the number of sheets of paper that composed it, not its dimensions or weight.[11] The paper was folded so as to leave room for the address to be written on one of the exposed sections, and it was then sealed with wax. Although, as we shall see, there were exceptions to this rule, *normally the same sheet of folded paper was both the letter and the envelope.* During this period most letters were thus materially different from the object that has become familiar to us since the nineteenth century, and which a modern dictionary defines as 'a written or printed message to a person or group, usually sent by mail in an envelope'.[12] For with the exception of those special letters that were placed *sous enveloppe* (wrapped in a sealed sheet of paper to further protect their secrecy or signify respect for one's superior), the same sheet of folded paper bore both the message and the address.[13] There was no difference between letter and envelope, between a letter's contents and its container.

8. In Article 10 of the 1698 postal treaty between England and France, a 'simple letter' was defined as a single folded and unsealed sheet, with the address written on part of the back; a 'double letter' was one that contained several sealed letters and weighed less than an ounce; while a 'packet' contained sealed letters weighing more than an ounce. Vaillé, *Histoire générale*, vol.5, p.411.
9. *Traité de la civilité, nouvellement dressé d'une manière exacte et méthodique et suivant les règles de l'usage vivant* (Lyon, Jean Certé, 1681), p.202. See *Le Nouveau secrétaire de la cour, ou Lettres familières sur toutes sortes de sujets, avec des réponses, une instruction pour se former dans le style épistolaire, le Cérémonial des lettres; et les règles de bienséance qu'il faut observer quand on écrit* (Paris, Théodore le Gras, 1732); *Le Nouveau secrétaire de la cour, ou Lettres familières sur toutes sortes de sujets; avec des réponses* (Nancy, L'Honoré et Chatelain, 1761). The latter edition begins with five proto-Oulipian letters, each composed without using one of the five vowels. Otherwise it is primarily a collection of model letters on various topics, with just five pages at the end composed of excerpts from previous editions of the *Nouveau secrétaire.*
10. 'Le cérémonial des lettres', in *Nouveau secrétaire de la cour* (1732), p.440.
11. Chauvet, *Introduction à l'histoire postale*, p.60, 61, n.1. My account of the functioning of the French postal system in the old regime is based primarily on Chauvet's concise exposition of these matters in the first volume of her invaluable book. Behringer's work on the Thurn and Taxis post contains a brief discussion of the functioning of a provincial post office in seventeenth-century Germany (*Thurn und Taxis*, p.94-95).
12. *Webster's New World dictionary of American English*, 3rd college edn (New York, 1988).
13. 'ENVELOPPE. s.f. Ce qui sert à envelopper. L'enveloppe d'un paquet. Ôter, défaire l'enveloppe d'un paquet. Enveloppe de cuir, de toile cirée. Sur l'enveloppe étoit écrit, à Monsieur [...] On dit, Ecrire sous l'enveloppe de quelqu'un, pour dire, Mettre sous l'adresse de quelqu'un des lettres qui sont pour un autre.' *Dictionnaire de l'Académie française*, 4th edn (Paris, Ve de Bernard Brunet, 1762).

Female letter-writers in eighteenth-century Paris could choose from a wide selection of papers of varying colors, qualities, sizes (small-format writing paper was particularly stylish) and uses, available at fashionable stationers.[14] The different paper formats bore charming names (such as *couronne* [crown], *raisin* [grape], *jésus* and *cloche* [bell]), derived from the design of the paper-maker's watermark; each format designated a sheet of a specific size (as is still the case today).[15] Nevertheless most letters were written on plain white paper, which was produced in batches of varying quality (the highest quality paper was imported from the Netherlands), each one of which also had a different name. In the eighteenth century, the ideal writing paper was:

> the whitest, thinnest paper that would sustain the action of a sharp quill and fold without tearing – a paper whose fine grain would guide the pen and whose finish would hold the brightest ink without blurring or absorbing it. The blackness of the best ink set off the whiteness of the finest paper. The smooth surface of fine writing paper allowed the writer's pen to glide over it gracefully: that grace would be apparent to the reader in the elegant hand in which words were formed.[16]

Pens, inks, envelopes

Another love letter from Diderot to Sophie Volland testifies to the fact that even the pen that was used to write a letter could contribute to its meaning. As he tells Sophie, he wrote this letter with a quill he had borrowed from the curate of a village near Langres:

> O l'heureux païs où il n'y a ni plume, ni encre, ni papier, que ce qu'il en faut au curé pour inscrire les noms des enfants qu'on y fait. Je suis à douze lieues de Langres, dans un village où c'est à la complaisance du pasteur que je dois le plaisir de causer avec ma Sophie. Jamais amant peut-être ne s'est trouvé ici; jamais du moins un aussi tendre. L'homme saint qui m'a prêté le seul tronçon de plume qu'il ait, me croit occupé de quelque grande affaire; et n'a-t-il pas raison? Quelle affaire plus grande pour moi que de vous apprendre que je revole vers vous avec une joye dont l'excès ne peut se comparer qu'à la peine que j'eus à vous quitter? Je vous reverrai donc. *Mais encore un mot de ce curé dont j'employe à vous dire que je vous aime à la folie, la même plume qui a griffonné*

14. Dena Goodman, *Becoming a woman in the Age of Letters* (Ithaca, NY, and London, 2009), p.184ff.
15. Although industrially-produced paper has no watermarks, these names (and others, such as *collier*, *écu* and *soleil*) are still used to designate paper of different sizes. For an evocation of various kinds of watermarks and laid paper used in eighteenth-century French writing paper, see John Grand-Carteret, *Vieux papiers, vieilles images; cartons d'un collectionneur* (Paris, Levasseur, 1896), vol.1, p.i. The same author's *Papeterie et papetiers* (Paris, 1913), p.39ff, lists the varieties and qualities of paper used for writing and other purposes.
16. Goodman, *Becoming a woman*, p.194.

les prônes où il damnoit ses pauvres idiots pour avoir écouté leurs cœurs qui les prêchoient bien mieux que lui.[17]

O the happy land where the only pen, or ink, or paper is what the parish priest needs to write down the names of the children that are made there. I am twelve leagues from Langres, in a village where it is thanks to the kindness of the pastor that I have the pleasure of chatting with my Sophie. Perhaps no lover has ever found himself here; certainly never such a tender one. The holy man who loaned me the only bit of quill he has believes that I am occupied with some weighty matter; and is he not right? What matter could be more important for me than to inform you that I am flying back to you with a joy whose excess can be compared only to the pain I felt upon leaving you? So, I shall see you again. *But one more word about this priest: to tell you that I love you madly I am using the same pen with which he scribbled the sermons in which he damned his poor idiots for having listened to their hearts that preached them better than he could.*

In Diderot's hand, the priest's 'bit of quill' symbolically draws a parallel between the adulterous love of Diderot and Sophie and the extra-marital affairs of the curate's parishioners. In the process, his phallic pen enables Diderot to share with Sophie a transgressive, sacrilegious pleasure, not unlike the pleasure in which Sade would invite his reader to partake when the anti-heroine of *Juliette* has sex with Pope Pius VI on Bernini's altarpiece in St Peter's Basilica.[18]

Metal pens had existed since Antiquity, but in the early modern era they were still expensive and unreliable. And although primitive fountain pens were in occasional use in the seventeenth century, in early modern Europe most letters were written with various kinds of feathers, usually goose feathers, using black ink derived from oak galls, with various additives.[19] In the sixteenth century, letters were normally folded and then wrapped in a silk thread whose ends were attached with sealing wax. Around 1640, it became more common simply to apply a cachet to the folded letter.[20] In France, as early as the sixteenth century official letters and letters from important persons were placed *sous enveloppe* (that is, wrapped in a sealed sheet of paper to protect their secrecy), as were letters addressed to one's superiors, as a sign of respect. A 1691 treatise on civility for children specifies that they should wrap letters addressed to a superior in an envelope; that letters addressed to ladies were to be wrapped in a sealed strand of silk, but that as a sign of even greater respect for the lady the letter so wrapped could also be placed in

17. Diderot to Sophie Volland, 16 August 1759, in Diderot, *Correspondance*, vol.2, p.217-18. Emphasis added.
18. Donatien-Alphonse-François, marquis de Sade, *Histoire de Juliette, ou Les Prospérites du vice* (Paris, 1987), part 4, p.156ff.
19. Grand-Carteret, *Papeterie et papetiers*, p.144ff. Grand-Carteret provides a standard recipe for writing ink, along with lovely images of ink merchants on p.137-39.
20. Alfred Franklin, *Dictionnaire historique des arts, métiers et professions exercés dans Paris depuis le treizième siècle* (New York, 1968 [orig. edn Paris and Leipzig 1906]), under 'Papetiers'.

an envelope.[21] The address was written on the back of the folded letter and repeated on the envelope. At first, the sender had to cut out such envelopes by hand from larger sheets of paper; but in the early seventeenth century French stationers began to sell *papier pour enveloppes de lettres*, paper that had been cut into dimensions such that they could be folded around a letter. Letters *sous enveloppe* were initially charged like sets of letters wrapped in a single envelope (*paquets*), since employees of the post office could not be absolutely sure – even if they held the letters up to a candle – how many sheets of paper (or how many letters) they contained.[22] The paper historian Grand-Carteret considers that it was only when when stationers began to offer folded envelope paper with hinges that could be cut open with a pocket knife that the first real 'envelopes' appeared.[23] Due to the high cost of paper, the use of such envelopes was far from standard practice before the nineteenth century, except among the privileged classes and (as a sign of respect) in letters addressed to them by their inferiors. Members of the elite sometimes used expensive imported paper with decorated borders and envelopes.[24] But it was not until the first half of the nineteenth century that a machine for folding envelopes was perfected in England by Edwin Hill, brother of Rowland Hill, secretary of the Post Office (1854-1865). Without mass-produced envelopes, uniform penny postage could not have functioned properly.[25] Mass-produced envelopes doubtless reinforced the sense, already widespread in eighteenth-century France, that the contents of a letter were private (that is, secret). When the list of grievances called *cahiers de doléances* were drawn up by the three Estates in March and April 1789, the second most frequent complaint of the French people (after the infamous *lettres de cachet*) concerned the so-called *Cabinet noir*, the government agency that was responsible (like today's NSA and GCHQ) for surveillance of private communications.

21. *Traité de la civilité*, p.216.
22. Vaillé, *Histoire des postes*, p.28; and Alain Tranquier, *Tarifs postaux 1644*, http://atrinquier.pagesperso-orange.fr/tarifs/bureau/t1644.html (last accessed 29 September 2015).
23. Grand-Carteret, *Papeterie et papetiers*, p.133.
24. In the middle of the eighteenth century, 'At the Porte-Feuille Anglais on the rue Dauphine, [the stationer] Salmon sold paper and envelopes decorated with spangles [*paillettes*], as well as "white envelopes ready-made for all formats of writing paper, morning notes, visiting cards"'. Goodman, *Becoming a woman*, p.190. I would like to thank Dena Goodman and Alden Gordon for bringing my attention to this practice.
25. 'Besides the novelty for the letter writer of 1840 of sending his letter for a penny and having that penny prepaid by a small piece of paper "with a glutinous wash at the back", an even greater change in habit was the use of an envelope to enclose the actual letter, in place of the centuries-old custom of folding the letter and writing an address on the outer face of the folded sheet. Previous to 1839 the use of an envelope would have meant a charge for it as an extra piece of paper. The "bon ton" were using them before 1840 to some extent.' Robinson, *The British Post Office*, p.299-300.

Folding, addressing, sealing

From the wide variety of methods of folding paper, a standard technique evolved, in which the paper was folded so as to yield a small rectangle, with two perpendicular flaps on the back that could be sealed with a wax cachet embossed with the arms or name of the sender.[26] The folding of a letter or envelope required time and skill, and the way in which an envelope was cut and folded could convey a great deal of information about its author. Abbé Galiani testifies to this fact in a mischievous passage of a letter to Mme Necker (the wife of Louis XV's finance minister, and Mme de Staël's mother):

> Vous m'avez promis de m'écrire souvent. Tiendrez-vous parole? Ecrivez-moi par la poste en droiture ici, mais chargez quelqu'un de faire les enveloppes. Vos lettres ressemblent à Socrate, la plus belle âme dans le corps le plus laid. Vos lettres sont aussi belles que l'enveloppe en est affreuse. Je dis cela pour faire plaisir à l'abbé Morellet et non pas pour vous humilier. Il ne vous conviendrait pas de bien faire les enveloppes. Cette matérialité ne sied pas au sublime de votre ineffable spiritualité.[27]

> You promised to write me often. Will you keep your word? Write me by post directly here, but have someone else make the envelopes. Your letters resemble Socrates, the most beautiful soul in the ugliest body. Your letters are as beautiful as the envelope is hideous. I say this to please abbé Morellet and not to humiliate you. This materiality does not suit the sublime nature of your ineffable spirituality.

Along with other matters to which I shall return, folding was part of what the 1732 edition of the *Nouveau secrétaire de la cour* – an anonymous letter manual that went through several editions in the eighteenth and nineteenth centuries – calls 'Le Cérémonial des lettres'. This it defines as 'les formalités que l'usage a établies, et par lesquelles on témoigne des égards de civilité, d'affection, d'honnêteté, et de respect pour les personnes à qui l'on écrit'.[28] (The formalities established by usage, through which one testifies to considerations of civility, affection, politeness and respect toward the persons to whom one writes.) The treatise describes three different ways of folding a letter, each of which is suitable to a particular social relationship. The first method, to be used when addressing one's superior, consisted of simply folding a sheet into four parts and wrapping it in an envelope. To write to a person who was one's social equal or inferior, an envelope was not needed, but in this case different techniques were required, depending on whether one was folding a letter or a *billet*. Folding a sheet [*feuille*] of in-quarto paper to make it into its own

26. See Vaillé, 'Le conditionnement de la lettre et les marques postales jusqu'à la Révolution', *Bulletin d'informations, de documentation et de statistique de la P.T.T.* 12 (1938), p.25-26.
27. Cited by Vaillé, in 'Le conditionnement de la lettre', p.29.
28. *Nouveau secrétaire de la cour* (1732), p.413.

envelope required a certain amount of practice, if one can judge by these instructions:

> [Q]uand on n'emploie point d'enveloppe [...] on plie [...] le premier feuillet dans sa largeur dans trois parties à peu près égales, puis les deux feuillets ensemble dans leur longueur dans trois autres parties dont les deux extrêmes se rapprochent, de sorte que celle du milieu est de même longueur que les deux autres ensemble; on renverse ce qui reste du second feuillet sur le premier, et au second pli qu'on y fait il ne reste qu'une bande dans laquelle on fait rentrer le tout, et où l'on applique le cachet. [...]
>
> Quand on veut plier une lettre de cette manière, il faut prendre si bien les mesures en écrivant, que la cire ou le pain à cacheter ne puisse mordre sur l'écriture.[29]
>
> [W]hen not using an envelope [...] one folds [...] the first half-sheet [feuillet] widthwise into three nearly equal parts, then folds the two pages together lengthwise into three more parts whose two ends almost touch, so that the middle part is as long as the two others together; one folds the rest of the second page back onto the first, and all that remains of the second fold is a strip into which one inserts the rest, and one applies the seal. [...]
>
> When one wishes to fold a letter in this way, one must get the precise measure of the entire sheet, so that the wax or bar or wax cannot touch the writing.

Folding a *billet* was much simpler; in fact, one was not even expected to seal it, but for this very reason a *billet* needed to be delivered by a trusted servant, and never by the post.[30]

As significant as the method of folding, the way in which a letter or envelope was sealed spoke eloquently of the sender's social values and standing. In December 1752, ten months after the Jesuits had managed to have the *Encyclopédie* of Diderot and d'Alembert condemned and its publication interrupted, Diderot sent a letter to La Condamine that bore a seal in the shape of a *fronde* (sling), the weapon that over the previous century had come to symbolize revolt or insurrection.[31] A seal (Latin *sigillum*) is literally a sign: a design or emblem imprinted upon molten wax in order to signify the authenticity of a document.[32] It took time and care, not to mention a certain artistic sense, to melt the end of a stick of sealing wax and emboss the wax (often scented, and available in an assortment of shapes and colors) with one's arms; this method of sealing was a token of gentility. In aristocratic circles, the most distinguished kind of seal bore one's coat of arms; monograms, monochromes and heraldic devices were also in use.[33] In contrast, the little bar of sealing

29. *Nouveau secrétaire de la cour* (1732), p.442-43.
30. *Nouveau secrétaire de la cour* (1732), p.441.
31. Diderot to La Condamine, 16 December 1752, *Correspondance*, vol.1, p.147-48.
32. Jean-Jacques Rousseau makes a strange allusion to the use of an *oublie* (seal of unleavened bread) as a security precaution. Jean-Jacques Rousseau to Pierre-Alexandre Du Peyrou, 8 September 1767, *CC*, vol.34, p.77 (6049).
33. *Nouveau secrétaire de la cour* (1732), p.443-44.

wax, which made its first appearance in the middle of the eighteenth century, made possible a much more expeditious method of sealing, which was also better suited to correspondents who did not have a great deal of time on their hands: one had only to moisten the bar and, pressing it into a concave shape (*en creux*), affix it to the folded flap and imprint one's seal. According to the 1732 'Cérémonial des lettres', it is most impolite to seal a letter to one's superior with an individual bar of wax (*pain à cacheter*).[34] Writing just before World War I, Grand-Carteret viewed the replacement in the previous century of sticks of sealing wax (*bâtons de cire*) by prepared individual bars as another regrettably democratizing effect of the French Revolution: 'And it was thus that the Revolution unknowingly caused the defeat of lovely scented wax sticks – an aristocratic mode of sealing – and brought about the triumph of individual bars – a democratic sealing method.'[35] Sealing wax was usually red but could also be black, the color that was used for letters to people in mourning.[36] Echoes of the time when letters were folded and closed with wax seals can still be heard in those European languages where a letter that has been closed for security is said to be 'sealed' (*versiegelt*, *cachetée*, etc.); in modern French, the word *pli* can mean not just 'fold' but also 'envelope' (as in the expression *une lettre sous pli*) and 'letter' (as in *recevoir un pli*).

In early modern Europe, every element (deliberate or not) that contributed to the preparation, composition and mailing of a letter had a rhetorical, social and esthetic function. For this reason, the letter manuals that began appearing at the end of the seventeenth century provided not only models of letters to be used in a wide range of situations, but advice on the formatting, appearance, folding and sealing of letters.[37] These are matters that, along with folding, compose part of the 'Cérémonial des lettres'. This text is followed by another treatise entirely devoted to the title by which one should address one's correspondent; in a society obsessively concerned with questions of rank, this was a particularly delicate question. One of the topics covered by 'Le Cérémonial des lettres' is the distinction between *billets* (short notes) and

34. *Nouveau secrétaire de la cour* (1732), p.444.

35. Grand-Carteret, *Papeterie et papetiers*, p.168.

36. *Nouveau secrétaire de la cour* (1732), p.444. In a letter to Pierre-Alexandre Du Peyrou, Jean-Jacques Rousseau mentions only the inferior quality of black sealing wax, but says nothing about its social meaning. Rousseau to Pierre-Alexandre Du Peyrou, 2 April 1767, *CC*, vol.33, p.4 (5809).

37. Bannet, *Empire of letters*, p.xiv. 'Abbreviated Secretaries or Letter-Writers were also inserted into even more compendious *vade mecums* [...] These taught numeracy, book-keeping, measuring and surveying and other practical skills as well as epistolography, and gave directions for making and preserving ink, for cutting the nibs on quill pens, and for writing secret letters', p.xv.

letters: the kind of paper to be used in each genre ('small' letter paper for *billets* and for letters addressed to one's inferiors; 'large' (in-quarto) letter paper for letters; larger (in-folio) paper when writing to the king or to members of the foreign nobility), the appropriate salutation (*inscription*, also called *suscription*) and closing (*souscription*) for each rank (as well as their placement: how far they should be located from the body of the text, on which side of the page, how much room there should be between the three conventional parts [for example, *Je suis* or *J'ai l'honneur d'être* + *de votre Altesse* + *Le très humble et très obéissant serviteur*] of the closing), to whom and in what circumstances each genre may be written (addressing a *billet* to one's superior is not done).

The treatise also deals with the polite conventions that govern the body of the letter (it is no longer necessary to leave a margin or to avoid writing on both sides of a sheet of paper; neither commonplaces, ambiguities, similes nor other forms of rhetorical self-indulgence are allowed; a cheerful tone is to be carefully avoided, as it can easily decline into joking; letters must be free of deletions and marginal notes). We are told that if some persons fool themselves into believing that their wealth entitles them to be treated with more respect than their equals, one should not take it upon oneself to disabuse them of this notion:

> Les grandes richesses sont de quelque considération, quand il est question d'examiner le rang; un homme riche se croit aisément au-dessus des ses égaux; il faut excuser son erreur,
>
> *Stultitiam patiuntur opes*[38]
>
> et lui écrire conformément à l'idée qu'il a de lui-même. Cette observation peut paraître frivole, mais elle ne l'est nullement, puisque ce n'est pas la peine d'écrire à quelqu'un pour l'offenser.[39]

> Great wealth is worthy of consideration when rank is examined: a rich man easily believes himself above his equals; his error must be excused
>
> *Stultitiam patiuntur opes*
>
> and he should be addressed according to the idea he has of himself. This observation may seem frivolous, but it is not in the least, since there is no point in writing to someone in order to offend him.

In court society, keen attention to distinctions of rank and close observation of others were required in the composition of a letter, as in all other aspects of daily life.[40]

In *Papetiers et papeterie* (1913) Grand-Carteret cites a lyrical evocation of this lost epistolary world by an unnamed contemporary, who was less concerned with the social dynamics that had preoccupied authors of

38. 'Riches allow one to be foolish.' Horace, *Epistles*, 1.18.29.
39. *Nouveau secrétaire de la cour* 1732, p.424.
40. See the classic analyses of these phenomena by Norbert Elias in *Court society* (Oxford, 1983).

letter-writing manuals in the eighteenth century than with the esthetic dimension of letters:

> Une lettre, en France, était un événement pour le destinataire, un plaisir pour celui ou celle qui l'envoyait. L'idée de parler au loin – qui est encore si agréable aux novices qui usent du téléphone – était délicieuse et aussi grande pour ceux qui se servaient de l'écriture, *extra muros*, hors des murs de leur demeure, de leur ville, ou de leur province.
>
> Un premier effort de pensée et de style, un second effort de calligraphie, un effort de salutations et hommages d'élite; il s'agissait encore d'un chef-d'œuvre de paraphe, de parfaire une signature rare et compliquée, à la fois majestueuse et intime, très cordiale et très noble. Et ce n'était pas fini. Il fallait épandre, d'une main exercée, la poudre de sable et d'or sur l'encre qu'il fallait sécher. Il fallait, en outre, et surtout, coucher doucement les mots, les uns sur les autres, hermétiquement.
>
> C'est ici que commençait le talent – et le génie. Les correspondants les plus pressés et les plus modestes pliaient leur lettre en trois parts égales, faisaient entrer un des derniers tiers dans l'autre, et fermaient le tout de deux – ou d'un – modestes pains à cacheter ou d'un ou deux cachets triomphaux, aux armes et sommés de couronnes, de crestes et de bêtes monstrueuses.
>
> Les plus raffinés, les plus patients, savaient ployer leur texte en trois dans le sens de la hauteur, en trois dans le sens de la largeur, fermer, en triptyque, les premiers plis, ramener sur les premiers, les derniers, mais, ici, il fallait, nécessairement, deux pains ou deux cachets, très sérieux. – et la missive était sacrée.
>
> C'est sous cette forme que furent closes et scellées les épitres et épistoles les plus illustres: celles de Voiture et de Balzac (lesquelles, au reste, étaient d'avance, des 'lettres ouvertes' et exercices de littérature), celles de Racine, de Fléchier, de La Fontaine, de Chapelle et de Bachaumont, de Fontenelle, de Voltaire, du président de Brosses, de Dupaty et de Paul-Louis Courier, même celles de Mme de Sévigné, de la Palatine et de Mlle de Lespinasse. C'était un art accessoire que de savoir donner à un chef- d'œuvre de lettre un aspect extérieur de chef-d'œuvre, avec une suscription digne d'un maître d'écriture et d'un maître à danser, déjà agréable, déjà révérence, avec un cachet qui se faisait saluer avant que d'être violé.

In France a letter was an event for the addressee, a pleasure for him or her who sent it. The idea of talking at a distance – which is still so pleasant for the novices who make use of the telephone – was delightful and also grand for those who used writing *extra muros*, outside of the walls of their home, their city, or their province.

A first effort of thought and style, a second effort of calligraphy, an effort of greetings and noble men; and then a masterpice of an autograph was called for, by perfecting a rare and complicated signature that was both majestic and intimate, at once most cordial and most noble. And all was not finished. A practiced hand was needed to spread the sand and gold powder on the fresh ink. It was necessary as well to inscribe the words upon each other gently, hermetically.

Here is where talent – and genius – began. The most hurried and modest correspondents folded their letter in three equal parts, slipped one of the last two thirds into the other, and closed the whole with two (or one) modest bars of wax or one or two triumphal seals, with arms and topped with crowns, crests and monstrous beasts.

> The most refined, the most patient, knew how to pleat their text in three vertically and horizontally, then close the first folds into a triptych and fold the last ones back on the first, but here two or three very serious bars or seals were needed, and the missive was sacred.
>
> It was in this form that the most illustrious epistles and letterets were closed and sealed: the letters of Voiture and Balzac, Fléchier, La Fontaine, Chapelle and Bachaumont, Fontenelle, Voltaire, Président de Brosses, Dupaty and Paul-Louis Courier, even those of Mme de Sévigné, the Princess Palatine and Mlle de Lespinasse. A secondary art was in knowing how to give a masterwork of a letter the exterior appearance of a masterwork, with a superscription worthy of a writing master and a dancing master, already pleasant, already a bow, with a seal that called forth a greeting before being violated.[41]

Paper and ink, calligraphy, folding, sealing: each of these elements was a potential source of social recognition and pleasure for addressor and addressee; each of them contributed to the representation of the sender, the receiver, and of the relationship between them. In many cases, once a letter was received, still another epistolary art would then be called upon: that of reading the letter aloud, 'naturally' or not, in a way that would heighten the pleasure of one's audience at receiving news from the sender. The practice of reading letters aloud was so ingrained that letter-writers who wanted to keep the contents of their letters (or portions of them) private had to resort to radical measures.[42] On the other hand, it was not considered proper for children to read aloud the letters they had received.[43]

Postage

Before the first postage stamps were issued in the 1840s, postage was usually paid by the receiver, for otherwise there would have been no incentive for employees of the post to convey them to their destination.[44] This convention also had the effect of discouraging anonymous letters, since addressees could refuse to pay for letters whose handwriting or seals they could not identify and for packages without a familiar countersignature.[45] The major drawback of this system was that, since senders had no incentive to restrict the number, size, or weight of items sent, the postal service could not recover the cost when recipients were

41. E. L. J. [Ernest La Jeunesse?], 'Le centenaire de l'enveloppe des lettres', in *Le Journal* cited by Grand-Carteret, *Papeterie et papetiers*, p.134-35, n.1.
42. Bannet, *Empire of letters*, p.89ff, p.256, 278-279.
43. *Traité de civilité*, p.218-19. On the history of reading aloud, see: Roger Chartier (ed.), *Histoires de la lecture: un bilan des recherches* (Paris, 1995), and Guglielmo Cavallo and Roger Chartier (eds), *A History of reading in the West* (Amherst, MA, 1999).
44. Vaillé, *Histoire générale*, vol.2, p.190; Ellis, *The Post Office in the eighteenth century*, p.38-39. See also Robinson, *The British Post Office*, p.120, and Zilliacus, *From pillar to post*, p.45-46.
45. As I show in Chapters 4, p.127-32, and 5, p.142-46, both Voltaire and Rousseau struggled with this dilemma.

unable or unwilling to pay for delivered items. When the receiver refused to accept a letter, the receiving post office could either write off its cost or refuse to deliver any further mail to the addressee until all the postage due had been paid off.[46]

Postage stamps would also obviate the need to consider the distance between two post offices in the calculation of postage rates. Prior to the introduction of stamps, domestic letter rates in France were based on the number of sheets, whether or not the sheets were wrapped in an 'envelope' (see below), the delivery speed (ordinary or extraordinary) and the destination (or distance to the destination) itself.[47] By the middle of the eighteenth century, if a mail carrier (in the relatively few places where home delivery of mail was provided prior to the creation of *petites postes*) was caught trying to increase his income by falsifying postal rates, he paid for his crime with public humiliation.[48] Although postage rates varied widely from country to country, sending a letter by post cost much more than it does today. In the sixteenth century, fees for the Taxis post were so high that relatively few private individuals could afford them, especially if they had to pay messengers to fetch letters and carry them to the nearest Taxis post office.[49] The same was true in Britain, where high postage costs were a serious problem from the very beginnings of public mail service in the 1630s until the introduction of postage stamps in 1840. Indeed from the beginning of the eighteenth century the American stamp tax was meant to offer the British government 'a way of limiting communication by increasing its costs'.[50] While it originally cost 2d to send a single sheet up to 80 miles, by the end of the eighteenth century the price for carrying that same sheet had risen to 3d for 15 miles. If one considers that 2d was the price of a bushel of the best oats in the

46. Vaillé, *Histoire générale*, vol.5, p.109.
47. Calculation of weight and distance was complicated by the existence of varying units of measurement in different areas of the country. For example, in calculating the cost of sending a letter from Paris to Dijon, the Parisian league (*lieue*) of 3.89 kms (2.41 miles) would be used; but since the Burgundy league was much longer (5.849 kms, 3.65 miles), it would presumably have cost less to send a letter in the opposite direction, from Dijon to Paris. This ambiguity was resolved in 1737 with the creation of a unit called the postal league (*lieue postale*: 3.98 kms, 2.47 miles). See http://atrinquier.pagesperso-orange.fr/tarifs/bureau/introtarif.html#tarifs (last accessed 29 September 2015).
48. A 'sovereign judgment' by Bertier de Sauvigny of the Chambre des Comptes, dated 1 April 1746, condemns 'Gilles Breton, a mail carrier of the Etampes letter post, to be bound and shackled on three consecutive market days, with a sign bearing these words, *Mail carrier, forger of false taxes*, and to banishment from the Paris generality for three years'. Bertier de Sauvigny, *Jugement souverain qui condamne Gilles Breton, facteur du bureau de la poste aux lettres d'Etampes à être mis au carcan et à un bannissement de la généralité de Paris pendant trois ans* (Paris, Imprimerie Royale, 1 April 1746).
49. Zilliacus, *From pillar to post*, p.49.
50. Bannet, *Empire of letters*, p.235.

Southampton market on 21 August 1625, one ninth of a carpenter's wages in 1633, and that 2d in 1630 is the rough equivalent of 75d in 2015, this concern is understandable.[51] Whyman notes that by that time, 'Even the rich kept detailed records of amounts of postage paid' and 'All ranks developed strategies to avoid postage, because mail had become a necessity'.[52] In October 1766, while Jean-Jacques Rousseau was staying at Wootton in Staffordshire, he kept an account of his expenses. It shows him spending 1 or 2d for domestic letters, 6d for letters from the continent, between 6 and 8d for a *paquet* (set of letters addressed to the same person), and as much as 11s 6d for a large package of books.[53] John Locke's journal shows that on 30 September 1776, during his prolonged stay in Provence, he paid more (10 sous) for the postage on a letter than for a fashionable pair of scented leather gloves (9 sous).[54] At the beginning of the seventeenth century in France, the addressee of a simple letter paid between 2 and 10 *sols* for it, while a mason earned between 8 and 10 *sols* a day.[55] The rate schedule for 1644 lists a range of prices for items sent from Paris: for 'simple letters', between 3 and 5 *sols*; for 'double letters with envelope below one ounce 1644', from 4 to 6 *sols*; and for 'packets above one ounce', 4 to 10 *sols*. Letters for cities or towns not named on the list were taxed at the rate of the nearest named city. Yet in Languedoc between 1640 and 1690, the average cost of a pound of mutton (a luxury meat) was between 2 *sols* 6 deniers and 2 *sols* 8 deniers. It is also worth noting that rates set in Paris were not always enforced in distant provinces such as Languedoc where postal farmers and other administrators sometimes chose to interpret the regulations to their own advantage.[56] The following table provides examples of the rates for letters in France, depending upon type of letter and distance, as established by the Royal Decree of 1703:[57]

51. Jan Luiten van Zanden, *Wages and the cost of living in southern England (London) 1450-1700*, http://www.iisg.nl/hpw/dover.php; The National Archives (last accessed 29 September 2015). Currency converter http://www.nationalarchives.gov.uk/currency/ (last accessed 29 September 2015). I would like to thank my colleague Margaret Hunt for referring me to these databases.
52. Whyman, *The Pen and the people*, p.63. See also Brant, *Empire of letters*, p.12.
53. Rousseau, *Dépenses à Wootton*, 15 October 1766, *CC*, vol.31, p.323-25 (A456).
54. *Locke's travels in France 1675-1679: as related in his journals, correspondence and other papers*, ed. and introduction by John Lough (Cambridge, 1953), p.111.
55. The price of 2 *sols* for a letter is given by Vaillé, *Histoire générale*, vol.5, p.189. In addition to the legal cost of postage, it was common for employees of the French post to demand additional fees, for which they provided more or less plausible justifications. *Histoire générale*, vol.5, p.107ff. (At this time the *livre*, *sol* and *denier* were accounting currency, not actual coins. See Locke's entry for 1 February 1776, *Locke's travels in France*, p.23-24.)
56. Biard, *Postes et messageries*, p.44ff.
57. Trinquier, http://atrinquier.pagesperso-orange.fr/tarifs/bureau/t1644.html (last accessed 29 September 2015). On the status of periodicals (which were carried by the post but

	Simple letter	Letter with envelope	Double letter	Ounce of paquets
Up to 20 leagues	3 *sols*	4 *sols*	5 *sols*	12 *sols*
20 to 40 leagues	4 *sols*	5 *sols*	7 *sols*	16 *sols*
40 to 60 leagues	5 *sols*	6 *sols*	9 *sols*	20 *sols*
60 to 80 leagues	6 *sols*	7 *sols*	10 *sols*	24 *sols*
80 to 100 leagues	7 *sols*	8 *sols*	12 *sols*	28 *sols*
100 to 120 leagues	8 *sols*	9 *sols*	14 *sols*	32 *sols*
120 to 150 leagues	9 *sols*	10 *sols*	15 *sols*	36 *sols*
More than 150 leagues	10 *sols*	11 *sols*	18 *sols*	40 *sols*
From Lyon to Perpignan and back	7 *sols*	8 *sols*	12 *sols*	28 *sols*

Table 1: Examples of the rates for letters in France by type / distance (as established by the Royal Decree of 1703)

This rate table would be revised in 1759, in order to keep up with inflation and pay for the costs of the Seven Years War.[58] In theory, the number of relays (*postes*) between two places played the most important role in the calculation of distance, but unregulated handling costs (especially for mail to foreign countries) could be added to the official rate.[59] Moreover letters to and from Paris were not assessed at the same rate as those between other destinations within the country. Measures of weight also varied from one *pays* (region) to another, so that, for example, it cost less to send a package from Toulouse to Paris than from Paris to Toulouse! To complicate matters more, the further regional postal officials were from Paris, the easier it seems to have been for them to get away with increasing their income by adding arbitrary and excessive processing fees to the official postage rate.[60] By compounding the cost of

---

not included in the rate schedule) see Chauvet, *Introduction à l'histoire postale*, p.64. Rates for rental of horses from the horse post were also subject to repeated revision by royal decree. See *Ordonnance [...] qui fixe à 30 sols par cheval pour chaque poste simple, les doubles postes et postes et demie à proportion, et les postes royales sur le pied de 3 l. par cheval, non compris les guides des postillons, à commencer du 1er juillet 1723 jusqu'au dernier juin 1724 [...]* (Paris, Louis-Denis Delatour and Pierre Simon, 24 June 1723); *Ordonnance du Roy qui fixe le prix qui sera payé pour les chevaux de poste, servant aux chaises à deux personnes, aux chaises à une personne seule, aux berlines, aux courriers allant en guide, et aux courriers de cabinet* (Paris, Louis-Denis Delatour, 17 June 1725); *Ordonnance..., qui à commencer du 1er janvier 1757, fixe à 25 sols par poste le prix de tous les chevaux de poste* [etc.], (Paris, L'Imprimerie Royale, 28 November 1756).

58. Biard, *Postes et messageries*, p.77. It has been shown that in the middle of the nineteenth century the cost of postage seems to have limited most written communication to distances between 20 and 100 kms. See Cécile Dauphin, Pierrette Lebrun-Pezerat and Danièle Poublan, with the collaboration of Michel Demonet, 'L'enquête postale de 1847', in Roger Chartier, *et al.*, *La Correspondance: les usages de la lettre aux XIXe siècle* (Paris, 1991), p.48. The situation was probably not much different in the three previous centuries.

59. *Postes et messageries*, p.76.

60. *Postes et messageries*, p.60, 68-70.

an already expensive public service, local abuses fostered popular support for centralized rationalization of postage rates.

Since in France it cost less to mail several letters as a *paquet*[61] (more than one letter enclosed in a single envelope) than to post them separately, it was not unusual for letters addressed to different people to be sent in a packet to a single person; the recipient of the *paquet* would distribute the other letters to their intended addressees. However in court circles putting more than one letter in an envelope was not the proper thing to do (doubtless because it betrayed a plebeian desire to save the addressee money), unless one was writing to a lady and her suspicious husband or to a nubile young lady and her parents.[62] As we shall see in a later chapter, Voltaire's nobiliary pretentions did not prevent him from having recourse to this device. For example, on 3 September 1760 M. de Voltaire sent his friend Damilaville in Paris a packet containing three letters: one for Diderot, one for Damilaville himself, and one to be sent to Madame Belot by the *petite poste* that had been established that very year:

> Je vous envoie, monsieur, une lettre à cachet volant pour m. Diderot. Je crois que vous vous intéressez autant que lui à tout ce que mon cœur lui dit; vous pensez tous deux de la même façon [...] Oserais je vous supplier de faire parvenir, par la petite poste, cette lettre à madame Belot? [63]

> I am sending you, Sir, a partially sealed letter for Mr Diderot. I think that you are as interested as he in everything that my heart tells him; you both think the same way [....] May I dare beg you to have this letter sent to Madame Belot by the *petite poste*?

On the other hand, since each additional letter in an envelope represented a loss of income for both the postal farmer (*maître des postes*) and the post master (*maître des courriers*), correspondents had to make sure not to abuse this expedient. In a letter to Sophie Volland written during one of his stays at baron d'Holbach's country estate in Grandval, Diderot advised her against sending him any more letters from Paris in an envelope:

> Mr Udet m'a fait dire que la première qui lui viendroit sous enveloppe seroit renvoyée à Paris. Je me hâte de vous prévenir; adressez dans la suite: *A Mr*

61. 'PAQUET se dit [...] d'Une ou de plusieurs lettres enfermées sous une enveloppe.' *Dictionnaire de l'Académie française*, 4th edn (1762). Although the modern sense of *paquet* as 'package' does not appear in any contemporary dictionaries that I have been able to consult, Voltaire sometimes uses it to designate a package (usually containing books) in the modern sense of the word. See Voltaire to Mme Du Deffand, 10 October 1760, D8535.
62. *Nouveau secrétaire de la cour* (1732), p.443-44.
63. Voltaire to Etienne Noël Damilaville, 3 September 1760, D8433. A *cachet volant* was an incomplete seal that that adhered only to the upper fold of a letter. The *femme de lettres* and translator Octavie Belot, née Guichard (1719-1805), was the second wife of presiding magistrate Jean-Baptiste François Durey de Meynières.

Hudet, pour remettre à Mr Diderot; ou envoyez chez le baron, ou chez Mr d'Aine, maître des requêtes, rue de l'Université, avec mon adresse au Grandval. Mais le plus sûr est Mr Udet, pourvu qu'il y n'ait point d'enveloppe. *L'enveloppe fait perdre le port au fermier et le bénéfice au directeur. Si ce n'est pas leur compte, ce n'est pas mon intention.*[64]

Mr Udet has sent me word that the next letter that reaches him in an envelope will be sent back to Paris. I hasten to warn you; from now on use this address: *To Mr Hudet, to be forwarded to Mr Diderot*; or send your letters to the baron or to Mr d'Aine,[65] Master of Requests, rue de l'Université, with my address at Grandval. But the most reliable is Mr Udet, as long as there is no envelope. *The envelope makes the farmer lose postage and deprives the maître des courriers of profit.* If it doesn't suit them, it is not my intention.

At this time there were no cross-country links in the French post road system, so that a letter sent from Caen (in Normandy) to Angers (several hundred kilometers south, in Anjou), was routed through Paris and postage therefore charged for the two routes – Caen to Paris, Paris to Angers – at a much greater cost than if it had been sent directly.[66] In England, since most mail passed through London, its cost was increased for the same reason.[67] In France, weight mattered only in the case of *paquets*, but the value of an ounce varied from city to city.[68] As previously noted, writing on a double (folded) sheet of in-quarto paper was considered to be more polite, even though postage on a double letter cost the addressee more. Hence one finds Voltaire apologizing to the marquis d'Argenson (who would soon become Louis XV's foreign minister) for writing on a half sheet [*feuillet*]: 'Pardon, il s'est trouvé une grande figure d'optique sur l'autre feuillet. Je l'ay déchiré. Adieu monsieur, respect, reconnaissance.' (Excuse me, there was a large optical diagram on the other half [feuillet]. I tore it up. Adieu, Sir, respect, gratitude.) [69] Indeed

64. Diderot to Sophie Volland, 20 October 1759, *Correspondance*, vol.2, p.293. Emphasis added.
65. Jean-Baptiste Nicolas d'Aine was Holbach's brother-in-law.
66. The fee schedule established in 1627 by the Postal General, Pierre d'Alméras, for mail posted in Paris applied only to regular mail deliveries. It 'made provision for four destinations and three taxes for each of them, one for a simple letter, one for small packets weighing up to one-half ounce, and one per ounce for packets weighing more than that.' (Vaillé, *Histoire générale*, vol.2, p.193).

    Fee schedules from 1685 and 1703 list four categories of postage: for simple letters, letters with envelopes, 'double' letters and packets: http://pagesperso-orange.fr/atrinquier/tarifs/bureau/t1676.html (last accessed 29 September 2015). Fees for mail addressed to foreign destinations were even more complex and variable. See *Continuation du Traité de la police* of de La Mare, vol.IV, title XIV, ch.VII.
67. 'Since postage was based on mileage, the customer paid twice: first for the journey to London; then outward to the addressee.' Whyman, *The Pen and the people*, p.55.
68. Vaillé, *Histoire générale*, vol.5, p.116ff. See Danielle Fauque, 'Mesure (systèmes et instruments de)', in Michel Delon (ed.), *Dictionnaire européen des Lumières* (Paris, 1997).
69. Voltaire to René-Louis, marquis d'Argenson, 26 January 1740, D2030. In his editorial note 2, Besterman remarks that 'It was regarded as more courteous to write on a double (folded) sheet; the second leaf of MS1 has in fact been removed'. Grand-Carteret cites the

the *Nouveau secrétaire de la cour* (1732) instructs its readers that it is most improper to prepay the postage on a letter addressed to one's superior, unless forced to do so when addressing the letter to a foreign country.[70] On the other hand, most recipients of mail were less concerned with *politesse* than with the cost of receiving letters. Whyman remarks that due to the cost of postage in Britain 'there was a taboo against letters of more than one sheet'.[71] And Brant cites the example of a correspondent of Thomas Percy 'who apologized at length for sending him a long and therefore expensive letter'.[72]

The eulogist for the philologist Georgius Graevius (1632-1703), declared that Graevius had spent one fifth of his wages on postage. In order to spare their correspondents the necessity of making such expenditures, members of the Republic of Letters would often have letters delivered to their recipients by friends and other private individuals. In a letter to his father, Pierre Bayle explains that he has entrusted it to a friend, so that the letter would arrive more surely and his father wouldn't have to pay for it: '[L]a quantité de paroles que je vous envoirai ne se perdra pas par les chemins, ni ne vous coûtera pas de l'argent, qui sont les deux inconvénients que l'on trouve par toutes des autres voies de vous donner des nouvelles.' ([T]he quantity of words I shall send you will not get lost on the way, nor will it cost you any money, which are the two drawbacks to be found by any other ways.)[73] In 1761 Jean-Jacques Rousseau's epistolary novel *Julie ou La Nouvelle Héloïse* enjoyed such phenomenal success that he was bombarded with manuscripts and letters and soon had to publish a public plea for mercy, in the form of a billet to the *Mercure de France* of March 1762.[74] Although Voltaire was much wealthier than Rousseau and went to great expense to pay the amount charged for the countless packages and letters he accepted, even he could not afford to pay for all the unsolicited packages that were sent

---

advice of Antoine de Courtin in 1695: 'It is also good to know that, to mark greater respect, a letter is placed in an envelope, with the address written on the outside. And for ladies, letters are sealed with silk; if it is simply as a sign of greater respect, a letter that already has been sealed with silk is placed in an envelope on which the address is written.' *Papeterie et papetiers*, p.133ff. The 1761 *Nouveau secrétaire de la cour* stipulates that 'It would be a lack of propriety to send a letter... without an envelope to a person above one'. p.442-43.

70. *Nouveau secrétaire de la cour* (1732), p.454.

71. Whyman, *The Pen and the people*, p.63.

72. Brant, *Empire of letters*, p.12.

73. Pierre Bayle to Jean Bayle, 21 September 1671. Cited by Antony McKenna, 'La correspondance de Pierre Bayle' in *Les Grands Intermédiaires culturels de la République des Lettres: études de correspondances du XVIe au XVIIIe siècles*, ed. Christiane Berkvens-Stevelinck, Hans Bots and Jens Häseler (Paris, 2005), p.320-21.

74. Rousseau aux Auteurs et aux Beaux Esprits, early March 1762, *CC*, vol.10, p.134 (1698). See Chapter 5, p.142-46, for the full text of this notice.

to him. For this reason he also published an announcement to that effect.[75] In addition, Voltaire had to concern himself with the burden of postage fees on his less affluent correspondents. In 1761 he gave the cost of postage as the reason (excuse for?) why he did not write more often to the actor Lekain: '[J]e vous écris rarement, la poste est trop chère pour vous faire payer des lettres inutiles.' ([I] write to you rarely; the post is too expensive to have you pay for useless letters.) [76]

Before the latter part of the eighteenth century (except during the few months in late 1653 when Villayer's system was available), in France one could only send mail from one part of a city to another by engaging the services of a messenger. Intraurban *petites postes* finally provided correspondents with another option, since the postage for these services was inexpensive and prepaid. As its name implies, Dockwra's penny post in London (1680) delivered letters for a penny. Its letters were stamped with the hour, day and office and delivered six to ten times a day.[77] When a *petite poste* was finally opened in Paris (1760) – after an unsuccessful attempt a century before – mail was collected as many as nine times a day.[78] It also provided people like Voltaire, who were at a great distance from the city, with an inconvenient but effective way of sparing their needy Parisian correspondents the cost of receiving their letters from the provinces. As we have seen, Voltaire had only to put letters in a *paquet* addressed to a friend in Paris (such as Damilaville or the d'Argentals) and ask him to forward them by the *petite poste*.[79] Like others who were in a position to do so, Voltaire sometimes freed his correspondents from the obligation to pay for postage by using the signature stamp (*contreseing*) and franking privilege (*franchise*) of his powerful relations, a device that also enabled him to communicate his thoughts more freely.[80] Despite such expedients as the *paquet* and the *franchise*, in France one still had to prepay the postage of letters to be sent abroad, as well as those addressed to important persons (such as magistrates, notaries and lawyers), who could not be expected to accept unpaid letters.[81] The franking privilege (instituted by Act of Parliament in 1660) may have been abused even more in England, where persons with franking privileges were allowed to

75. This announcement and the other steps Voltaire took to limit what he and his correspondents paid for postage are discussed in Chapter 4, p.127-32.
76. Voltaire to Henri Louis Lekain, *c.*7 August 1761, D9149. In fact, there are 93 letters from Voltaire to Lekain in the Besterman edition of the correspondence.
77. Whyman, *The Pen and the people*, p.52.
78. Hubert Cappart, 'La petite poste de Paris', http://e.boonafoux-amvd.chez-alice.fr/jadis/jadis1/cappart.htm (last accessed 29 September 2015).
79. Between 15 June 1760 and 5 July 1762, Voltaire had recourse to this expedient eight times.
80. On the proliferation of franking privileges in the eighteenth century and the efforts of postal farmers to limit them, see Vaillé, *Histoire générale*, vol.5, p.125ff.
81. Lenain, *La Poste de l'ancienne France*, p.43.

frank letters for any business with which they were connected.[82] However for persons without the privileges of an MP or a Voltaire the necessity of paying for the letters one received could impose an intolerable burden.[83]

Collection and conveyance

As noted in the Introduction, the modern postal service is more than a system of relays (or 'posts'): it is also a collection and delivery agency. In *The Pen and the people*, Susan Whyman briefly summarizes the journey of a letter after it was handed into the General Letter Office.[84] Here I shall focus on how letters were collected and delivered in France. Depending upon where the sender lived and whether or not the sender and the recipient lived in the same city or town, there were three ways of making a letter available for collection by the post: leaving it at the counter of a post office, putting it in a mail box, or paying a foot messenger (called a *piéton*) to carry the letter to the nearest post office.[85] In addition, when the *petites postes* made town delivery of mail available in the late eighteenth century and some large offices of the (interurban) *poste aux lettres* began offering residential delivery of mail, one could ask the letter carrier (*facteur*) – whose job was to deliver mail, not collect it – to carry letters to the post office. Daily postal service was offered rarely (and almost exclusively in the North), and the mail coach usually scheduled its departures only a few times a week: Marchand reports that only 10% of the cities with postal connections offered service more than two or three times a week.[86] The *Almanach royal* of 1755 supports this observation. It indicates that most cities and towns in France (and many cities abroad) had postal service two or three times a week, but that even some small

82. 'Peers and Officers of State were also privileged, holders of this right were allowed to frank letters for their friends or for any business with which they were connected; MPs were in great demand on the Boards of the Banks and large commercial houses. The system was abused to an increasing extent. In 1776 the loss of revenue from franked letters reached the sum of £119,000. It is on record that no fewer than 100,000 franked bankers' letters passed through the London Office during a single day in October, 1794.' Horace N. Soper, *The Mails: history, organization and methods of payment* (London, 1946), p.4. On the evolution of franking privileges, see Vaillé, *Histoire générale*, vol.4, p.44ff; Whyman, *The Pen and the people*, p.52, 65-71.
83. After the Seven Years War, Frederick II of Prussia appointed 1500 French finance officials to regularize and rationalize the postal system, thus increasing the postage rates. These officials became an object of popular hatred. The 'französiche Postregie' entailed a system of reciprocal spying and denunciation between the public and the postal officials. North, *Die Post*, p.37.
84. Whyman, *The Pen and the people*, p.50-53.
85. Chauvet, *Introduction à l'histoire postale*, p.81. Although *piéton* means 'pedestrian' in modern French, in the context of the early modern post it was a technical expression.
86. Marchand, *Le Maître de poste*, p.144.

towns in the North (such as Bavay: population 1339 in 1793) had daily service, while Lyon was the only city south of the Loire – doubtless because of its strategic location – to be so privileged (except on Sundays); even the larger cities in the South had only two-day (Bordeaux) or three-day (Marseille, Toulouse) service. The post served towns in the least accessible regions of the country (such as the Auvergne and the Limousin) only once a week. The same North/South hierarchy generally obtained for departures from abroad: cities such as Berlin, Bremen and Geneva (every day except Sunday) enjoyed daily mail service, whereas the post left Bologna, Rome and Madrid just once weekly; a significant exception to the rule was Barcelona, from which there were three weekly departures.[87]

Although the French postal farm had established an efficient mechanism for collection of mail and transport from one city to another, in the middle of the eighteenth century the only way for urban dwellers to discover whether they had any mail was to go (or have someone else go) to a post office and ask. The *petites postes* thus provided a solution to the problem of mail delivery within cities. In addition, Louis-Sébastien Mercier (in his *Tableau de Paris* [1781]) and others would soon give the mailmen of the Parisian *petite poste* a reputation as conveyors of billets-doux (so-called *poulets*, see fig.4, p.77):

> C'était autrefois en Italie les vendeurs de poulets qui portaient les billets doux aux femmes; ils glissaient le billet sous l'aile du plus gros, & la dame avertie ne manquait pas de le prendre. Ce manège ayant été découvert, le premier messager d'amour qui fut pris, fut puni par l'estrapade, avec des poulets vivants attachés aux pieds. Depuis ce temps, poulet est synonyme à billet doux. Les commis ambulants de la petite poste en portent et rapportent sans cesse; mais une cire fragile et respectée tient sous le voile ces secrets amoureux; le mari prudent n'ouvre jamais les billets adressés à sa femme.[88]

> In Italy it used to be chicken vendors who would carry love notes to women; they slipped the letter under the wing of the largest one, and the informed lady never failed to remove it. This ploy having been discovered, the first love messenger who was caught was punished with the strappado, with chickens attached to his legs. Since that time *poulet* [chicken] has been synonymous with billet-doux. The walking employees of the *petite poste* continually carry them back and forth; but a fragile and respected bit of sealing wax keeps these love secrets under the veil; the prudent husband never opens the notes addressed to his wife.

Nevertheless most people had no choice but to pay a messenger to carry letters to the post office, since as late as 1830 there were 35,000 towns in France that had no post office and hence no mail boxes, either (see fig.5, p.78). The first mail boxes in France were installed on the initiative of the *conseiller d'Etat* Renouard de Villayer (or Valayer), who (as we have seen in

87. *Almanach royal* (Paris, Le Breton, 1755).
88. *Tableau de Paris*, ch.296, p.261.

Figure 2: *Bureau de poste* 1760 / A French post office in 1760.

Chapter 1, p.42) in 1653 attempted to set up an intraurban mail system in Paris. Although the business quickly failed, some of its mail boxes were taken over by the interurban *poste aux lettres*. Located either at the exterior of the post office or in certain urban neighborhoods, mail boxes were used if the postage was to be paid by the addressee. In 1722, there were seven neighborhood mail boxes in Paris, ten of them in 1759, and seventy-seven in 1788. By the 1780s *petite poste* deliveries were being made in Paris twelve times a day (at a rate of 2 *sols* per letter) and twice a day in the suburbs (3 *sols* per letter).[89] In the second half of the eighteenth century, *petites postes* finally established themselves in French cities. In 1795, after it had become general practice to send intraurban letters postage due, the boxes were taken over by the state and could again be used for mail within a municipality. Prior to that date, one could hand a local letter to the intraurban mailman, who would then inscribe his postmark.[90] In France it does not seem to have been possible to leave letters in cafés or shops for collection or forwarding, as was the case in England.[91]

In France, letters that were prepaid or required special treatment were handed to an employee at the counter of the post office. After being sorted, letters were tied into large packages (*melons*) and transported either on horseback (at modest speed by regular couriers or at the accelerated speed of royal *courriers de cabinet* and *courriers extraordinaires*), by a horse-drawn carriage, or on foot by *piétons*.[92] These foot messengers were professionals, whose technique enabled them to travel 30-40 km a day. Accompanied by postilions (guards) from the *poste aux chevaux*, regular couriers on horseback could travel at 35-40 km an hour at full speed. 'Grand couriers' were required to cover a 'post' (8 km) in 35 to 50 minutes. But normally considerations such as the state of the roads, the region (service was more frequent and more rapid in the North), and the need to make detours to reach towns located off the main post roads could considerably diminish the speed of a postal connection.[93] Mounted on his horse, the postilion, who was recruited by the post master and belonged to the relay, would accompany the letter courier to the next relay and then take the horses back to their original relay.[94] On

89. Jean-Luc de La Croix and Luc-Vincent Thierry, *Almanach du voyageur à Paris, et dans les lieux les plus remarquables du royaume* (Paris, Robert-André Hardouin, 1783). Similar conditions obtained for the London Penny Post, which had been founded much earlier (1680) than the Paris *petite poste*. Whyman, *The Pen and the people*, p.52-53.
90. Chauvet, *Introduction à l'histoire postale*, p.81.
91. Whyman, *The Pen and the people*, p.62.
92. Chauvet, *Introduction à l'histoire postale*, p.112.
93. Marchand, *Le Maître de poste*, p.145ff.
94. Chauvet, *Introduction à l'histoire postale*, p.30-31. In some circumstances, the postilion could be charged with transporting correspondence by himself.

Figure 3: *1ère expérience de petite poste* / The first *petite poste* experiment was a failure.

Figure 4: La petite poste / Sending a *poulet*.

Figure 5: *Carte des Postes de France* 1748 / Post offices in France 1748.

post roads (so called because they were equipped with postal relays) only these riders, along with the mail coach (*malle-poste*) and express coach (*diligence*) had the right to gallop or pass other vehicles.[95] Because it posed a direct threat to the *maîtres de poste*, express coach service was not tolerated until 1775, when Turgot (who was both Controller General of Finances and General Superintendent of the Post) finally imposed it. From that point on, the horses of postmasters (*maîtres des postes*) could be harnessed to *diligences* (express coaches).[96]

Still the post was far from the only way of conveying a letter to its destination. Correspondents could choose from a range of options for dispatching a message, according to the importance they granted to speed, reliability and cost. It was expensive to send a letter by post and (as we shall see in Chapter 3) letters entrusted to it were vulnerable to search, but for the general public it was also the fastest means of sending a letter. Letters conveyed *en poste* were carried by a courier of the letter post, accompanied by a postilion from the horse post and using horses that belonged to the latter. Throughout Europe the delivery of mail seems to have been the exclusive province of men, although this may not have been the case in Sweden.[97] Unfortunately during most of this period the Postal Farm did not employ many couriers and covered a very limited number of routes. A second, less expensive and much more popular option consisted of engaging a private dispatching service; however service by message contractors was widely considered to be unreliable. On the other hand, those messengers who were friends or acquaintances, rather than contractual employees, were more reliable and presumably did not charge for the service. Pierre Bayle, for example,

95. Christophe Studeny, *L'Invention de la vitesse: XVIIIe-XXe siècles* (Paris, 1995), p.178ff, and Marchand, *Le Maître de poste*, p.29ff.

96. 'The generalization of stage coaches meant [...] the loss of a professional privilege [for postmasters] that had previously been jealously guarded: speed.' Marchand, *Le Maître de poste*, p.36. *Diligence* originally referred to an accelerated service for transport of voyagers, not a type of vehicle. *(Coche de) Diligence* was a generic term for express coaches, from the most uncomfortable and rudimentary to the *carrosse* that appeared at the beginning of the seventeenth century; from the lighter and faster *chaise de poste* of the 1660s (with room for only one or two passengers), to the roomier but heavy *turgotine* (with separate compartments within the vehicle for different social classes and an uncovered spot on the roof for the poorest voyagers) and the *malle-poste* (mail coach) of the late eighteenth century.

97. I have found almost no information on the gender of European postal workers. In Michèle Chauvet's *Introduction à l'histoire postale*, the sections devoted to staffing of the horse post and letter post are entitled 'Les hommes'. However in the *Chronique de l'œil-de-bœuf*, Georges Touchard-Lafosse alleges that the bellicose policies of Charles XII had led to the death of so many Swedish men that by the end of his reign normally male jobs were being performed by 'the weak hand of women, [and] timid virgins had to learn to mount post horses in order to perform the painful work of couriers'. *Chronique de l'œil-de-bœuf, des petits appartements de la cour et des salons de Paris, sous Louis XIV, la Régence, Louis XV et Louis XVI* (Paris, 1860 [1st edn 1800]), p.34.

Figure 6: *Turgotine* 1775 / A *turgotine* stagecoach.

frequently asked merchants (especially book sellers) in 'the Huguenot network' (as McKenna calls it) to carry his letters from Geneva to Puylaurens and Montauban in the South, and from there to his home town of Le Carla.[98] If no one from one's social network was available, it was possible to hire a messenger to carry letters to the addressee, avail oneself (for certain routes) of a regularly-scheduled messenger service, or have recourse to the kind of illegal postal service that Thomas Pynchon imagines in *The Crying of lot 49*.[99] Throughout Europe employing private messengers also meant that one's letters would be safe from scrutiny by the agents of the state, who routinely opened, read and copied extracts of letters carried by the post.[100] The postal administration also offered its users a third option, called transport *en estafette*, in which letters were carried by employees of the horse post; this method was often employed by the various ministries, even though its reliability was questionable.[101] In addition, members of the social elite like Grotius and Leibniz could have letters carried to their destination in the diplomatic pouch. During the old regime, the king's household and government had yet another possibility at their disposal, the *courriers de cabinet* and (starting with the reign of Louis XIV) *courriers extraordinaires*. These couriers, who operated independently of the post, were charged with personally delivering messages to their addressees as quickly as possible, changing horses on the way.[102] However the post would eventually offer most correspondents a fairly convenient and reliable system for collection, sorting and delivery of mail, with the sole exception of very large packages, which had to be sent by messenger.[103]

The wretched state of roads and bridges in the France of Louis XIV, especially in the poorest regions of the country (the South, Brittany and the Vendée) made delivery of mail notoriously unreliable.[104] The routes

98. McKenna, 'La correspondance de Pierre Bayle,' p.319-20.
99. 'When high costs and slow speeds thwarted letter-writing, people created alternative methods, many of them illegal, to ensure mail was received.' Whyman, *The Pen and the people*, p.58
100. See Chapter 3, p.95-123.
101. For a fuller account of the various options for transport of letters that were available during the old regime, see Marchand, *Le Maître de poste*, p.121ff.
102. Chauvet, *Introduction à l'histoire postale*, p.112. The requirement that postmasters furnish royal couriers with horses was a chronic source of grievance.
103. Both Rousseau and Voltaire refer to this distinction. 'Les épreuves lües, refermées à mon adresse, et mises à la poste me parviendront exactement. Si les pacquets étoient fort gros, nous avons un Messager qui va quatre fois la semaine à Paris, et dont l'entrepos est à *l'hôtel de Grammont, rue St Germain l'Auxerrois*.' Jean-Jacques Rousseau to Chrétien-Guillaume de Lamoignon de Malesherbes, 6 March 1760, *CC*, vol.7, p.54 (953). Emphasis in text. See 'Il se pourrait que le paquet étant trop gros, on l'eût laisse à la poste, ou qu'on l'eût ouvert', Voltaire to Etienne Noël Damilaville, 27 November 1767, D14553.
104. For a vivid evocation of traveling conditions in early modern France, see Studeny, *L'Invention de la vitesse*, ch.2.

on which mail coaches traveled consisted of mostly local mazes of circuitous and poorly-maintained roads. In England, France and the Hapsburg territories, delivery times on such roads were longer in winter, when daylight was limited and the weather often foul. The converse was true in Scandinavian countries, where in the winter months postal sleds could be driven straight across frozen lakes. In the early 1670s the philosopher Pierre Bayle (1647-1706) compares the letters he has been trying to send his family in southwestern France from Geneva to boats embarking on a perilous journey across a stormy sea:

> [J]'ai passé déjà dans ces quartiers près de deux ans sans recevoir de vos nouvelles que deux fois [...] [P]our ne rien perdre, je vous envoye des lettres que je vous avais écrites il y a quelque temps. Elles avaient déjà commencé leur navigation pour vous aller trouver, mais un vent contraire les remit au port tout aussitôt, si bien que ce n'est qu'après 8 mois de séjour qu'elles se mettent en mer pour la deuxième fois.[105]

> [I] have already spent nearly two years in this area without receiving news from you more than twice... [I]n order not to lose anything, I am sending you letters that I had written to you a good while ago. They had already begun to sail in your direction, but a contrary wind sent them straight back to port, so that it is only after a stay of eight months that they are once again setting out to sea.

The correspondence of Mme de Sévigné (1626-1696), with her daughter in Provence was exposed to similar hazards. It was from her residences in Brittany and Paris that Sévigné sent the comtesse de Grignan over two-thirds of her 1120 extant letters. But the marquise had to accept the fact that their letters could easily go astray, if the mail coach got stuck in a quagmire or fell into a ditch:

> 'Vraiment, ma bonne', she tells her daughter, 'vous me contez une histoire bien lamentable de vos pauvres lettres perdues [...] On est gaie, gaillarde, on croit avoir entretenu tous ses bons amis, et il se trouve que toute la peine qu'on a prise, c'est pour être dans un bourbier.[106]

> Really, my dear, you tell me a sad story of your poor lost letters [...] We are gay, sprightly, we think we have been conversing with our good friends, and it turns out that all the pains we have taken have wound up in a ditch.

As late as 1782, the road between St-Martin-d'Estréaux and St-Germain-Lespinasse (today in the Rhône-Alpes region) was so poor that the

105. Pierre Bayle to Jean Bayle, 1 July 1672. Cited by Antony McKenna, 'La correspondance de Pierre Bayle', p.320.

106. Marie de Rabutin-Chantal, marquise de Sévigné to Françoise Marguerite de Sévigné, comtesse de Grignan, 6 October 1675, *Correspondance* (Paris, 1972), vol.2, p.118. Cited and translated by Roland Racevskis, *Time and ways of knowing under Louis XIV: Molière, Sévigné, Lafayette* (Lewisburg, PA, and London, 2003), p.121-22. During the same period La Fontaine and Racine also complained about the state of the roads in France. See Vaillé, *Histoire générale*, vol.3, p.312.

strength of seventeen horses and six oxen did not suffice to pull the diligence back onto the road; the roads in Burgundy were not any better.[107]

The delivery of mail would remain unreliable throughout Europe until improvements were made in the roads and vehicles that formed part of postal infrastructure.[108] As Behringer has remarked, since postal vehicles (unlike travelers on foot or horses) could not simply hop over obstacles in their way, for a system that functioned on timetables it was absolutely necessary to make improvements in the roads.[109] Such changes came more quickly to England than to France. In England they arrived with the construction of the first turnpikes, starting in 1674. In France the alternative to traveling on land, transportation by water, long remained irregular and unreliable in most of the country. However the Canal Royal in Languedoc constituted a notable exception to the general undependability of travel by mail boat in France. Built during the early years (1666-1681) of Louis XIV's reign, the canal (since 1789 the Canal du Midi) runs for 150 miles (241 kilometers) to Toulouse from the Etang de Thau near the Mediterranean.[110] Mrs Anna Francesca Cradock, an Englishwoman traveling with her husband on the post boat from Béziers to Toulouse in 1785, gives a very favorable account of their leisurely passage. In her journal she records that the boat, which carried the Cradocks in their own chaise, 'is large, clean and well fitted out for passengers, who disembark for dinner and to spend the night. The journey from Béziers to Toulouse takes four days, and each passenger is allowed to bring his wine and the food that he might require during this time.'[111] In the late seventeenth century, the average speed of mail delivery in England was three to four miles per hour; but Ralph Allen's reforms (1720-1764) of the Royal Mail enabled posts to attain average speeds of five miles per hour on some routes.[112] The speed and reliability of mail delivery in France eventually improved in the eighteenth century, thanks to mercantilist policies that promoted the development of highways and canal systems. Anne Bretagnolle and Nicolas Verdier have used statistical analysis and computer simulations to document the topographical and geographical dynamics in the development of a

107. Mience, *Histoire des postes du Rhône*, vol.1, p.43.

108. On the state of European roads in the seventeenth and eighteenth centuries, see Jean-Marcel Goger, 'Transport', in *Dictionnaire européen des Lumières* (Paris, 1997).

109. 'Communications revolutions', p.360.

110. 'Communications revolutions', p.337.

111. Anna Francesca Cradock, *La Vie française à la veille de la Révolution (1783-1786): journal inédit de Madame Cradock, traduit d'après le manuscrit original par Mme O. Delphin-Balleyguier* (Paris, 1911), p.167-68. My retranslation of the French. The original English manuscript does not seem to have been published.

112. Whyman, *The Pen and the people*, p.53 and 56.

network of postal roads in pre-industrial France.[113] In addition, while there had been fewer than 800 postal relays in the country at the beginning of the eighteenth century, there were 1426 in 1788.[114] The establishment of the Ecole des Ponts et Chaussées in 1747 testifies to the importance that the royal administration attached to transportation infrastructure. With these improved roads came greater security, higher speeds, lower delivery prices and the possibility of reliable planning, which increased the frequency of mail.

Even so, differences in postal regulations among the various provinces could make sending letters from one part of France to another a long and frustrating process, and an often impossible task in the case of books. Voltaire laments this situation in a letter to Mme Champbonin:

> Je voudrais pouvoir vous envoyer des livres. On ne sait comment faire. La poste ne veut pas s'en charger. Les formalités sont le poison de la société. Il faut passer par cent mains avant d'arriver à sa destination; et puis on n'y arrive point. Il semble que d'une province à une autre on soit en pays ennemi.[115]

> I would like to be able to send you books. One knows not how. The post does not want to take care of them. Formalities are the poison of society. One has to pass through a hundred hands before reaching one's destination; and then one doesn't reach it. It is as if from one province to another one were in enemy territory.

Technological developments soon gave France a leadership position in bridge and road construction. The French road network was significantly improved in the eighteenth century, with the development of *chaussées*, roads built in straight lines, with little concern for geographical circumstances. Writing in the 1780s, Mercier observed that the kingdom of France was '*coupé comme un damier*' (cut like a checkerboard) by excellent roads.[116] The most important of these roads, some of which (the so-called *grandes routes*) were as much as 60 feet wide, had firm bases and smooth surfaces, in the middle of which horses and carriages could confidently trot. On these improved roads, faster and more comfortable carriages, such as the improved mail coach (*malle-poste*, first provided in 1793, see fig.6, p.80, and fig.7, p.88) and the express coach or *diligence* could even reach a gallop and pass other vehicles; they also had priority at postal relays.[117] Thanks to these vast improvements in the quality of the French

113. 'Images d'un réseau en évolution: les routes de poste dans la France préindustrielle', *M@ppemonde* 79:3 (2005), http://mappemonde.mgm.fr/num7/articles/art05301.html (last accessed 29 September 2015). See also Guy Arbelot, *Autour des routes de poste: les premières cartes routières de la France XVIIe-XIXe siècle* (Paris, 1992) and Marchand, *Le Maître de poste*.

114. Jean-Pierre Poussou, 'Transports', in Michel Figeac (ed.), *L'Ancienne France au quotidien: vie et choses de la vie sous l'Ancien Régime* (Paris, 2007), p.1061-65.

115. Voltaire to Mme de Champbonin, 15(?) November 1761, D9364.

116. *Tableau de Paris*, ch.1003, 'Chaise de poste'. De La Mare, *Continuation du traité de la police*, p.569) presents the so-called *soufflet* as a predecessor of the post chaise.

117. Studeny, *L'Invention de la vitesse*, p.71ff and 178ff.

road system and regulations prohibiting lengthy stops, the speed of postal coaches dramatically increased.[118]

Express coaches in France were considered to be comfortable, but only relative to the poorly sprung mail coaches that preceded them. In fact, only a 20-foot lane in the middle of these 60-foot highways was actually graveled or paved; it was flanked on both sides by earthen bands of equal width (the *bermes*), on which voyagers found it more comfortable to travel in the summer months.[119] Even so, a long journey in a post chaise could be an excruciating ordeal at any time for a passenger like Jean-Jacques Rousseau, who was beset with urinary complaints:

> M. Hume dit fort bien que j'ai supporté la chaise en venant de Paris mais il ne dit pas que j'y fus forcé, ni combien j'en souffris, ni que c'étoit la plus belle saison et le plus beau tems de l'année, ni enfin que mon mal et moi avions alors trois ans et demi de moins. Il est certain que je suis hors d'état de soutenir la Diligence, encore moins le carrosse, et que je n'ai point de chaise pour aller en poste.[120]

> Mr Hume rightly says that I tolerated the post chaise on the way from Paris but he doesn't say that I was forced to do so, nor how much I suffered from it, nor that it was the most beautiful season and weather of the year, nor finally that my illness and I were three and a half years younger at the time. It is certain that I am in no condition to bear the Diligence, and the coach even less and that I have no chaise to travel by post.

Thanks to improvements in the quality of mail service in the eighteenth and early nineteenth centuries, the post eventually became a model of easy and reliable service, as illustrated by the French idiom for something's being easily accomplished, *passer comme une lettre à la poste*, first attested by the *Robert* dictionary in 1825.[121]

Arriving in post

The express coach or *(carrosse de) diligence*, so called because of its speed, was a coach that had been greatly improved around 1760 by the coach maker Roubo. According to Foville (1876), cited in the supplement (1873-1877) to the Littré *Dictionnaire de la langue française* (1863-1872):

118. Schnaitl, *La Poste française*, p.102ff.

119. The *routes nationales* in France have retained this 60-foot width. Marchand, *Le Maître de poste*, p.76.

120. Rousseau to Marie-Madeleine de Brémond d'Ars, marquise de Verdelin, 3 November 1765, *CC*, vol.27, p.214 (4788).

121. '*Passer comme une lettre à la poste*, facilement et sans incident; être facilement digéré (aliment, repas); être facilement admis.' Josette Rey-Debove and Alain Rey, *Le Petit Robert de la langue française 2010* (Paris, 2010) henceforth *Petit Robert*.

> Sous Louis XV, ce n'était plus en carrosse, mais en coche qu'on voyageait... 5 jours en été, 6 jours en hiver suffisaient désormais pour arriver de Paris à Lyon (125 lieues); cela faisait, dans la belle saison, 25 lieues par jour; et on trouvait cela si beau que le nom flatteur de diligence fut inventé précisément pour cette voiture.[122]
>
> Under Louis XV one no longer traveled by carriage, but by coach... 5 days in summer, 6 days in winter sufficed thenceforth for travel from Paris to Lyon (125 leagues); in summer, that meant covering 25 leagues a day, which was thought so fine that the flattering name of diligence was invented precisely for this vehicle.

Brought into service expressly for travelers, the diligence traveled the route from Paris to Lyon twice as fast as had been needed to cover the same route in a carriage.[123] The term *malle-poste* (mail coach) originally referred to a wheelbarrow that was modified to carry the mail trunk, or *malle* (in English, the word 'mail(e)' also referred by metonymy to its contents). After 1793, it designated a covered vehicle that was capable of carrying a few voyagers and traveled even faster than the *diligence*. The *malle-poste* ran only on post roads, where it always had the right of way.[124] Having been reduced by half under Louis XV, postal delivery time was nearly halved again during the following seventy-five years, as the following table[125] shows:

Route	Year	Number of days
Paris-Lyon	1664	10-11
Paris-Lyon	1760	6
Paris-Bordeaux	1660	10
Paris-Bordeaux	1789	5½-6
Paris-Bordeaux	1831	3
Paris-Rouen	17th c.	3
Paris-Rouen	18th c.	1-2

Table 2: Reduction in postal delivery times, mid-seventeenth to late eighteenth centuries.

Starting in 1765, the creation of solidly built roads in England had comparable effects upon the speed of postal deliveries.[126] Still the horses that drew mail coaches were saddle horses, bred for their ability to bear considerable weight, and they typically did not cover any more distance in a day than did foot messengers.[127] On the initiative of John Palmer,

122. French-made post coaches were introduced to England by the postal reformer John Palmer of Bath (1742-1818). Whyman, *The Pen and the people*, p.57.
123. Chauvet, *Introduction à l'histoire postale*, p.141.
124. *Introduction à l'histoire postale*, p.142; Marchand, *Le Maître de poste*, p.132.
125. Schnaitl, *La Poste française*, p.121.
126. Robinson, *The British Post Office*, p.130.
127. Chauvet, *Introduction à l'histoire postale*, p.141-42.

French-made high-speed post coaches were introduced to the Royal Mail in the 1780s, with similar results. By the early nineteenth century, average speeds on post roads had increased to eight to nine miles per hour.[128]

In his study of clocks and modern temporal orders, Gerhard Dohrn-van Rossum has recounted how the development of land routes and waterways in the eighteenth century made possible an increase in, among other things, the transport of letters. Due to improved road construction techniques and new carriage designs, wheeled traffic on eighteenth-century truck roads gradually reached the speed (Paris to Brussels in two days) of mounted messengers and couriers in the sixteenth century.[129] While noting that the general tempo of transmission of news (for example, two weeks from Paris to Venice) hardly changed over the same period, Dohrn-van Rossum maintains that 'The new postal systems were... preconditions for the letter culture of the Age of Enlightenment'.[130]

In the final years of the *ancien régime* the exhilarating speed (around 6-7 km/hr!) that could be reached by riding 'in post' was mostly the privilege of the wealthy elite.[131] At the beginning of *Les Liaisons dangereuses* (1781) the marquise de Merteuil teases the vicomte de Valmont about his timid courtship of Mme de Tourvel by asking him: '[D]epuis quand voyagez-vous à petites journées et par des chemins de traverse? Mon ami, quand on veut arriver, des chevaux de poste et la grande route!'[132] (Since when have you enjoyed traveling in short stages and on by-roads? My dear man, when people are keen to get somewhere, they travel with post horses and on main roads.) In Beaumarchais's frenetically-paced play *The Marriage of Figaro* (1784), when Figaro (II, 2) wants to say that his marriage is imminent, he says that it is 'arriving in post'. Still, not everyone welcomed the advent of high-speed postal coaches. Stendhal's *Mémoires d'un touriste*

128. Robinson, *The British Post Office*, p.130ff; Whyman, *The Pen and the people*, p.57-58.

129. A table published by Behringer shows the times (in hours) guaranteed by Franz von Taxis in 1505 and 1516 for delivery of mail between Brussels and other major European cities. 'Communications revolutions', p.344.

130. Dohrn-van Rossum, *The History of the hour*, p.344. The author is referring to the maps in Braudel, *Civilization and capitalism, 15th-18th century*, vol.1: *The Structures of everyday life*, translated by Siân Reynolds (New York, 1981), p.426-27. Brigitte Schnaitl (*La Poste française*, p.7ff) has also commented on the relationship between the marked increase in postal activities in the middle of the eighteenth century and improvements made to the French road system. See Whyman, *The Post and the people*, p.55-58.

131. On this topic Studeny (*L'Invention de la vitesse*) refers to Charles Morazé, *La Politique routière en France de 1716 à 1815* (Paris, 1988), p.397-402.

132. Choderlos de Laclos, *Les Liaisons dangereuses* (London, 1961), p.x, 68. English translation by P. W. K. Stone, modified. In a footnote to this passage, Delon, in his preface to the French edition, p.68, n.1, comments on this comparison and refers the reader to Jean-Louis Cornille, *La Lettre française: de Crébillon fils à Rousseau, Laclos, Sade* (Paris, 2001), p.65-92.

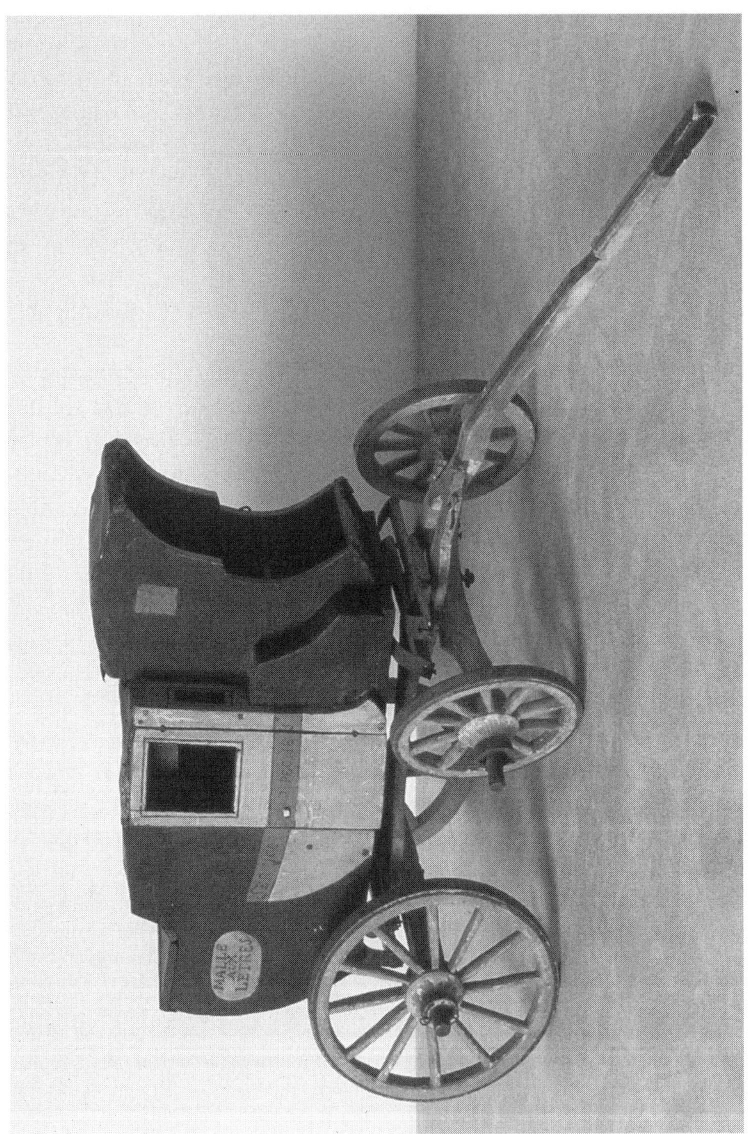

Figure 7: *Malle aux lettres* / A speedy *malle-poste*.

(1838) evokes the experience of traveling in a *malle-poste* with a mixture of admiration and horror (not unlike the feelings of an automobile passenger today on the German *autobahn*): 'Pendant les douze années que je fus marchand, je n'ai voyagé que par la malle-poste. Trois jours de Paris à Marseille! c'est beau; mais aussi l'homme est réduit à l'état d'animal: on mange du pâté ou l'on dort la moitíe de la journée.' (For the twelve years that I was a merchant, I traveled only by postal coach. Three days from Paris to Marseilles! This is fine indeed, but man is also reduced to the state of an animal: one eats pâté or sleeps half the day.)[133] Despite dramatic improvements in much of the country, in the poorer regions of France roads remained poor and mail delivery still infrequent and unreliable.[134] For the most part, however, the technologies that enabled the construction of the French road and postal systems made travel easier and facilitated the spread of knowledge, both of foreign countries and of the colonies.

Address, sorting, distribution

Epistolary address involves at least two related matters. The first is that of interlocution: who writes a letter, and to whom is it being written? Even if one does not share Kafka's anxiety about epistolary vampirism, one can recognize that in the early modern period letters were often not messages addressed by a single person to another. They could form part of a network of group and interfamilial communication: during this period and long after, letter-writers often collected and transmitted information about various members of a family group, while successively addressing themselves to various members of another group. In addition, letters frequently contained information written in different hands, as correspondents took their turn making additions to the text.[135]

The 'address' of a letter also designated the writing on the exposed surface of the folded letter (or envelope, if there was one) that provided instructions about where the letter should be sent.[136] To address a letter properly during this period, one first had to know the precise name of the post office nearest to the addressee, which was not always a simple matter. One had to specify the name of the province, since towns in

133. Stendhal, *Mémoires d'un touriste* (Paris, 1891), p.77.

134. Schnaitl, *La Poste française*, 83ff. Daniel Roche makes the same point in the 'Avant-propos' to Pierre-Yves Beaurepaire (ed.), *La Plume et la toile*, p.14-15. See also Marchand, *Le Maître de poste*, p.144.

135. Cécile Dauphin, *et al.*, 'L'Enquête postale de 1847', p.37.

136. By carefully examining the multivolume postal inquiry of 1847, Dauphin *et al.* were able to establish that in the middle of the nineteenth century postal communication between Paris and the provinces tended to go in only one direction (outward), and that relatively few local letters were sent or received. Dauphin, 'L'Enquête postale de 1847', p.46.

different provinces could have the same name. In France many towns did not have post offices, so that one also had to know the name of the office that was nearest to the addressee. Starting in 1754, various editions of the *Dictionnaire des postes* aimed to solve these and other practical problems, such as what happened in fairly large towns where two people (especially those of different social classes) had the same name, a situation that could lead to confusion for which the post could wrongly be held responsible.[137] In England, collection and delivery of mail were carried out in much the same fashion as in France, but letters were not delivered to the houses of the addressees. Except when postmasters took the initiative of hiring themselves out to deliver letters, letter-writers had to make their own arrangements for posting or fetching them. This task was often shouldered by servants, such as Voltaire's long-suffering agent Dalloz, who was charged with carrying large quantities of postal material back and forth, in all kinds of weather, between Ferney and the post offices in Geneva and Versoix.[138] Stealing letters was punishable by death both in England and France.[139] In France, when the courier had delivered the mail to the destination post office, the postmaster (after 1762, the 'director') and his employees (*commis*) would sort it. However in both countries distribution of mail was impeded by the absence of any means of notifying addressees that they had mail. Fairs and markets provided good opportunities for seeking out people whose mail had not

137. Edmé-Gilles Guyot, *Dictionnaire des Postes, Contenant le nom de toutes les Villes, Bourgs, Paroisses, Abbayes et Principaux Châteaux du Royaume de France & du Duché de Lorraine, les Provinces où ils sont situés et la distinction pour celles pour lesquelles il faut affranchir* (Paris, Chez la Veuve Delatour, rue de La Harpe, aux trois tours, 1754), p.ii.

The *Dictionnaire des Postes* is primarily devoted to an alphabetical list of localities, provinces and post offices to which mail should be addressed. Ambiguity of names also caused problems within cities. According to Anton Tantner '[A]t the end of the eighteenth century, there were six buildings in downtown Vienna and another twenty three located in the suburbs named "*Zum Goldenen Adler*" (At the Golden Eagle); thus, all together there were twenty-nine houses that could be mixed up under a name-based addressing system.' 'Addressing the houses: the introduction of house numbering in Europe', *Histoire et mesure* [on line] 24:2 (2009), p.6, http://histoiremesure.revues.org/3942 (last accessed 29 September 2015).

138. See Chapter 4, p.129-30. In *Les Liaisons dangereuses* Valmont orders his *chasseur* to ingratiate himself with the man who carries Mme de Tourvel's letters to the post: 'Songez aussi à vous rendre l'ami de celui qui porte ses Lettres à la Poste. Offrez-vous souvent à lui pour faire cette commission à sa place; et quand il acceptera, ne faites partir que celles qui vous paraîtront indifférentes, et envoyez-moi les autres; surtout celles à Mme de Volanges, si vous en rencontrez.' Letter CI, p.320. Formerly a servant in charge of the hunt, a *chasseur* was at this time a servant who wore hunting gear.

139. Soper, *The Mails*, p.4; According to Soper the last time a man was hanged for stealing letters was in 1832. See Edmé de La Poix de Fréminville, *Dictionnaire ou Traité de la police générale des villes, bourgs, paroisses, et seigneuries de la campagne. Dans lequel on trouvera tout ce qui est nécessaire de savoir & de pratiquer en cette partie, par un procureur fiscal [...]* (Paris, chez les associés du privilège des ouvrages de l'auteur, 1778), p.377.

been distributed.[140] As early as the first half of the eighteenth century home delivery of mail was furnished in some French towns outside of Paris, but it was usually necessary to pick up one's mail (or have it picked up by friends or servants) at the post office. Later in the century, home delivery of intraurban mail became available in those cities that had provided themselves with *petites postes*, as well as in their suburbs.[141] Even where home delivery of mail was available, its reliability and security were impeded by the fact that so many mailmen were illiterate, leading some of them to deliver mail to the wrong persons, a situation that could have serious legal consequences.[142] Before that time (except in 1653 during Villayer's brief experiment in Paris) delivery of intraurban mail was actively discouraged, doubtless because it was thought a waste of time and money. The royal almanac of 1760 specified that: 'Letters that are popped into Paris [mail] boxes for Paris will not be carried to their addresses; they will be discarded.'[143]

A house number was not part of the address, since few European houses and other buildings were numbered until the late eighteenth century. Numbering was first introduced as a way of enabling the state to oversee and tax the contents of houses or conscript their inhabitants, lodge soldiers and monitor illegal housing: it was not initially meant to help people orient themselves in cities or to help strangers find their way.[144] But the gradual institution of house numbering certainly did facilitate the task of the letter carrier, as well as make it easier for the police to find people and conduct surveillance.[145] In the absence of house numbering and, in some cases, even of street names, it was not always easy or even possible in Europe to deliver a letter to its ad-

140. Marchand, *Le Maître de poste*, p.113.

141. Chauvet, *Introduction à l'histoire postale*, p.37 and p.201. 'Of the 1323 post offices listed in 1791, about twelve to fifteen percent seem to provide various kinds of home delivery.' p.202; see Marchand, *Le Maître de poste*, p.114.

142. Fréminville, *Dictionnaire ou Traité de la police*, p.377.

143. Marchand, *Le Maître de poste*, p.113.

144. Recent research on house numbering is summarized by Tantner, 'Addressing the houses', p.83-103. More recently, Vincent Denis has published the results of his study of address declarations in Paris police archives, 'Les Parisiens, la police et les numérotages des maisons, du XVIIIe siècle à l'Empire', *French historical studies* 38:1 (February 2015), p.83-103. See 'The numbering of houses,' *New York times*, 16 July, 1898, http://query.nytimes.com/mem/archive-free/pdf?_r=2&res=9803EEDB1139E433A25755C1A9619C94699ED7CF&oref=slogin (last accessed 29 September 2015). The sixty-eight identical brick and stone houses on the Pont-Notre-Dame (1500-1511) were the first to be numbered in Paris. See 'Notre-Dame (pont', Jacques Hillairet, *Dictionnaire historique des rues de Paris,* vol. 2 (Paris, 1963).

145. From the perspective of Michel Foucault, house numbering is a way for states to make their subjects more 'governable'. See Reuben S. Rose-Redwood, 'Governmentality, geography, and the geo-coded world', in *Progress in human geography* 30:4 (2006), p.469-86.

dressee.[146] Delivering letters involved much interpreting of the address and search for the right house and person. Often the mere mention of the name and qualities of the addressee would suffice, as in a letter sent by Voltaire to Elie Bertrand in Bern:

> A Monsieur
> Monsieur Bertrand
> 1er pasteur de l'Eglise française
> à Berne.[147]

If one were in France and needed to address a letter to the king, the queen or the dauphin, respect for their exalted position required one to put only the words 'To the King [the Queen, the Dauphin]' at the bottom of the envelope, taking care to respect their absolute, unqualifiable essences by inscribing these words at the very bottom of the envelope ('de sorte qu'il n'y ait plus d'espace pour écrire' – so that there be no more room for writing).[148]

Until house numbering began, an equally common format included the name of the addressee, the home where he or she was residing and the street or square where that home was located. For example, a letter from Horace Walpole in Reims to Thomas Ashton in London arrived at its destination with the following address: 'To Mr Ashton at Messrs Lewes's Hanover Square London. Franc à Paris. pour l'Angleterre.'[149] Even if the name of the addressee's street was known, one could not always be sure that it would be delivered. And that uncertainty was compounded if, like Jean-Jacques Rousseau, one did not trust the post to do its job. On 14 March 1768 he asked the printer and bookseller Pierre Guy to find out whether a letter Rousseau had written to thank the astronomer Lalande for a favorable review of the *Dictionnaire de musique* had reached its destination:

> M. de Lalande m'ayant donné dans la lettre qu'il m'a fait l'honneur de m'écrire l'adresse de la rue Saint-Honoré, je lui ai répondu sous cette adresse; mais comme la rue Saint-Honoré est bien grande, je ne sais si, quelque connu qu'il soit, ma lettre lui sera parvenue; lorsque vous aurez occasion de le voir, vous m'obligerez de le lui demander en lui faisant bien des salutations de ma part.[150]

146. Codogno's *Nuovo itinerario delle poste per tutto il mondo* (1608) already refers to this problem. Cited by Rübsam, 'Zur Geschichte', p.71.
147. Voltaire to Elie Bertrand, 7 January 1760, D7968.
148. *Nouveau secrétaire de la cour* (1732), p.454.
149. Thomas Gray, *Correspondence of Thomas Gray: 1734-1755,* ed. Paget Toynbee *et al.*, 3 vols (Oxford, 1935), vol.1, p.114–15, letter 65.
150. Jean Jacques Rousseau to Pierre Guy, 14 March 1768, *CC*, vol.35, p.199 (6293). On Rousseau's mistrust of postal communication, see Chapter 5, p.141-66.

> Mr de Lalande having given me the rue Saint-Honoré address in the letter he honored me by writing, I answered him at that address; but since the rue Saint-Honoré is quite long, I do not know if, as well-known as he is, my letter actually reached him; when you have the opportunity to see him, please do me the favor of asking him about it and greeting him with many salutations on my behalf.

When street names were not known, houses were often identified in terms of proximity to landmarks. Thus when the sailor Thomas Bowrey wrote from Bermuda to his family in London, he addressed the letters 'at different times to Wellclose Square, Marine Square, and "near the tower"'.[151] Other correspondents simply provided the mailman with directions, as in this Parisian example from 1778: 'de Sahuguet d'Espagnac, rue Meslé, la quatrième porte à droite en entrant par la rue du Temple.'[152] A Paris guidebook published in Year VII (1798) notes that 'It is impossible to calculate the loss of time, the mistakes and innumerable predicaments caused by the confusion of street numbers [...] In the infinitesimal streets, such as the rues du Bac, Saint-Martin, Saint-Denis, etc., one is completely lost, it is a veritable maze.'[153] On one occasion the Royal Post received a letter whose address contained neither names nor directions of any kind, but just a fantastic list of the addressee's myriad qualities:

> Au prince des poètes, phénomène perpétuel de gloire, philosophe des nations, mercure de l'Europe, orateur de la patrie, promoteur des citoyens, historien des rois, panégyriste des héros, Aristarque des Zoïles, arbitre du goût, peintre en tout genre, le même à tout âge, protecteur des arts, bienfaiteur des talents, ainsi que du vrai mérite, admirateur du génie, fléau des persécuteurs, ennemi des fanatiques, défenseur des opprimés, père des orphelins, modèle des riches, appui des indigents, exemple des sublimes vertus.[154]

> To the prince of poets, perpetual phenomenon of glory, philosopher of the nations, Mercury of Europe, orator of the homeland, promoter of citizens, historian of kings, panegyrist of heroes, Aristarchus of the Zoilists, arbiter of taste, painter in all genres, the same at all ages, protector of the arts, benefactor of talents as well as true merit, admirer of genius, scourge of persecutors, enemy of fanatics, defender of the oppressed, father of orphans, model for the rich, supporter of the indigent, example of the sublime virtues.

151. Whyman, *The Post and the people*, p.62.
152. Catherine Farvacque-Vitkovic, Lucien Godin, Hugues Leroux, Florence Verdet, Roberto Chavez, *Adressage et gestion des villes* (World Bank, Washington, DC, 2005), p.9.
153. *Tableau général du goût, des modes et costumes de Paris, par une société d'artistes et de gens de lettres* (Paris, An VII), vol.I, p.55. Cited in Studeny, *L'Invention de la vitesse*, p.65-66.
154. *Mémoires de Bauchaumont*, 1 November 1769 ; cited by André Magnan, 'Postes', in Jean Goulemot, André Magnan and Didier Masseau (eds), *Inventaire Voltaire* (Paris, 1995). In polite circles it was considered most improper to burden the exterior surface of a letter: 'Il est contraire au bel usage de charger le dessus d'une lettre d'une légende des qualités des personnes à qui l'on écrit.' *Nouveau secrétaire de la cour* (1732), p.447.

After careful deliberation by employees of the post office, the letter was sent to the only person to whom all these qualities applied: Voltaire sent the extravagant letter back unopened. It was opened at the post office and its author discovered to have been a certain abbé de Launay, a mediocre, destitute poet and cadger who had just been released from prison.

3. Surveillance and secrecy: the Black Cabinets

> Le secret postal est l'œil de Jupiter, la trappe par laquelle ce dieu voit ce qui se passe dans le cœur des hommes. En vérité, cette faculté inquisitoriale de la royauté sent moins le père de famille que le despote (Postal secrecy is Jupiter's eye, the trapdoor through which this god sees what transpires in the hearts of men. In truth, this inquisitorial faculty of royalty smacks less of the pater familias than of the despot)
>
> *Journal et mémoires du marquis d'Argenson*[1]

The marquis d'Argenson, Louis XV's Minister of Foreign Affairs from 1744 to 1747, wrote his memoirs with inside knowledge of the violation of postal secrecy, since his younger brother had been both Minister of War and Superintendent of the Posts. Although state-controlled postal services were not established solely for reasons of security, European governments immediately began using them for surveillance, as a means of unearthing conspiracies. Indeed, as Siegried Grillmeyer has remarked, 'The history of postal espionage and postal surveillance is as old as the history of transport of letters itself'.[2] The institution of public mail systems provided a much-needed service to the general public, while at the same time furnishing rulers with a source of substantial revenue and a terrifyingly effective surveillance mechanism, in the form of the so-called Black Cabinets or Black Chambers. At the same time illegal services, like the one imagined by Thomas Pynchon in *The Crying of lot 49*, arose to challenge the state monopoly on postal service.[3] A comprehensive history of the Black Chambers has yet to be written, in part because of the scarcity of reliable information on the subject.[4]

1. *Journal et mémoires du marquis d'Argenson, publiés pour la première fois d'après les manuscrits autographes de la Bibliothèque du Louvre* (Paris, 1866), vol.VIII, p.423.
2. Grillmeyer, *Habsburgs Diener*, p.54.
3. One such illegal system may have been created by the Society of Friends. See Liza Picard, *Restoration London* (London, 1997), p.72. Cited by James How, *Epistolary spaces*, p.57-58. In *The Pen and the people*, p.48-49, 64-65, Whyman discusses early challenges to the Royal Mail and alternatives to using the post. On the postal system in *The Crying of lot 49*, see Chapter 6, p.189-93.
4. Karl de Leeuw refers to this problem at the beginning of 'The Black Chamber in the Dutch Republic during the War of the Spanish Succession and its aftermath, 1707-1715', *The Historical journal* 42:1 (March 1999), p.133-56. The archival resources of the Geheime Ziffernkanzlei in Vienna were destroyed in 1805 (when Napoleon first occupied the city) and again in 1848. See also König, *Schwarze Cabinette*; however the author does not indicate

Antecedents to the Black Cabinets were functioning in England and France early in the seventeenth century, but de Leeuw is right to see them as 'basically an eighteenth century phenomenon' that should be understood in terms of its role in the developing European state system.[5] Prior to the opening of state-controlled postal systems to private correspondence, European princes could only gain access to other people's letters by having couriers arrested or letters stolen. Systems that were open to the public enabled rulers to violate the secrecy of correspondence more efficiently, more systematically and in the best of cases, secretly as well.[6] *Raison d'Etat* provided them with a convenient justification for doing so. European states sought to distinguish between justifiable violations of the secrecy of correspondence, committed by the state in the national interest and therefore not punishable by law, and unjustifiable violations, committed by individuals (usually employees of the post) in their private interest and punishable by sanctions ranging from public flogging and expulsion (in Germany) to death (in France).[7]

Belief in the inviolable secrecy of correspondence conflicted with state control of the postal service.[8] According to the theory of intellectual property proposed by the jurist Michel de Servan, the seal was (in

the sources for his assertions. See also: Franz Stix, 'Geschichte der Wiener Geheimen Ziffernkanzlei von ihrend Anfängen bis zum Jahre 1848', *Mitteilungen* 51 (Institut für Geschichtsforschung, Vienna) (1937), p.131-60; Kalmus, *Weltgeschichte*, p.404-25; Vaillé, *Le Cabinet noir*; and Arthur de Boislisle, 'Le secret de la poste sous le règne de Louis XIV', *Annuaire-bulletin de la Société de l'histoire de France* (1890), p.229-45. Grillmeyer discusses this problem in *Habsburgs Diener*, p.55, and provides additional bibliographical references in notes 193-95. Boislisle ('Le secret de la poste', p.233, 235) cites evidence of postal surveillance in Spain; I have not been able to discover any extended discussions of this topic.

5. De Leeuw, 'The Black Chamber', p.134. See also Bennington, *Legislations*, p.244.
6. 'The nationalization of the Austrian post [by Charles VI] is doubtless at least partly the consequence of its having been charged with [surveillance of mail].' Kalmus, *Weltgeschichte*, p.406. A struggle for control of state power is also a contest for the right to conduct surveillance of the mail. During the disturbances of the Fronde (1648-1653) there was a moment when the conspirators convinced the postal administrator to intercept communications between Chief Minister Mazarin, who had been forced into exile, and the Queen Mother (and Regent), who had taken refuge outside of Paris with her son, the young Louis XIV. Boislisle, 'Le secret de la poste', p.230.
7. 'Briefgeheimniß,' in *Brockhaus' Conversations-Lexicon*, 13th edn (Leipzig, 1882-1887), vol.3. See also Vaillé, *Le Cabinet noir* and *Histoire générale*, vol.4, p.108ff. Boislisle ('Le secret de la poste', p.235) cites a case during the reign of Louis XIV when a postmaster was sent to the Bastille 'for the sake of form' for having aided an agent of the state by violating the secrecy of correspondence.
8. Goodman remarks that 'The tension between state control and public service was at the very heart of the postal system, just as it was at the heart of the state itself', *The Republic of letters*, p.19. The historian Lucien Bély explores the relationship between secrecy and the exercise of 'absolute' power during the reign of Louis XIV in *Les Secrets de Louis XIV: mystères d'état et pouvoir absolu* (Paris, 2015). His discussion of the Black Cabinet (p.241-48) relies primarily on *Le Cabinet noir* of Vaillé.

Dena Goodman's words) 'the mark of the confidence with which the public entrusted their private thoughts to the public servants of the state' and 'The *Cabinet noir* was the violation of that confidence'.[9] Doubtless one reason for this conflict was practical, because 'epistolary networks [...] embody the ambiguity of a public sphere made up of private persons'.[10] But the conflict also had its roots in principle. The irresolvable tension between state secrecy and individual conscience clearly manifests itself in the operation of the Black Cabinets. As Susan Whyman has observed, in eighteenth-century England the Post Office both encouraged free speech – by providing the public with mail service and using franking to encourage the distribution of newspapers – and repressed it by opening people's letters, leading to protests by private individuals and in the House of Commons.[11] In France that tension was embodied by Marc-Pierre de Voyer de Paulmy, comte d'Argenson (1696-1764), who not only served as Minister of War and Superintendent of the Posts, but was also a protector of the *philosophes* and the dedicatee of Diderot and d'Alembert's *Encylopédie.* The development of the European state system gave rise to both the Black Cabinets and the widespread belief that state violation of the confidentiality of correspondence was an intolerable practice. In France, when the 1789 *cahiers de doléances* were drawn up, the second most frequent popular grievance of the French people (after the infamous *lettres de cachet*) concerned the *Cabinet noir.*[12] Indeed, when Count Stanislas de Clermont-Tonnerre summarized the *cahiers* to the Estates General, he denounced these two abuses as equally 'absurd and infamous': 'La Nation française s'élève avec indignation contre les lettres de cachet, qui disposaient arbitrairement des personnes, et contre la violation du secret de la poste, l'une des plus absurdes et des plus infâmes inventions du despotisme.'[13] (The French Nation rises up with indignation against the *lettres de cachet*, which arbitrarily took advantage of persons, and against the violation of the secrecy of the post, one of the most absurd and infamous inventions of despotism.) All three Estates

9. Goodman, 'Epistolary property', p.353.
10. Goodman, 'Epistolary property', p.340.
11. Whyman, *The Pen and the people*, p.66-68.
12. The title of a constitutional monarchist brochure published in 1789 underscores the common association between *lettres de cachet* and the lack of postal security. [M. D. B. G. D. S. D. F.] *La Liberté du peuple, lettres de cachet, espionage abolis, et sûreté des lettres de la poste* (Paris, Imprimerie de la Grangé, 1789).
13. *Archives parlementaires, 1re série, tome VIII*, p.284, séance du 27 juillet 1789. See Alexis Belloc, *Les Postes françaises: recherches historiques sur leur origine, leur développement, leur législation* (Paris, 1886), p.254ff; and Vaillé, *Le Cabinet noir*, p.207. During the debates at the National Assembly of 21-24 December 1789 on the status of Jews in France, the same comte de Clermont-Tonnere (1757-1789) famously argued that 'Il faut tout refuser aux juifs comme nation et tout accorder aux juifs comme individus'. Source: Pierre Birnbaum, *La République et le cochon* (Paris, 2013), p.180.

condemned the interception of private letters and called for the abolition of the so-called *Bureau du secret.*[14] Such universal condemnation implied that, at the end of the old regime there was (in all literate sectors of the French population) a firmly established belief that the contents of letters were private, and that therefore the secrecy of correspondence should be inviolable.[15]

Secret places

Siegert maintains that Enlightenment defenses of the confidentiality of correspondence were derived from natural law: 'Advocates of the Enlightenment [defended] the confidentiality of the letter, which they derived from natural law, against all such state policies and [defined] it as the private space of bourgeois freedom.'[16] Yet although learned arguments for the inviolability of correspondence were sometimes couched in terms of natural law, an important condition for belief in the secrecy of correspondence lay in the separation between politics and ethics, as posited by absolutist doctrine of the previous century. As Reinhart Koselleck has argued, the memory of fratricidal religious wars led Hobbes to insist that peace could only be assured if subjects obeyed the law, regardless of their private convictions. The prince would not concern himself with the beliefs of his subjects, provided that the latter conceded to him the right to take whatever actions he judged necessary to secure the interests of the state. Hobbes therefore argued for a separation between the private individual ('Private, is in secret free')[17] and the law-obeying subject, between a person's mind and her or his course of action. As citizens, people were bound to obey the law, but as private individuals they were also entitled to their convictions (which Hobbes reduced to the status of *opinions*), as long as they kept them secret.[18]

14. 'The Nobility, the Third Estate, and the Clergy joined in the same reprobation and expressed their will and faith in the abolition of a practice that shocked the nobility of heart and the independence of mind of an enthusiastic generation called upon to build a new world.' Vaillé, *Le Cabinet noir*, p.201. König affirms the same belief on the first page of *Schwarze Cabinette.*
15. Michèle Perrot traces the growth of the belief in a right to the secrecy of correspondence. 'Le secret de la correspondance au XIXe siècle', in *L'Epistolarité à travers les siècles* (Stuttgart, 1990), p.184-88. See also: Rémi Duchêne, 'Le secret de la correspondance', in *Correspondances: mélanges offerts à Roger Duchêne* (Tübingen and Aix-en-Provence, 1992), p.267-75; Geneviève Haroche-Bouzinac, *L'Epistolaire* (Paris, 1995), p.45-50. There was no copyright law during the Enlightenment. However, as Dena Goodman has shown in 'Epistolary property', the jurist Michel de Servan argued that the contents of a letter belong to its author, if not to both the author and the addressee. See also Vaillé, *Le Cabinet noir*, p.120, n.2.
16. Siegert, *Relays*, p.14.
17. Thomas Hobbes, *Leviathan*, ed. Noel Malcolm (Oxford, 2012), vol. 1, p.564.
18. Koselleck formulates the situation this way: 'So bricht der Mensch bei Hobbes entzwei, er

In Hobbes's theory, the break between conscience and politics affects only the individual subject, who is split between what Koselleck calls the human being [*Mensch*] and the citizen [*Staatsbürger*]. The sovereign, at least as a concept, is self-identical, standing unified, whole and above the law: 'It is true that they that have soveraigne power may commit Iniquitie, but not Injustice.'[19] In principle, the unity of the sovereign guaranteed that he would act in the interest of the state, rather than that of a private interest or moral or religious conviction (including her or his own).[20] During the Thirty Years War, for example, the fact that Louis XIII of France was a Catholic did not prevent him from deciding that, to counter the hegemony of the Spanish Habsburgs, the interest of the French state required him to form an alliance with Protestant Sweden; likewise in theory it was not personal conviction, but *raison d'Etat* that led him to contest the political and military privileges that Protestants within his kingdom had enjoyed since the Religious Wars.

But what enabled the sovereign to determine the interest of the state? How could he have done so without performing a necessarily secret calculation of that interest? Hobbes does not explicitly address these questions, although his concept of sovereignty would seem to imply that, like his subjects, the sovereign is a divided entity, and that he also has a zone of secrecy. In effect, absolutist theory posits two realms of secrecy: it explicitly grants the sovereign's subjects a secret realm, where they are free to entertain their own opinions of his actions, provided they keep those opinions to themselves; and it implicitly requires another secret place where the sovereign can calculate the course of action that is in the interest of the state. For without retreating into such a realm of secrecy, where could he arrive at a rational determination of a course of action that expressed neither private opinion nor private interest (and for which he would be responsible only to God), but only the interest of the state? Unlike the secret place he granted to his subjects, the sovereign's locus of secrecy (which, borrowing the name of an institution created by Louis XV, one might call 'the king's secret') was not a place where he kept

---

wird geteilt in eine private une in einie öffentliche Hällfte: Handlungen und Taten unterliegen restlos dem Staatsgesetz, die Gesinnung ist frei, 'in secret free'. [...] Die Aufspaltung des Menschen in das Private und das Etatistische ist konstitutiv für die Genese des Geheimnisses', *Kultur und Krise: Eine Studie zur Pathogenese der bürgerlichen Welt* (Frankfurt am Main, 1973, p.29; first publication Freiburg/München, 1959); 'Hobbes's man is fractured, split into private and public halves: his actions are totally subject to the law of the land while his mind remains free, "in secret free." [...] The dichotomy of man into the private and the public was intrinsic to the genesis of secrecy [*des Geheimnisses*]', Reinhart Koselleck, *Critique and crisis: Enlightenment and the pathogenesis of modern society* (Cambridge, MA, 1988), p.37-38. Translation modified.

19. *Leviathan*, vol.2, p.272, quoted in Koselleck, *Critique and crisis*, p.36.

20. Koselleck, *Critique and crisis*, p.36.

his private convictions, but a place for deliberation.[21] For if kings and queens had private convictions and desires as individuals, as sovereigns they could have none, at least theoretically. Moreover, unlike the private convictions of their subjects, which were not allowed to affect their behavior, the deliberations secretly conducted by the sovereign necessarily resulted in action (or inaction, when appropriate).

Between these two secret realms lay the sphere of public action, where the king imposed the law and his subjects obeyed it.[22] In principle, these two secret realms guaranteed and authorized each other; in practice, the boundaries between the two were not always clearly defined. In theory, political action was the exclusive domain of the prince, and morality was that of his subjects. But in practice, secret of state and secret conviction encroached upon each other's boundaries; and each could threaten the existence of the other. Was it not the prince's duty to take whatever steps – such as censoring books and having his subjects' mail opened – that might be necessary to protect the interest of the state?[23] And once his subjects had been granted the right to their own opinions, would they not eventually seek to extend the realm of conscience to its absolute limits, by demanding that the state itself become a moral agent?[24] The ambiguous status of postal communication at this time stems from the way in which letters could be held to extend the right to secrecy from the realm of private conscience or opinion to that of written communication (which, along with conversation, was the central mode of discourse among eighteenth-century elites). At the same time that conversation could expand the sphere of conscience beyond the apparently immediate sphere of

21. The *Secret du Roi* was a secret organization founded by Louis XV during the War of Austrian Succession, to promote the candidacy of the Prince de Conti to the Polish throne. Headed by Charles-François de Broglie and with agents such as the Chevalier d'Eon and Pierre Caron de Beaumarchais, the King's Secret continued to pursue unofficial diplomatic initiatives until it was dissolved by Louis XVI in 1774. After the dissolution of the network, its agents played a role in the American Revolution. It would appear that, unlike the Black Cabinet, the King's Secret actually did remain secret during all the years of its operation. See Gilles Perrault, *Le Secret du Roi* (Paris, 1993), 3 vols; and Vaillé, *Le Cabinet noir*, p.175.

22. In *L'Europe absolutiste: raison et raison d'état (1649-1775)* (Paris, 1977), Robert Mandrou argues that after 1649 two models of absolutism emerged in Europe.

23. 'Sixthly, it is annexed to the sovereign to be judge of what opinions and doctrines are averse, what doctrines are conducive to peace; and consequently, on what occasions, how far, and what men are to be trusted withal in speaking to multitudes of people; and who shall examine the doctrines of all books before they are published. For the actions of men proceed from their opinions, and in the well governing of opinions consisteth the well governing of men's actions in order to their peace and concord.' *Leviathan*, vol.18, p.109-10.

24. 'As evident in Hobbes, the moral inner space that had been excised from the State and reserved for man as human being meant (even rudimentarily) a source of the unrest that was originally exclusive to the Absolutist system. The authority of conscience remained an unconquered remnant of the state of nature, protruding into the formally protected State.' Koselleck, *Critique and crisis*, p.38.

self-presence to more open and vulnerable areas, so did correspondence provide the dynamic mechanism whereby the private sphere of conscience could expand to a broader field. Moreover, when correspondence was published (excerpts from Mme de Sévigné's letters first appeared in 1725), that field became potentially infinite.[25] At the same time, the tremendous popular success of epistolary novels testified to an intense desire for access to private opinions and feelings.[26] It was as if a vast reading public wished to share the sovereign's godlike access to postal secrecy, which the marquis d'Argenson called 'Jupiter's eye, the trapdoor through which this god sees what transpires in the hearts of men'.[27]

The paradoxical logic of secrecy under absolutism is perfectly exemplified by the 'lodge', a term which in the eighteenth century designated two secret places: one controlled by the sovereign and the other by certain of his subjects. The lodge was, on the one hand, a place operated by the state for the purpose of intercepting correspondence. In 1711, when a certain Rochus Stella, Count Santa Croce, came from Spain with the new Holy Roman Emperor Charles VI to head the Black Cabinet in Vienna, he not only gave the institution the basic shape that it would maintain in the Habsburg Empire under various names until 1848,[28] but he set up secret offices, or 'post lodges' (*Postlogen*; sometimes called *Brieflogen* or 'letter lodges'), in post offices all over the country. On the other hand, when modern Freemasonry arose at the beginning of the eighteenth century, the term 'Lodge' referred to the organization's basic organizational units and, by extension, it designated the place where Freemasons met to conduct secret rituals and impart esoteric knowledge.[29] Recalling Hobbes's distinction between the law-abiding citizen and the private individual, Koselleck remarks that, 'The intellectual fact "to be in secret free" received its social concretion in the lodges'.[30] Later in the century, when Freemasonry had spread throughout Europe, its secretive nature caused it to be suspected of various kinds of conspiracies. The contested status of the lodge secret had become comparable to that of the letter, insofar as both were a legitimate concern of the state and a form of legitimate private expression. As Siegert puts it, 'The postal counterpart of the lodge secret was the confidentiality of the letter.'[31] In both

25. I would like to thank an anonymous reader of this manuscript for having made these last two points.
26. Robert Darnton has argued that Rousseau's *Julie* 'was perhaps the biggest best-seller of the century', *The Great cat massacre and other episodes in French cultural history* (New York, 1984), p.242. Goethe's *Werther* triggered a 'Werther fever' in male dress, as well as copycat suicides.
27. *Journal et Mémoires du marquis d'Argenson*, vol.VIII, p.423.
28. Stix, 'Geschichte der Wiener Geheimen Ziffernkanzlei', p.132-33.
29. Technically speaking, Freemasons meet *as* a Lodge, not *in* a Lodge.
30. Koselleck, *Critique and crisis*, p.75.
31. Siegert, *Relays*, p.13.

areas, the Enlightenment 'lodge' gave institutional form to the sovereign's power to regulate the private expression of opinion and to the power of private individuals to express their opinions.

Eve Tavor Bannet has shown that in eighteenth-century communications between Britain and British America the tension between public and private (that is, secret) realms of communication – insofar as it is possible to make a clear distinction between the two – manifested itself in other ways, too.[32] One way was in the production of both public and hidden transcripts of administrative proceedings on both sides of the Atlantic; another indication can be found in the importance that trans-Atlantic correspondents, whatever their economic or political interests, attached to using their letters to transmit and receive intelligence and otherwise cultivate private relations with their correspondents.[33] The interaction between public and ostensibly private communication can also be discerned in the relationship between newspapers, which could be read by the general public, and newsletters, which were addressed to a more or less restricted audience. The concern with keeping one's private opinions secret expressed itself in the rhetorical and practical precautions that letter-writers took to ensure that the information contained in their letters would be kept secret, as well as in the various forms of 'secret writing' that were taught by Anglo-American letter manuals and *vade mecum*s in the eighteenth century. Bannet shows that, behind the 'external letter' for which these books provided models, there was often another 'internal letter' in which correspondents expressed their private opinions.[34]

In its very existence as a material object the letter also exhibited the tension between state control and public service. As we have seen, a letter usually consisted of a sheet (or more) of paper with a message written on one side, which was then folded so as to leave room for the address on one of the exposed sides, and sealed with wax on the other. As most letters were not enclosed in envelopes, the seal did not so much describe

32. Bannet, *Empire of letters*, p.225ff. '[T]he binary of "private" and "public" was [...] constantly being destabilized by the overlap in the same correspondences of private and public concerns.' *Empire of letters*, p.256.

33. 'For British officials and British-American colonists alike [...] getting essential political, commercial, legal and personal business done resembled nothing so much as a game of cards in which each of the players tried to keep the hand that he and his partner of the moment were playing hidden close to his chest, while trying to determine from the cards publicly and ceremoniously laid upon the table how the game was going and what card to play next.' Bannet, *Empire of letters*, p.241.

34. 'This introduced another level of writing and reading [...] Here the commonplaces and conventions of different classes of letter became a means of making letters look ordinary that were not in reality so. The epistolary models merely served as useful masks for politically or commercially riskier messages that correspondents wished to conceal from third parties of various sorts.' Bannet, *Empire of letters*, p.226.

a continuously closed boundary or separate an 'outside' from an 'inside', as it marked a point that lay between what necessarily concerned the public mail service and what concerned only the private addressee. By virtue of its exposed address, without which employees of the state-controlled mail service could not direct and carry it to its destination, a letter opened itself to public scrutiny; while hidden behind within the folds, its message remained private, at least in principle.

By the end of the eighteenth century, nearly all literate French citizens believed that the realm of private opinion (conscience) consisted not just of unexpressed thoughts and private conversations, but also their written expression in letters. Indeed throughout Europe epistolary exchanges would eventually come to be viewed as exchanges of secrets. In England, as Whyman remarks, although the violation of the secrecy of correspondence had been frequently condemned throughout the eighteenth century, it was not until 1844 that the opening of letters was disclosed by Parliament. Whereupon *The Sun* printed the following angry reaction: 'When a man puts a letter into the post-office here, he confidently believes [it] [...] will not be read either by Postmaster-General, or penny postman, or Secretary of State, and that no human being will venture to break a seal which has hitherto, in this free country, been regarded a sacred as the door of his own private residence.'[35] This belief in the sacred character of the seal is perhaps most strikingly formulated in a book published in Weimar in 1814, which posits the seal of a letter as the postal equivalent of the seal of confession:

> What is locked up most carefully in the heart, in one's own living room, is entrusted without hesitation to the postal service by everyone, by hundreds of thousands every day. The postman's satchel thus holds incomparably more secrets, and no less securely under proper administration, than the seal of confession, and the symbol of discretion is none other than that of the postal service.[36]

In this view, the seal is the sign of a sacred pledge that the secret, private 'conversation' it secured would remain confidential. For the jurist Michel de Servan (1737-1807), who used images of violation, especially rape, to describe breaches of epistolary property, the seal was like a maiden's hymen. For the general public, the seal authenticated the identity of the sender and marked, if not always 'the confidence with which the public entrusted their private thoughts to the public servants of the state', then at least a limit that no one but the addressee could legitimately

35. RMA POST 23:7, Newspaper Cuttings file I, *The Sun*, 15 June 1844. Cited by Whyman in *The Pen and the people*, p.68.

36. Johann Ludwig Klüber, *Patriotische Wünsche das Postwesen in Teutschland betreffend* (Weimar, 1814) p.6-7; cited by Siegert, *Relays*, p.38. Before referring to this quotation in Siegert, Henkin calls mail bags 'public repositories of private expression', *The Postal age*, p.99.

cross.[37] Yet precisely because it guaranteed the identity of the sender, the seal made it easier for employees of the Black Cabinets to know whose correspondence they should be opening. In a letter written at Les Délices in the summer of 1762 to Claude Philippe Fyot de la Marche, First Presiding Magistrate of the Burgundy Parliament (law court), Voltaire warns his childhood friend not to put his seal on packages addressed to him:

> [V]ous devez être averti que Mrs des postes ont décachetez plusieurs paquets adressez à mr Dargental sous l'envelope de mr de Courteille. Si vous m'adressez quelque chose par cette voye, ne mettez point de cachet au paquet qui m'est destiné. C'est ce cachet senti par les mains funestes des commis qui autorize leur insolence.[38]

> [Y]ou should be warned that the Gentlemen of the posts have broken the seals of several packages addressed to M. d'Argental under the cover of M. de Courteille. If you send me anything by post, do not put a seal on the package destined for me. It is this seal, perceived by the baneful hands of the clerks, that authorizes their insolence.

Espionage and counterespionage

Indeed, despite the common belief in the 'sacred' character of private correspondence, only the most naïve letter-writers assumed that the contents of their letters could be kept secret.[39] The interception of letters was a practical reality with which everyone had to deal, and throughout the early modern period the various Black Cabinets of Europe competed with each other in the art of ciphering and deciphering messages.[40] In seventeenth-century France violation of postal secrecy was already such a common occurrence in spheres of power that Jules Mazarin, Louis XIII's chief minister, offered the following advice to budding politicians:

> In a letter never write anything that might have repercussions if it were seen by a third party. On the other hand, it is never a bad idea to slip in a bit of praise for someone who you suspect might read it. From time to time it is useful to intercept the letters destined for your subordinates. After having read them attentively, be careful to send the letters on to them so that they suspect nothing.[41]

37. Goodman, 'Epistolary property', p.354.
38. Voltaire to Claude Philippe Fyot de La Marche, 9 June [1762], D9698.
39. Bély (*Espions et ambassadeurs*, p.143) underlines this point by quoting from a canonical text by François de Callières 'Few things can remain secret among men who have dealings over a long period of time, intercepted letters and several other unforeseen accidents often discover them...', *De la manière de négocier avec les souverains* (Paris, Michel Brunet, 1716), p.304.
40. Vaillé, *Le Cabinet noir*, p.187, n.2.
41. Jules Mazarin, *Bréviaire des politiciens* (Paris, 1996), p.24. Originally published in Latin. Cited by Geneviève Haroche-Bouzinac, in 'Les lettres qu'on ne brûle pas', *Revue d'histoire littéraire*

After all, no state could accept the notion that its security was compatible with the unrestricted expression of private thoughts, either in print or in the public mails. From this standpoint it was therefore necessary to intercept letters and break the seal that secured their contents. The Black Cabinets were created to do this delicate and distasteful job, and if possible without leaving any trace of their passage. This last task was not easy, since most sealing wax was not made of beeswax, but of a compound of chalk, resin, plaster, shellac, turpentine and coloring matter and (unlike beeswax) it could therefore not be softened with water vapor. According to the Princess Palatine (Elisabeth Charlotte von der Pfalz), who got the information from her son the French Regent, the *Cabinet noir* softened the seals of intercepted letters with a mixture called *gamma* (or *gama*), made of quicksilver and other substances today unknown.[42] Once relevant passages of a letter had been copied, the missive was more or less artfully resealed, so as to leave as little evidence as possible that the secrecy of correspondence had been violated, and the letter was quickly dispatched to its addressee.

Just as relations between nations were fraught with love, hate, jealousy and desire, correspondence between monarchs more or less related by blood resembled love letters by the feelings they elicited.[43] In his study of espionage and counterespionage during the reign of Louis XIV (1661-1715), Lucien Bély has chronicled the tactics employed by European powers of the time to intercept political and military communications – even those of their allies – and keep their own epistolary communications secure.[44] In Russia, letters from foreign diplomats to their governments and dispatches from those governments to their envoys were regularly subject to 'perlustration' by Catherine II's secretary.[45] A particularly well-documented example of tactical interception of mail is that of Celle (in Lower Saxony) at the end of the seventeenth century.[46] Since postal communications between France, on the one hand, and Denmark and Sweden on the other, passed through Celle, the Duke of Brunswick took advantage of the city's strategic position to have

de la France 103:2 (2003), p.301. In *Epistolarité*, p.46-47, Haroche-Bouzinac cites Puget de la Serre's 1680 manual, *Le Secrétaire du Cabinet*, which advises its readers 'not to lightly write anything that may harm us or our friends if it came to light'.

42. Vaillé, *Le Cabinet noir*, p.104. The information is taken from the Princess Palatine's letter dated 2 December 1717.
43. Bély, *Espions et ambassadeurs*, p.138.
44. Bély, *Espions et ambassadeurs*, p.134ff.
45. König, *Schwarze Cabinette*, p.54ff.
46. Stephen. P. Oakley, 'The interception of posts in Celle, 1694-1710', in *William III and Louis XIV: essays 1680-1720, by and for Mark A. Thomson*, Ragnhild Hatton and J. S. Bromley (eds) (Liverpool, 1968), p.95-116.

diplomatic communications between these countries intercepted by the post office. Thanks to this arrangement, William III of Orange-Nassau (*Stadtholder* of much of the Lowlands and King of England) and Heinsius (Grand Pensionary of the States of Holland) were informed of decisions taken at Versailles before the news reached French representatives in Scandinavia. The standard tactic for avoiding interception of letters was the use of false addresses. Spies would be instructed to send their reports (usually in a second envelope) to false addresses, and a list of these addresses would then be communicated to allied postmasters, who were given forwarding addresses for these letters.[47]

In addition to the use of false addresses, the Black Cabinets were confronted with a number of other practical problems, the first of which was that of determining which letters, among the mass of correspondence that passed through post offices, were worthy of their attention. Letters from foreigners or converts, as well as letters with manifestly forged handwriting were obvious candidates for inspection. Correspondents who had secret information to convey would try to avoid suspicion by writing in ways that would not attract the attention of the authorities or ensuring that 'at least [it] could not be proved against one'.[48] As soon as persons fell under suspicion, their correspondence was set aside and closely examined for clues or coded messages; it could then eventually be used to trace an entire espionage network.[49] There was also the problem of discreetly opening and resealing letters. Diplomats, negotiators and secret agents often employed code names for the parties to whom they referred in their letters. They also used invisible ink or lemon juice to write messages between the lines of the visible message. But if the message was long, and especially if it was entirely written in cipher, the secret letter-opening offices could have the greatest difficulty in carrying out their assignments while still maintaining the necessary appearance of respect for the secrecy of correspondence. Indeed it was no more than an appearance, since the existence of these offices was an open secret, and letters often reached their addressees with traces of having been opened and resealed.[50] Indeed, because all parties to diplomatic and military communications were aware that their messages were likely to be intercepted, the Black Cabinets also had to contend with the additional problem of distinguishing information from disinformation.

During the Renaissance a revival of the ancient art of political cryptology accompanied the emergence of postal systems sponsored by

47. Bély, *Espions et ambassadeurs*, p.157-60.
48. Bély, *Espions et ambassadeurs*, p.269; see also p.270-73.
49. Bély (*Espions et ambassadeurs*, p.88ff, 148ff.) describes the dismantling of the extensive Marseilles network, organized in 1694 by a Protestant apologist named Jurieu.
50. Boislisle, 'Le secret de la poste', p.237-39.

Italian city-states and emerging nation-states.[51] Cryptology (Greek *kruptós*: hidden, secret + *logos*: word, discourse) has two components: cryptography, or the coding and ciphering of messages; and cryptanalysis, the decoding and deciphering of same. In the *Dictionnaire philosophique*, Voltaire portrays cryptanalysts as mere charlatans:

> Ceux qui se vantent de déchiffrer une lettre sans être instruits des affaires qu'on y traite, et sans avoir des secours préliminaires, sont de plus grands charlatans que ceux qui se vanteraient d'entendre une langue qu'ils n'ont point apprise.[52]

> Those who boast of deciphering a letter without having knowledge of the affairs treated in it, and without having some preliminary assistance, are greater charlatans than those who boast of understanding a language that they have never learned.

It was indeed extremely difficult for a cryptanalyst to decipher a message of whose contents he was ignorant, unless a traitor had supplied him with the key; and even then, employees of the Black Cabinets would not have dared to 'boast' of their accomplishments. If the key was changed frequently enough (which was not always the case), messages could remain secure from all but the most gifted analysts.[53]

The employees of these secret departments opened, read and, when necessary, deciphered letters in all European languages, copied (in part or in whole) and resealed them, and sometimes even forged letters. When governments were accused of doing such horrible things, they either feigned ignorance or responded in a tone of outraged virtue. Earlier in the same article, Voltaire makes an ironic comment on this practice:

> [J]amais le ministère qui a eu le département des postes n'a ouvert les lettres d'aucun particulier, excepté quand il a un besoin de savoir ce qu'elles contenaient. Il n'en est pas ainsi, dit-on, dans d'autre pays. On a prétendu qu'en Allemagne vos lettres, en passant par cinq ou six dominations différentes, étaient lues cinq ou six fois, et qu'à la fin le cachet était si rompu, qu'on était obligé d'en remettre un autre.

51. There is an excellent general discussion of cryptology in David Kahn, *The Codebreakers: the story of secret writing* (New York, 1967). Kahn summarizes the emergence of modern political cryptology and the Black Cabinets in ch.3 and 5 respectively. See also König, *Schwarze Cabinette*; Stix, 'Geschichte der Wiener Geheimen Ziffernkanzlei', and Vaillé, *Le Cabinet noir*.
52. Voltaire, 'Poste', in *QE*, *OCV*, vol.42B, p.472-73. Derrida comments on this passage in *The Post card*, p.71.
53. In the seventeenth century, the mathematician John Wallis and his grandson William Blencowe in England, along with Rossignol in France, were prodigiously gifted cryptanalysts. Leibniz also excelled at it. 'The entire rationalist tradition found in it a concrete and practical application, a sort of intellectual exercise. The era of Descartes and Newton disposed of a diplomatic chess game to which it devoted itself with passion.' Bély, *Espions et ambassadeurs*, p.154.

> [T]he minister in charge of the postal department has never opened the letters of a private individual, except when he needs to know what they contain. Things are not the same, apparently, in other countries. It has been claimed that in Germany your letters, while passing through five or six different dominions, were read five or six times, and that its seal ultimately became so fractured that it became necessary to put on a new one.

As we shall see, what Voltaire says about Germany was entirely plausible. Voltaire wrote these lines in the early 1770s, but he had been especially concerned with postal surveillance ever since taking refuge with Mme Du Châtelet at Cirey in 1734, after the publication of the *Lettres philosophiques* (originally published in 1733 as *Letters on the English nation*) caused a *lettre de cachet* to be issued against him.[54]

England

Queen Elizabeth I of England refused to allow any improvements in the roads and postal facilities of her kingdom: discouraging communication was a fairly effective, if somewhat shortsighted method (still in use in some parts of the world) of preventing conspiracies, as was raising postal rates to discourage communication among one's subjects.[55] When Oliver Cromwell finally agreed to put the Post Office directly under state control in 1655, he did so primarily to get wind of subversive plots, not to provide a public service.[56] John Thurloe, Cromwell's Secretary of State and spymaster, had decided that intercepting letters was a far more effective tactic than preventing communication.[57] Surveillance and censorship were facilitated by the fact that most mail passed through London.[58] The Royal Mail had become 'the pulse of all political move-

54. The earliest of his myriad references to surveillance of his mail can be found in a love letter to Olympe du Noyer ('Pimpette'), written when François-Marie Arouet was nineteen years old: 28 November 1713, D7. During his sojourn at Cirey, Voltaire's first explicit reference to state surveillance of his mail occurs on 3 November 1737, when he informs Thieriot that 'N'osant pas vous écrire par la poste, je me sers de cet homme qui part de Cirey et qui se charge de ma lettre'. Voltaire to Nicolas Claude Thieriot, D1383.
55. Robinson, *The British Post Office*, p.11. During this period, one of the more imaginative attempts at organizing a conspiracy against the crown involved hiding messages inside beer kegs. *The British Post Office*, p.13.
56. Prior to 1655 the Post Office had been operated as a farm, as in France. According to Cromwell's decree, the erection of 'one general Post Office' would 'discover and prevent many dangerous and wicked designs, which have been, and are daily contrived against the Peace and Welfare of the Commonwealth, the intelligence whereof cannot well be Communicated but by letter', Firth and Rait, *Acts and ordinances of the Interregnum*, vol.II, 1110-13; cited in Robinson, *The British Post Office*, p.46. See also Robinson, *The British Post Office*, p.44-45, and Kahn, *The Codebreakers*, p.171.
57. How, *Epistolary space*, p.12. Moreover, according to Alan Marshall (*Intelligence and espionage in the reign of Charles II, 1680-1685* (Cambridge, 1994), p.78), the practice continued in the late seventeenth century: 'In the late seventeenth century the postal service was at the forefront of the Stuart intelligence system.' Cited in How, *Epistolary space*, p.57.
58. Whyman, *The Post and the people*, p.51.

ments, the deputy postmasters in the country serving as a hydra-headed agency for the State – seeing, hearing, and reporting everything of importance'.[59] During and after the Civil War, Parliament asked the great mathematician John Wallis to decipher messages sent by Charles I (in 1643) and later (in 1660) by Charles II. Wallis's talents as a cryptanalyst were so prodigious that after the Restoration, even though he had worked for the enemy, Charles II (and later William and Mary) did not hesitate to employ and reward him.[60] After the Restoration, Wallis and his colleagues worked in a secret room adjacent to the General Letter office, where from 11:00 p.m. to 3:00 or 4:00 a.m. they used special techniques to open, copy and reseal letters: 'It was said employees could open letters, take impressions of seals, imitate writing perfectly, and copy a letter in one minute, using an "offset process of pressing damp tissue paper against the ink".'[61] Wallis's successors were known collectively as the Deciphering Branch. They worked at home and received their material by special messenger from two subdivisions of the Post Office: the Secret Office, for foreign interceptions; and the Private Office, for domestic ones.[62] The practice of preventing letter carriers from leaving the General Letter Office until the king's mail was sent gave officers in the secret room time to open and reseal letters.[63]

After the Glorious Revolution of 1688, when the balance of power in Great Britain shifted definitively from the monarch to Parliament, members of both Houses were free to voice their objections to violations of postal secrecy, but the practice increased nonetheless. At the same time, the privacy of correspondence had come to be viewed as a fundamental liberty. Thus the Act of 1711 gave the Post Office precise directions about the conditions in which letters could be opened, specifying that whatever their provenance, letters could be examined only by express warrant. All the same private correspondents and members of Parliament often complained about the abuse of warrants, though to

59. James Hyde, *The Post in grant and farm* (1894), p.238. Cited by Whyman, *The Post and the people*, p.49.

60. Kahn, *The Codebreakers*, p.119, 166ff; Ellis, *The Post Office in the eighteenth century*, p.127-128

61. Whyman, *The Pen and the people*, p.49, citing H. W. Dickinson, *Sir Samuel Morland* (Cambridge, 1970), p.95. See also Robinson, *The British Post Office*, p.119-20; Ellis, *The Post Office in the eighteenth century*, p.67ff.

62. See Kahn, *The Codebreakers*, p.171-72. As Kahn points out, these warrants provide the legal precedent for the modern tapping of telephones (and today, presumably, for the interception of electronic communications) in England.

63. Whyman, *The Pen and the people*, p.51. Secretary of State Lord Arlington's deputy, Joseph Williamson 'also forged links between the Royal Mail and the newspaper. He used the Post to gather news from domestic informers and foreign contacts, who reported on shipping, trade and military affairs. Then he circulated what he wished in the government's official newspaper, *The London gazette* (1666-1688)'. *The Pen and the people*, p.50.

little effect.[64] In 1735 the House of Commons appointed a committee to report on the 'abuses of the Post Office', provided that no inquiries were made into anything tending to discover the secrets of government.[65]

In the eighteenth century, the opening of private correspondence formed an important part of the British state's intelligence operations.[66] After the succession to the throne of George I (Elector of Hanover) in 1711, the British Secret Office collaborated with the Hanoverian Black Cabinet, based in three towns within the Electorate. In one of these towns, Nienburg, members of the same family were hereditary decipherers throughout the eighteenth century.[67] On the domestic front, British letter-writers of the eighteenth century complained frequently about the examination of their correspondence.[68] Authors as diverse as John Gay, Bolingbroke, Horace Walpole, Jonathan Swift and their correspondents knew full well that their letters were being opened and forwarded to the secretaries of state. In a postscript to a letter of 1737 to a Mrs Whiteway, William King addresses himself to one of the letter-openers:

> To the gentleman of the Post Office, who intercepted my last letter addressed to Mrs Whiteway at her house in Abbey Street, together with a letter enclosed and addressed to the Dean of St. Patrick's [Jonathan Swift]. When you have sufficiently perused this letter, I beg the favour of you to send it to the lady to whom it is directed. I shall not take it ill though you should not give yourself the trouble to seal it [...] I shall think myself obliged to you if, at the same time, you will be pleased to send Mrs Whiteway those letters which are now in your hands, with such alterations and amendments as you will think proper, but I cannot believe that your order will justify in detaining letters of business, as [...] I conceive you have not a license to rob on the highway.[69]

The need to return intercepted mail to the Post Office on the same day that it was received placed extreme pressure on the clerks of the Secret

64. Robinson, *The British Post Office*, p.119ff.
65. Ellis, *The Post Office in the eighteenth century*, p.76. In 1844, after it was admitted that the Foreign Office had revealed the correspondence of the Italian patriot Giuseppe Mazzini to the Neapolitan government, both Houses of Parliament set up secret committees to inquire into the illegal opening of letters, past and present. Robinson (*The British Post Office*, p.122) summarizes the published report of the House of Commons committee. See also David Vincent, *The Culture of secrecy: Britain, 1832-1998* (Oxford and New York, 1998), p.1-9.
66. Ellis, *The Post Office in the eighteenth century*, p.60ff. 'Huge volumes of intercepted letters in The National Archives and British Library are evidence of the office's effectiveness.' Whyman, *The Pen and the people*, p.67, 280, n.234.
67. Kenneth Ellis, 'The administrative connections between Britain and Hanover' in *Journal of the Society of Archivists* 3 (1969), p.559ff. See also Kahn, *The Codebreakers*, p.172; Ellis, *The Post Office in the eighteenth century*, p.74.
68. Robinson, *The British Post Office*, p.120ff.
69. Cited by Robinson, *The British Post Office*, p.123.

Office, with the result that intercepted letters were sometimes placed in the wrong envelopes. Or at least that was the inference drawn by Jean-Jacques Rousseau's friend and protector George (Lord) Keith:

> Votre lettre m'est parvenue sans avoir été ouverte à ce me semble; je ne crois pas qu'on pense à ouvrir ni les votres ni les mienes; j'ay trouvé cependant l'autre jour dans une des mienes venant d'Ecosse, une ecrite à Dublin par un Marchand à son correspondent à Barcelone, comment est-elle entré sous une envelope à moy, j'ignore. Je soubsonne que c'est par une bevue des ouvreurs de lettres à la poste; on veut quelque fois savoir la correspondance de quelcun, on ouvre alors toutes les lettres; et peutetre la lettre que j'attens de mon home d'afaire en Ecosse est allé a Barcelone. Ceci est un mal general, c'est une etiquette des Cours, tres etablie par tout.[70]

> Your letter reached me without having been opened, so it would seem; I do not think that anyone means to open your letters or mine; the other day in one of mine that came from Scotland I found a letter written from Dublin by a merchant to a correspondent in Barcelona. How had it gotten inside of an envelope for me? I know not. I suspect it was through a blunder by the letter-openers at the Post; sometimes they want to know what is in someone's correspondence, and they open all the letters and perhaps the letter I am expecting from my man of affairs went to Barcelona. This is a general evil, it is a matter of court etiquette, everywhere established.

France

Unlike the king of England, the princes of continental Europe did not have to contend with parliaments or commissions of inquiry. As early as 1507, long before the French state officially allowed its post to carry private letters, Louis XII was having letters and travelers stopped and searched by postmasters. But as the state gradually acquired a monopoly over the post, surveillance of private communications became easier. A *Cabinet noir* (also known as the *Secret de la poste* and the *Bureau du dedans*) already operated under Richelieu, whose redoubtable decipherer, one Antoine Rossignol, had a reputation that discouraged conspiracies.[71] While Louvois served as Louis XIV's Minister of War and General Superintendent of the Post, his *Cabinet noir* regularly opened domestic mail. Indeed the practice was so widespread that (as in England) some letter-writers inserted into their letters comments directed to the indiscreet third parties of the post. In a letter dated 18 March 1671, Mme de Sévigné tells her daughter:

70. George Keith, 10th Earl Marischal, to Jean-Jacques Rousseau, 26 April 1766, *CC*, vol.29, p.152.

71. Vaillé, *Le Cabinet noir*, p.52. See also Boislisle, 'Le secret de la poste', p.229, and Kahn, *The Codebreakers*, p.157ff. Although Rossignol's proper name is the same as the French word (*rossignol*: literally, nightingale) for a lock-picking device, there is no etymological connection between them. As Kahn points out (*The Codebreakers*, n.160), the word *rossignol* appears as criminal slang in police documents as early as 1406.

> Mais je veux revenir à mes lettres qu'on ne vous envoie point; j'en suis au désespoir. Croyez-vous qu'on les ouvre? Croyez-vous qu'on les garde? Hélas, je conjure ceux qui prennent cette peine de considérer le peu de plaisir qu'ils ont à cette lecture, et le chagrin qu'ils nous donnent. Messieurs, du moins ayez soin de les faire recacheter, afin qu'elles arrivent tôt ou tard.[72]
>
> I should like to return to my letters that are not being sent to you, I despair of them. Do you think they are being opened? Do you think they are being kept? Alas! I beseech those who are taking this trouble to consider how little pleasure they derive from reading them and the distress they cause us. Gentlemen, at least take care to reseal them, so that they eventually arrive.

Louvois instructed his men to pay special attention to foreign correspondence.[73] As Funck-Brentano points out, given the rank and German origins of the Palatine Princess (Elisabeth Charlotte of Bavaria was the second wife of Philippe d'Orléans), it was understandable that the Foreign Affairs Council should have wanted to keep an eye on her correspondence. Even if she had not been the second-highest ranking woman at the court of Louis XIV, the simple fact that Liselotte (as she was called) maintained regular and often intense correspondence with friends and relatives in Germany would have been sufficient reason to intercept her letters.[74] However the Princess had no tolerance for such precautions. In the middle of a letter to her aunt, Duchess Sophie of Hanover, she abuses and threatens the employees of the *Cabinet noir*:

> I would very much like to know what they imagine that Your Ladyship and I could write to each other that matters so much to them. They had better not put me in a temper, since they could put me in a mood to tell them a few truths in what I write Your Ladyship that would snuff out their delight in opening letters. I shall always maintain the respect that I owe the King, I cannot and will not ever say anything against H. M., but as for the toadeaters

72. Madame de Sévigné to Madame de Grignan, 18 March 1761, *Correspondance*, vol.1, p.192. Vaillé quotes from a letter of 18 September 1692, in which the Princess Palatine tells the following anecdote to the Duchess of Hanover: 'Speaking of letters opened by the post, I must tell you a story that happened a few years ago. The Grande Mademoiselle [Anne Marie Louise d'Orléans (1627-1693)] received letters from her business people and clearly saw that they had been opened. She answered everything, and then she added: Since M. de Louvois has a fine mind and will see this letter before all of you, I beg him, when he opens my packet to insert a word of advice on my business, it can only profit from it.' (Quoted by Vaillé in French translation, without date, *Le Cabinet noir*, p.77).
73. After Louvois, (Colbert de) Torcy was both Superintendent of the Posts and Minister of Foreign Affairs. During the reign of Louis XV, the comte d'Argenson, the marquis d'Argenson's brother, was (like Louvois) both Minister of War and Superintendent of the Post. When the hostile relations between him and Mme de Pompadour became public knowledge, he was replaced as Superintendent in 1757. Vaillé, *Le Cabinet noir*, p.151 and p.161.
74. Frantz Funck-Brentano, *Liselotte, duchesse d'Orléans, mère du Régent* (Paris, 1936), p.123; Bély, *Espions et ambassadeurs*, p.144-45.

> [*die Furschwenker undt Furschwenkerinne*] who surround the King and who amuse themselves by opening our letters, I shall confront them with terrible proof of their own infamy if they persist in this exercise.[75]

And in a post-scriptum, she adds: 'Written to pass before the eyes of the letter openers.' In her letters, the Palatine did her very best to embarrass Torcy, who oversaw the operations of the *Cabinet noir* as Minister of Foreign Affairs (1696-1715) and until 1723 as Superintendant of the Posts. In another letter nominally addressed to her aunt, Liselotte complains that the clerks in the *Cabinet noir* are not just reading her letters to family and friends in Germany, but completely mislaying them on occasion. In typically lively terms, she wishes an appropriate punishment upon them:

> Indeed they are going a bit far with my letters, all my Hanover mail is missing. My room is full of wasps, more than 30 of them at the window, and I wished that those who open my letters could have all of them up their behind, so that they would have something else to think about besides my letters.[76]

Louis XIV had letters intercepted for personal and political reasons, and punished those who criticized him too wittily; and occasionally he would personally concern himself with finding the guilty parties.[77]

After the death of Louvois in 1691, it was the Pajot and Rouillé families (the primary financial backers of the postal farm from 1672 to 1738) who ran the *Cabinet noir* in France, under the command of the General Superintendant.[78] At that time, the 'Inside Office' was located in the Hôtel de Villeroy, which belonged to those families; it communicated by a corridor with the Arrivals Office. The General Superintendent personally ordered its employees to keep track of this or that correspondence. In the 1750s, one of the arguments made to justify the creation of a *petite poste* in Paris was that it would facilitate interception of letters in

75. Elisabeth Charlotte von der Pfalz to Sophie of Hanover, 22 November 1692. *Aus den Briefen der Herzogin an die Kurfürstin Sophie von Hannover: ein Beitrag zur Kulturgeschichte des 17. Und 18. Jahrhunderts*, ed. Eduard Bodemann (Hanover, 1891). Judging from a recent article on the portions of Eric Hobsbawm's MI5 file that have been made public, it would appear that as late as the 1950s the relationship between 'secret' postal inspectors and their witting quarry had not changed. See Frances Stonor Saunders, 'Stuck on the flypaper', *London review of books* 37:7 (9 April 2015), p.8.
76. *Aus den Briefen der Herzogin an die Kurfürstin Sophie von Hannover*, 3 September 1702. In a letter to the duc de Grammont, dated 6 March 1721, she evaluates the competency of the various translators and ministers who have read her mail over the years: 'M. de Louvois read all my letters, but he had very knowledgeable translators... Torcy never had any who were as skilled. Abbé Dubois imitates these two ministers. As the French proverb says: he is a little dog imitating big ones, he pisses on the walls because he sees others doing it.' 6 March 1721. Cited in French by Vaillé, *Le Cabinet noir*,.p.115.
77. Vaillé, *Le Cabinet noir*, p.80, 88, 92.
78. See Boislisle, 'Le secret de la poste', p.236-37.

Paris.[79] Although the personnel of the Inside Office was composed of men whose discretion the guarantors could trust, a number of precautions were taken to ensure that they did not communicate with the regular staff of the postal farm.[80] The Pajot-Rouillé dynasty had access to secrets which, according to Saint-Simon, provided them with the means of staying in power for so many years:

> [L]a plus cruelle de toutes les voies par laquelle le roi fut instruit bien des années avant qu'on s'en fut aperçu, et par laquelle l'ignorance et l'imprudence de beaucoup de gens continua toujours de l'instruire, fut celle de l'ouverture des lettres. C'est ce qui donna tant de crédit aux Pajot et aux Rouillé, qui en avaient la ferme, qu'on ne put jamais ôter ni les faire augmenter par cette raison si longtemps inconnue, et qui s'y enrichirent si énormément tous, aux dépens du public et du Roi même. On ne saurait comprendre la promptitude et la dextérité de cette exécution. Le Roi voyait l'extrait de toutes les lettres où il y avait des articles que les chefs de la poste, puis le ministre qui les gouvernait, jugeaient devoir aller jusqu'à lui, et les lettres entières quand elles en valaient la peine par leur tissu, ou par la considération de ceux qui étaient en commerce.[81]

> [T]he cruelest of all the means by which the king was informed years before it was noticed and by which the ignorance and imprudence of many continued to inform him, was the opening of letters. This is what gave so much credit to the Pajots and Rouillés who had the postal farm, which could never be taken away from them any more than their payments could be increased, for this reason that was so long unknown to the public and who enriched themselves so enormously at the expense of the public and the King himself. The promptness and dexterity of their operations was incomprehensible. The King saw excerpts from all the letters that the director of the post and then the minister in charge of it thought should be forwarded to him, as well as entire letters if this was justified by either their content or the rank of the correspondents.

Although he believed that *raison d'Etat* could justify intercepting private correspondence and bringing its contents to the attention of the king, what shocked Saint-Simon was the fact that knowledge of private matters gave unlimited power to mere officials of the postal service. For not only did these people reveal to the monarch what his publicly loyal subjects were saying about him in private, they also had the power to take these remarks out of context, and alter or even invent them with impunity:

> Par là les gens principaux de la poste, maîtres et commis, furent en Etat de supposer tout ce qu'il leur plut et à qui il leur plut, et, comme peu de chose perdait sans ressource, ils n'avaient pas besoin de forger ni de suivre un intrigue. Un mot de mépris sur le Roi ou sur le gouvernement, une raillerie, en un mot un article de lettre spécieux et détaché, noyait sans ressource, sans

79. Vaillé, *Le Cabinet noir*, p.166 and n.1.
80. Vaillé, *Le Cabinet noir*, p.99ff.
81. Louis de Rouvroy, duc de Saint-Simon, *Mémoires* (Paris, 1985), vol.5, p.526. According to Saint-Simon and Luynes, the Cabinet noir burned its account books at the end of every year, in order to keep its enormous profits a secret. Vaillé, *Le Cabinet noir*, p.140.

perquisition aucune et ce moyen était continuellement entre leurs mains. Aussi à vrai et à faux est-il incroyable combien de gens de toutes les sortes en furent plus ou moins perdus. *Le secret était impénétrable*, et jamais rien ne coûta moins au Roi de se taire profondément, et de dissimuler de même.[82]

In this way the principal people at the post, masters and employees, were in a position to libel whomever they pleased however they pleased, and since not much was required to irremediably ruin someone, they did not need to forge or follow the course of a plot. A scornful remark about the King or governance, a gibe, in brief just a specious line from a letter, taken out of context, was enough to irreparably destroy one, without any investigation, and this instrument was continuously in their hands. It is therefore incredible how many people of all sorts were more or less ruined by this means. *Secrecy was impenetrable*, and nothing ever cost the king less effort than to wrap himself in profound silence and dissimulation.

Whether true or invented, information transmitted to Louis XIV could be used, careers broken and people ruined. The king could keep the reasons for his actions hermetically sealed behind his inscrutable mask, in his own 'impenetrable secrecy'. For just as the king had the unlimited, absolute power to reward or punish whom he pleased, postal officials – in principle, his obedient subjects – had the secret, unchecked and absolute power to ruin whom they pleased, effectively making the king himself subject to the whims of commoners. As a consequence, Louis XIV unwittingly became at times the occasional instrument of an institution that had been created to serve him. He may have thought of the *Cabinet noir* as a kind of primitive listening device, which would enable him to capture the secret thoughts of his subjects, but at times he probably heard only what his surveillance operatives wanted him to hear. The very technology that the Sun King had caused to be installed in order to acquire knowledge of his subjects and thereby wield even greater power over them also had the potential to do just the opposite: to feed him disinformation and give his subjects power over him and over each other. In this fashion, what Saint-Simon believed to be a justifiable violation of secrecy, for reasons of state, gave rise to the manipulation of secrecy for private ends, to what he decried as 'the poison of fortunes':

Ce pernicieux usage de livrer le public et la fortune de chacun aux commis de la poste, même aux ministres, doit donc faire frémir et pour les fortunes n'est pas différent de l'usage du poison pour les corps avec cette différence qu'on ne peut empoisonner sans hasard de se commettre et sans des occasions qui se trouvent parfois bien difficiles, outre la crainte des suites et du péril d'être à la fin découvert par les événements les moins susceptibles d'être prévenus, au lieu que *le poison des fortunes* est à couvert de toute crainte, de toute suite et se peut donner tous les jours à qui on veut dans la sécurité la plus démontrée.[83]

82. Saint-Simon, *Mémoires*, vol.5, p.526. Emphasis added.

83. 'Projet de gouvernement du duc de Bourgogne' (Paris, 1859). Cited by Vaillé, *Le Cabinet noir*, p.95. Emphasis added.

> This pernicious habit of handing the public and everyone's fortune over to the employees of the post, even to the ministers, should make one shudder and is no different for fortunes than poison for bodies, except for the fact that no one can poison without the risk of compromising himself and without opportunities that can be very delicate indeed, not to mention the fear of consequences and the risk of being discovered by the most unforeseeable events, whereas *the poison of fortunes* is safe from all fears and consequences and it can be administered every day to whom one wishes in the most proven security.

Thus it was that officials of the *Bureau du dedans*, as it was euphemistically called, always had at their disposal both the means and the opportunity to administer a lethal dose of misfortune to anyone, and at no risk to themselves.

After the death of Louis XIV, the *Cabinet noir* continued to open letters in the interest of state security, but its scope expanded in order to satisfy the curiosity of Philippe d'Orléans and Louis XV about the private opinions of their ministers, not to mention the love life and family secrets of influential persons at court and in town. It began intercepting private letters on a nearly systematic basis. The journal of abbé de Véri (1724-1799), the influential friend of both Maurepas (the king's 'mentor') and Turgot (Louis XV's Controller-General of Finances) testifies to the fact that even Louis XV's most powerful ministers knew that their correspondence was subject to inspection. In the entry for 21 August 1775, Véri refers to two letters that he has received, one from Mme Maurepas and the other from Turgot, both of which deal with the bitter struggles over Turgot's attempts at financial reform. He quotes at length from Mme Maurepas (whose influence over her husband was reputedly almost as powerful as Turgot's influence over her), and then adds: 'La seconde lettre est de M. Turgot. Elle ne me parle pas avec la même clarté, parce qu'il craint l'ouverture des lettres de la poste.' (The second letter is from M. Turgot. It does not speak to me with the same clarity, because he fears that the post will open his letters.)[84] In 1775, during his bitterly contested efforts at financial reform, Turgot was so afraid of having his letters opened that he only dared express himself in veiled terms. While all of the other Black Cabinets in Europe seem to have concerned themselves exclusively with protecting state security, Louis XV took particular delight in reading about the savory details of important people's lives. While initially created for the same reason as the other Black Cabinets of Europe, in the eighteenth century the *Cabinet noir* now began to serve a different end: namely, to satisfy the voyeuristic desires of the *man* in power rather than the security concerns of the sovereign.[85] In

84. *Journal de l'abbé de Véri*, published with an introduction and notes by Le Bon Jehan de Witte (Paris, 1928), p.327.
85. Vaillé believed that Louis XV's desire to learn about other people's secrets betrayed an 'unhealthy curiosity'. The popularity of such genres as novels and memoirs suggests that

the chapter on the *petite poste* in the *Tableau de Paris* (1782-1788), Mercier devises his own voyeuristic fantasy about the post. Imagine, he says, being able to read all the letters carried by the *petite poste* in a single day:

> On a publié une mince brochure, intitulée, *La Petite Poste dévalisée*. Ces lettres sont fictives; mais s'il était permis de lever par simple curiosité les cachets, et de parcourir la correspondance d'un seul jour, Dieu! que de choses curieuses et intéressantes à lire! La certitude que ces lettres n'ont été écrites que pour une seule personne, que l'âme s'est épanchée en liberté, formerait un contraste singulier et une lecture unique; jamais l'imagination d'un auteur ne produira rien qui s'en approche; la détresse, l'infortune, la misère, l'amour, la jalousie, l'orgueil, donneraient des tableaux piquants; et comme on ne pourrait douter de la réalité, l'intérêt deviendrait plus vif. Quel plaisir de voir à nu le style de l'homme d'affaires, du marquis, de la courtisane, de la jeune fille amoureuse, de l'habitué de paroisse, de l'emprunteur, du tartuffe dans toutes les classes! Que ne donnerait-on pas pour les lettres d'un Desrues, pour tenir un billet de tel homme célèbre dans telle circonstance de la vie![86]

> A thin brochure has been published entitled *The Petite Poste burglarized*. These letters are fictive; but were it permitted to remove the seals and to peruse the correspondence of a single day, Lord! How many curious and interesting things there would be to read! The certainty that these letters were written for one person, that a heart and soul have candidly poured out their feelings, would make for a singular contrast and unique reading; an author's imagination will never produce anything that approaches it; distress, misfortune, love, jealousy, pride, would add piquant features; and since one could not doubt the reality of these letters, they would be all the more interesting. What a pleasure to see the style of the man of business laid bare, of the courtesan, the amorous young girl, the fervent churchgoer, the borrower, the Tartuffe in every class! What would one not give for the letters of a Desrues, to possess a letter from such-and-such a man in such-and-such a circumstance in life!

Antoine-François Desrues was an infamous poisoner, who was put on the wheel (*roué*) in Paris in 1777. Mercier's words recall those of Saint-Simon, who also associated the post with poison. However for Mercier, the *petite poste* is a fundamentally good and useful institution, certainly not the 'poison of fortunes'; it is a source of information that could have enabled one to see the mind of a real, literal poisoner at work. Just as the entire *Tableau de Paris* was meant to present the reader with a meticulously drawn picture of Parisian society in all its motley forms, so Mercier imagined that a day's letters from the *petite poste* would reveal to *him* (this is a dominating and penetrating 'male' perspective) the subjective reality behind those appearances.[87] He would be able to view the full array of

---

Louis XV shared with many of his contemporaries a curiosity about the intimate details of other people's lives.

86. Mercier, *Le Tableau de Paris*, vol.I, p.762-63. Vaillé, *Le Cabinet noir* 342-43.

87. In 'Vue des Alpes' Mercier locates his narrative perspective at the top of a mountain in the Alps. *Tableau de Paris*, vol.II, dclxxv, p.496-502.

human passions, as well as the 'stile' of persons in all social categories 'laid bare' (*à nu*); he would be able to see the entire human comedy of his century in a form much truer than anything that authors of fiction can imagine. There is, he assures us, nothing unseemly about this fantasy, since removing the seals on all those letters would be merely the expression of 'simple curiosity'. When he stresses the fact that letters from the *petite poste* 'have been written for a single person', without constraint, Mercier makes an implicit contrast between letters sent through this system and many of the letters sent by regular (interurban) post, which have been written with the understanding that they will or might be read aloud, to a wider audience.

Louis XV's awareness of the ease with which the post could supply him with other people's secrets made him fear that his own letters might be intercepted. During the War of Austrian Succession, when he took it into his head to adopt a policy that contradicted the official policy of his Minister of Foreign Affairs, he created a network of secret agents (the so-called *Secret du Roi* or King's Secret) and ensured the security of his correspondence with them by instituting his own secret mail service.[88] Diplomatic papers from this service were kept at Versailles in the secret drawers of the famous roll-top secretary (*Bureau du Roi*), whose only key the king always carried with him. By instituting this secret mail service, he completely reversed the historical relationship between surveillance and secrecy. Black Cabinets had been established for the purpose of discovering conspiracies against the state, but by creating his own secret mail service, Louis XV assumed the role of conspirator: 'Thus the correspondence of an absolute sovereign in his own kingdom was organized with all the precautions that conspirators would have taken to prepare a crime of State.'[89]

Habsburg territories

The War of Spanish Succession (1701-1714) marked a turning point in the history of postal surveillance on the continent. During that conflict, the French used postal intercepts to such great advantage that Prince Eugene of Savoy and the Holy Roman Emperor Charles VI decided to organize their own surveillance services, after which all of the European

88. Perrault, *Le Secret du Roi*. See n.21 (p.100).

89. Albert de Broglie, *Le Secret du Roi: correspondance secrète de Louis XV avec ses agents diplomatiques, 1752-1774* (Paris, 1879), vol.2, p.9. Quoted by Vaillé, *Le Cabinet noir*, p.180. At the beginning of his reign, Louis XVI expressed moral objections to the operation of the *Cabinet noir*, but he was finally convinced of its political necessity. During the Affair of the Diamond Necklace the *Cabinet noir* reached its fullest development, with twelve employees and a director who was paid 20,000 *livres* a year. Vaillé, *Le Cabinet noir*, p.185, 195.

powers established their own Black Cabinets.[90] As we have seen, when Charles VI became Holy Roman Emperor in 1711, he brought with him Count Santa Croce, who gave its basic shape to the Austrian Black Cabinet. Under orders from the Austrian Hapsburgs, the Thurn and Taxis post operated the most renowned and active Black Cabinet in Europe, with secret 'lodges' staffed by handsomely paid employees, on all major German roads.[91] From that point on, the secrecy of correspondence was merely a legal formality in the Hapsburg Empire: only the secrecy of the sovereign's correspondence was respected.[92] There were Black Cabinet offices at all the postal relays: Eisenach, Frankfurt, Nuremberg, Augsburg and Regensburg, in the Hanseatic cities and in the capitals of the ecclesiastical electors, notably at Mainz.[93] In the 1730s not a single piece of diplomatic correspondence from Holland, England and France escaped interception by a branch of the Austrian surveillance services. To keep this service as secret as possible, the Hapsburgs allowed the positions to become hereditary, as in the Electorate of Hanover. Count Kaunitz, Empress Maria-Teresa's chancellor of state and minister of foreign affairs (1753-1793), was not one to neglect the Black Cabinet. He directed the various secret agents and spies who labored in the *Geheime Ziffkanzlei* (Secret Chancellery) and who formed 'a sort of second-class aristocracy': in fact, it would appear that many of these gentlemen were actually ennobled.[94] The Hapsburgs had corrupted most of the German couriers, so that it was a simple matter for them to intercept the mail:

> On the Bohemian border near Pirna, a house had been specially built in a conveniently chosen place for the use of [the postal administration's] confederates, who were the only ones allowed to enter: several of them even lived there. Here these Gentlemen awaited the courier from Berlin, had him get into their post chaise, and opened his bag; while the horses galloped, they deftly unsealed the dispatches, read them and copied the important passages. When their work was done, the letters were resealed and put back in the bag. Finally the chaise reached a mysterious house just before

90. Kalmus, *Weltgeschichte*, p.377ff. In principle, for the sake of security all states must have monitored postal communications. However, as noted at the beginning of this chapter, the inherently secretive nature of Black Cabinets can make it difficult to find reliable evidence of their operation. For example, both Kalmus and Vaillé consider interception of mail by the Spanish Court as an established fact, but only Vaillé (*Le Cabinet noir*, p.119ff, 159) provides evidence for this practice.
91. Nodé-Langlois, 'La poste internationale', p.307; König, *Schwarze Cabinette*, p.69ff; Stix, 'Geschichte der Wiener Geheimen Ziffernkanzlei', p.132ff. As the feudal lord of Prince Thurn and Taxis, the Kaiser could force him to do this job for him; moreover, the post could not operate without the Kaiser's permission. Kalmus, *Weltgeschichte*, p.407.
92. Kalmus, *Weltgeschichte*, p.407.
93. Vaillé, *Le Cabinet noir*, p.187.
94. Vaillé, *Le Cabinet noir*, p.187; König, *Schwarze Cabinette*, p.72.

> Langenzersdorf, the last postal relay on the road to Vienna. The good folk separated, and three hours later the Prussian ambassador received dispatches of which Austria already possessed copies.[95]

Bags of mail for the embassies in Vienna were taken to the office of the *Geheime Ziffkanzlei* at 7:00 a.m. where the letters were opened. Important parts of letters were quickly taken down by teams of copyists, translated (if necessary) and the letters replaced in their envelopes, resealed and returned to the post office by 9:30 a.m.[96] The craftsmen of the Vienna Black Cabinet could also imitate handwriting and give false advice, duping senders and receivers alike. An entire wing of the Hofburg was devoted to the labors of the 'letter inquisitors', as König calls them. He alleges that 'It was mainly Neapolitans and Frenchmen who were used for this dirty business, since experience had proven them masters of dexterity and cunning'.[97] In addition to making translations and copies of suspicious correspondence, the Secret Chancellery prided itself on possessing the best-trained and most skilled decipherers in Europe, who also applied their craft to the encoding of confidential documents. Stix evokes their labors with reverent admiration:

> Only an intelligent choice of Chancellery personnel, a brotherly cloistered relationship, enabling an uninterrupted exchange of ideas and mutual assistance, the fact that several generations of the same family thus incessantly devoted themselves to a branch of the service that so quickly exhausted their physical and intellectual powers – such that father and son labored in the same department, and not least the lively interest that the sovereign took in the secret service – could produce such results.[98]

The employees of the Secret Chancellery were generously rewarded for their services, and, when the occasion warranted it (when a clerk unlocked a new code, for example), by the Kaiser himself. Nevertheless the workers in these secret offices seem to have been treated more like prisoners than employees; in the workplace and around their homes, police surveillance was constant. The work required such meticulous accuracy and speed that even though cryptanalysts worked only every other week, it was not uncommon for them to suffer nervous break-

95. Belloc, *Les Postes françaises*, 208-209 ; König, *Schwarze Cabinette*, p.74. Both authors seem to rely on the same (uncited) source.
96. See Kahn, *The Codebreakers*, p.163-64. Here Kahn paraphrases Stix ('Geschichte der Wiener Geheimen Ziffernkanzlei', p.138ff), whose slightly implausible account is based upon an 1852 report by Aloïs Cobelli.
97. König, *Schwarze Cabinett*, p.74. Stix's hypothesis ('Geschichte der Wiener Geheimen Ziffernkanzlei', p.133) that Santa Croce, the apparent founder of the Viennese Black Cabinet, was trained in France, as well as the pleasure that Rübßam derives ('Zur Geschichte des internationalen Postwesens', p.59) from criticizing the research of his French contemporary Alexis Belloc, are also symptoms of francophobia.
98. Stix, 'Geschichte der Wiener Geheimen Ziffernkanzlei', p.142.

downs.[99] When German princes became aware that the Hapsburgs were using the Thurn and Taxis system to intercept their mail, they established their own offices for the opening and forwarding of mail, with their own *Brieflogen*.[100] In the 'Poste' article of the *Questions sur l'Encyclopédie*, Voltaire ironically noted that a letter passing through the German states could easily be opened several times before it reached its destination. Writing from Potsdam in 1751, he had suggested to Charles Emmanuel de Crussol, duc d'Uzès, a way of avoiding having his letters opened several times in transit:

> Ayez la bonté de recommander d'adresser les paquets par Nuremberg et par les chariots de poste, comme on envoie les marchandises; car les gros paquets de lettres qui sont portés par les courriers, sont toujours ouverts dans trois ou quatre bureaux de l'empire. Chaque prince se donne ce petit plaisir; ces messieurs là sont fort curieux.[101]

> Be so kind as to recommend that *paquets* be sent like merchandise, via Nuremberg and postal carts; for the large *paquets* of letters that are carried by couriers are always opened in three or four offices of the empire. Each prince offers himself his little pleasure; these gentlemen are curious indeed.

Denmark

In Denmark, as in the rest of Europe, it was not local postmasters who opened suspicious letters, but employees of special offices in Copenhagen and a few other important cities, such as Hamburg, where a Danish-Prussian post office was located.[102] As in the Hapsburg territories, the Danish government was primarily concerned with communications that might provide information about plans and operations against Denmark by foreign powers. During the Great Northern War (1700-1721), Christian Erlund (1673-1754) performed feats of spy craft that made him a legend of the Danish Black Cabinet. His secret technique for forging the seals of the letters enabled him to send hundreds of letters on their way without anyone's being the wiser. Erlund pulled off his greatest coup in 1714, when he intercepted, read, decoded and

99. König, *Schwarze Cabinette*, p.74; Stix, 'Geschichte der Wiener Geheimen Ziffernkanzlei', p.142-43; Kahn, *The Codebreakers*, p.64.
100. König, *Schwarze Cabinette*, p.75.
101. Voltaire to Charles Emmanuel de Crussol, duc d'Uzès, 4 December 1751, D4021.
102. What follows is a second-hand account. Since I do not read Danish, I am relying on two English-language commentaries on Sune Christian Pedersen's *Brudte Segl: Spionage og censur i enevældens Danmark* [Broken seals: espionage and censorship in absolutist Denmark] (Copenhagen, 2008). The first is a review by Finn Ehrard Johannessen (in *Scandinavian journal of history* 34:4 (December 2009), p.459-61); the other is a blog post (http://thehandwrittenletter.blogspot.com/2009/02/broken-seals.html; last accessed 17 August 2015), by a person named Joanna.

modified the correspondence of the Swedish field marshal Magnus Stenbock, who had been placed under house arrest in Copenhagen. More remarkably, by making changes in some of Stenbock's letters to a shopkeeper in Hamburg who held secret Swedish documents and packages and by forging others, Erlund fooled the shopkeeper into handing the materials over to one of Erlund's agents.

The ends of surveillance

As we have seen, the institution of public mail services provided European princes with both a source of substantial revenue and a frighteningly effective surveillance mechanism, in the form of the Black Cabinets. Whether or not Voltaire's discourse on the post was 'haunted', as Derrida claims, by a king and his police, by those who did their redoubtable work in the so-called Black Cabinets, the *philosophe*'s correspondence certainly was under surveillance.[103] In fact, the only extant manuscript of one of Voltaire's letters is a partial copy that was made by the Black Cabinet.[104] Since Voltaire knew that his correspondence was under surveillance, he did his best – by dictating letters to strangers and servants, using codes, borrowing the countersignature of allies such as Damilaville and asking friends and visitors to deliver letters for him – to frustrate the curiosity of the king's agents.[105] When Frederick the Great

103. Derrida, *The Post card*, p.71. 'It had become more difficult than for the Ancients to venture on grand undertakings; it is difficult to hide them because communication between Nations is such that each Prince has ministers in all the Courts and can have traitors in all the Cabinets. The invention of the Post has meant that news flies so to speak and comes from everywhere.' Montesquieu, *Considérations sur les causes de la grandeur des Romains et de leur décadence...* (Paris, 1879), p.251. Quoted by Vaillé, *Le Cabinet noir*, p.45, n.1. See Vaillé, *Le Cabinet noir*, p.201.

104. Voltaire to Charles-Augustin Fériol, comte d'Argental, 19 April 1773 D18323. In the first editorial note on this manuscript Besterman remarks that: 'MS1 is the c[opy] taken by the "cabinet noir", which intercepted suspect letters; it is quite possible that all Voltaire's were so intercepted, but if so it is not clear why this one has survived in the files, especially as the most compromising passages were not transcribed; it seems that Voltaire had a most valuable friend in the "cabinet noir", who expurgated his letters before transmitting them to the ministry; but this hypothesis is quite disconcerting, for no such person is known.' However as Cronk and Mervaud note: '[D]ans ce manuscrit, les passages les plus compromettants ont été supprimés, non parce que Voltaire aurait bénéficié de l'aide bienveillante d'un employé du Cabinet noir [...], mais pour protéger Marin, qui était mis en cause.' *OCV*, vol.42B, p.471, n.4.

105. Even a countersignature did not always keep the Black Cabinet from opening his correspondence. See below, Chapter 4, p.135-37. When Voltaire's *Lettres philosophiques* were published in French in 1734, he was forced to flee Paris and take refuge at Cirey, on the border of Lorraine (which was until 1766 part of the Holy Roman Empire), at the home of M. and Mme Du Châtelet. There Emilie Du Châtelet tried to protect the occasionally imprudent Voltaire fby creating what André Maurel would call a 'gentil Cabinet noir'. It led to a bitter quarrel with Mme de Graffigny. André Maurel, *La Marquise*

sent Voltaire an ode that attacked Louis XV, the *philosophe* saw that the letter had already been opened and later claimed that he had feared for his life.[106] However by endowing the employees of their Black Cabinets with the power to penetrate secrets, the princes of Europe unwittingly triggered a chain of events that would result in a diminishment of the power and profits that the post and its surveillance mechanisms were designed to assure. Once the operation of these originally secret institutions became public knowledge, not only did encryption techniques become more sophisticated and difficult to unravel, but other rulers created their own, rival postal services, with their own Black Cabinets. Moreover, by delegating surveillance power to the employees of the Black Cabinets, the rulers made themselves and their subjects vulnerable to abuses of that power. Although these artists were allowed to forge letters in the interest of national security, they could also seek to exploit their knowledge for their own private reasons. And since people in the business of discovering secrets could divulge those secrets, willingly or not, it became necessary to oversee the surveillants by hiring more surveillants, who themselves were theoretically vulnerable to the same abuses as the people they were employed to watch. Nevertheless, despite the unintended and ultimately self-destructive consequences of creating Black Cabinets and similar institutions, it remains to be seen whether state-sponsored postal systems could have done without them and, more generally, whether any nation-state can dispense with surveillance of communications.[107]

Du Châtelet: amie de Voltaire (Paris, 1930), p.65-70. See also René Vaillot, *Avec Mme Du Châtelet*, in Rene Pomeau (ed.), *Voltaire en son temps* (Oxford, 1988), vol.2, p.99, 102ff.

106. Voltaire to comte d'Argental, 6 April 1759, D7531. In an editorial note to the passage, Besterman views this claim with skepticism.

107. In the United States, where all electronic communications are now recorded by the National Security Agency, the United States Postal Service may now be the most secure means of communication available to the public.

4. Voltaire's post: 1760-1770

In previous chapters I have considered Voltaire's existential investment in the post as a medium and examined his wary relationship with the Black Cabinets that intercepted and monitored mail. Here I shall provide some context for these and other aspects of Voltaire's relationship with the post by focusing on the 1760s, the first decade of Voltaire's residence at Ferney, and his most active decade as a correspondent. As someone who spent most of his life in exile and perpetual fear of arrest, Voltaire urgently needed the post to maintain his relationships with the outside world. It was mainly thanks to the post that throughout the course of a life spent mostly far from Paris and other great centers of power Voltaire managed to put himself at the center of one of the most important networks in the Republic of Letters. It was in December 1760 that Voltaire took up residence just over the border from the Republic of Geneva, at Ferney, a property that he had purchased in 1758. Despite his conflicted relations with Geneva, he could always flee to relative safety there if he again felt himself threatened by the king's police.[1] This was a realistic precaution, since during the 1760s Voltaire would publish some of his most virulently anti-clerical works – among them, *La Pucelle d'Orléans* (1762) and the *Dictionnaire philosophique* (1st edn, 1764) – and (through his involvement in a series of 'affairs') fashion the image of himself as a tireless campaigner against intolerance and fanaticism.[2] During this decade Voltaire quarreled and broke with Rousseau; he also began his fifteen-year correspondence with Catherine II of Russia. Ferney became a sort of pilgrimage site, whose location on the important communications axis between Northern Europe and Italy made it easy and even convenient for the social and intellectual elite of eighteenth-century Europe to pay a visit to 'the great man'.[3]

Voltaire did not rely exclusively on the post to deliver his letters. Knowing that agents of the Black Cabinet were opening his mail, he

1. 'A king and his police, with all its lieutenants, is what haunts Voltaire's discourse. Each time that it is a question of *courrier* [messenger, courier; mail], in one guise or another, there is police, royal police – and a basilica, a royal house, an edifice or edification of the law, the place in which justice is rendered (with merchants near the lower porticos) or a temple, a religious metropolis. All of it, if possible, in the service of the king who disposes of the *courrier*, the seals, of the emissaries as well as of the addressees, his subjects.' Derrida, *The Post card*, p.71.
2. Calas, beginning in 1762; Sirven, starting in February 1765; la Barre, 1766.
3. See René Pomeau *et al.*, *Ecraser l'infâme* (Oxford, 1994), p.348ff; Didier Masseau, 'Ferney', in *Inventaire Voltaire*, p.541.

would sometimes arrange to have friends and other visitors to Ferney carry letters to their destination. In addition, his correspondence with royalty (Frederick II, Catherine II, Gustave III of Sweden and others), seems to have been handled largely, if not exclusively, by private couriers.[4] However when royal messengers carried letters and packages across borders and over long distances, even they could not always ensure the security of the contents.[5] He also availed himself of private delivery services for parcels that were too large for the post or that contained either valuable objects or bound books. There were times when the royal post would not accept books or any printed matter, regardless of size, especially when it was addressed to Paris from abroad, where most books condemned by royal French censors were published. In 1734, after the unauthorized publication of the *Lettres philosophiques*, when Voltaire took refuge from a second *lettre de cachet* at Cirey on the border of Lorraine, he began to use his Paris business agent and factotum Bonaventure Moussinot as a kind of informal post office, sending him packet after packet of letters to be relayed to their addressees. Since there was no intraurban mail service in France until 1760, when a *petite poste* was created in Paris, Moussinot presumably had either to deliver these letters himself or entrust them to a messenger.[6] All the same, Voltaire could certainly not have become known as 'King of Ferney' without reliable and regular public mail services and the 'epistolary space' that they opened up.[7]

Tactics

In the *Questions sur L'Encyclopédie* (1770-1772) Voltaire portrays the post as a source of vital consolation: '[L]a poste est le lien de toutes les affaires, de toutes les négociations; les absents deviennent par elle présents; elle est la consolation de la vie.' ([T]he post is what binds all transactions, all

4. Theodore Besterman's critical edition of Voltaire's correspondence does not indicate whether letters have been sent by post or by messenger, but Besterman occasionally alludes to the question. For example, in a textual note about the dating of a letter to Catherine II, he remarks that: 'if a messenger happened to be leaving and travelling direct to the destination the time taken would be drastically reduced'. Voltaire to Catherine II, *c.*November 1765, D12973. In this and subsequent quotations from Voltaire's correspondence the original spelling and punctuation have been retained.
5. 'L'impératrice de Russie m'avait envoyé son portrait avec de gros diamants: le paquet a été volé sur la route.' Voltaire to Marie Elisabeth de Dompierre de Fontaine, 1 April 1761, D9717.
6. 'P. S. Portez je vous en suplie cette lettre à mr Pugeau, et renvoyez la moy répondue.' Voltaire to Bonaventure Moussinot, 24 February 1739, D1903.
7. On James How's notion of 'epistolary space', see Introduction and Chapter 6, p.173-75. For a discussion of other aspects of Voltaire's claim to royalty, see my *In the king's wake* (Chicago, IL, and London, 1999), p.139ff.

negotiations, through it the absent become present; it is the consolation of life.)[8] That consolation was not easily granted him. In his correspondence he refers on over two hundred occasions to the multifarious ways in which the post impedes postal communication.[9] Voltaire also complained, and not without reason, about how much he himself spent for mail. Every week he had to pay for vast quantities of letters, books, maps, documents and other printed material that arrived for him at the French post offices in Geneva and Versoix. To limit his expenditures on postage, he left a register at the post office containing the names of the two hundred or so correspondents whose letters and packages he would accept, along with samples of their signs and seals, and published an announcement to this effect:

> AVERTISSEMENT DE M. DE VOLTAIRE. Plusieurs personnes s'étant plaintes de n'avoir pas reçu de réponse à des paquets envoyés, soit à Ferney, soit à Tourney, soit aux Délices, on est obligé d'avertir, qu'attendu la multiplicité immense de ces paquets, on a été contraint de renvoyer tous ceux qui n'étaient pas adressés par des personnes avec qui on a l'honneur d'être en correspondance.
>
> *Annonces, affiches et avis divers* (Paris), Monday 6 November 1761.[10]

> NOTICE FROM M. DE VOLTAIRE. Several persons having complained about not having received a response to packages sent either to Ferney, to Tourney or to Les Délices, we are required to give notice that, given the immense multiplicity of these packages, one has been forced to return all that were not addressed by persons with whom one has the honor of having a relation.

In a letter to his former teacher, the abbot Pierre Joseph Thoulier d'Olivet, he alludes to this filtering mechanism:

> Vos lettres sont venues à bon port mon très cher maître. Les veredarii [*courriers*] sont exacts par ce qu'il leur en revient quelque chose. Il est vray que j'ay été obligé d'avertir que je ne recevais point de lettres d'inconnus; et vous trouverez que j'ay raison quand vous saurez que très souvent la poste m'apportait pour cent francs de paquets de gens discrets qui m'envoyaient leurs manuscrits à corriger ou à admirer. Le nombre des fous mes confrères quos scribendi cacoetes tenet est immense. Celuy des autres fous à lettres anonimes n'est pas moins considérable...[11]

8. *OCV*, vol.42B, p.471.
9. The Index to the Besterman edition of Voltaire's correspondence contains an exhaustive list of these references to the royal post under the heading 'Post, postal service.'
10. Cited by André Magnan, in 'Poste', *Inventaire Voltaire*, p.1088. The opening paragraphs of my discussion are based on this article. A copy of the register is housed at the Voltaire Institute and Museum in Geneva.
11. Voltaire to Pierre Joseph Thoulier d'Olivet, 19 March 1761, D8904. The Latin is adapted from Juvenal, *Satires*, vii, p.51-52. Claire Brant remarks that 'Many letter-writers pathologised their epistolary productiveness: if an "itch for scribbling" had been a

> Your letters have arrived intact, my most dear master. The veredarii [*couriers*] are punctual because there is some profit to be made from it. It is true that I had to give notice that I would not receive letters from unknown persons; you will find that I am right when you learn that the post often brought me one hundred francs worth of packages from discreet people who sent me their manuscripts to correct or admire. The number of my mad colleagues *quos scribendi cacoetes tenet* [who are possessed by the itch for writing] is immense. The number of other madmen who send anonymous letters is no less considerable...

The register unfortunately does not seem to have achieved the desired effect. For not only did it sometimes delay the delivery of items he wanted to receive

> Il est arrivé un singulier inconvénient au paquet de Mr le Kain; comme nous avions déclaré que nous ne recevrions aucun gros paquet qui ne fût contresigné, il était demeuré à la poste, nous ne l'avons reçu qu'aujourd'hui.[12]

> Mr le Kain's package succumbed to a singular mishap; since we had declared that we would not receive any large packages that were not countersigned, it had remained at the post office, and we received it only today.

but it also failed to prevent vast quantities of unwanted mail from arriving. In April 1770, almost nine years after the announcement was published, he complained to Jean François René Tabareau, director (postmaster) of the post office in Lyon, that he was being 'assassiné de Lettres d'inconnus que je suis obligé de renvoier'[13] (assassinated by unknown Letters that I am forced to return).

In order to obtain favorable treatment of his correspondence, Voltaire sought to ingratiate himself with various postal administrators, the most powerful of whom was Louis XV's unofficial prime minister Choiseul, also Superintendent of the Post from 1760 until his disgrace in 1770.[14] Voltaire cultivated a relationship with Tabareau and his assistant, Jean-Joseph Vasselier, both of whom were sympathetic to the philosophical camp. To thank them for their help in facilitating the dispatch of his mail (and for offering him the occasional gift of fresh fish, melons or chickens), he regularly sent them copies of his latest pamphlets and books.[15] In the same letter in which he complained to Tabareau about

---

medical condition, it would have displaced gout as the archetypal eighteenth-century complaint.' Brant, *Eighteenth-century letters*, p.20.

12. Voltaire to Henri Louis Lekain, 26 January 1762, D9490.
13. Voltaire to Jean François Louis Tabareau, 6 April 1770, D15224. Magnan comments on this ineffective screening mechanism in 'Poste' (*Inventaire Voltaire*).
14. Voltaire to Charles Augustin Fériol, comte d'Argental, 10 November 1760, D8626. On the other hand, in the same year Choiseul also lent his support to *Les Philosophes* (1760), the satirical sendup of the philosophes by Palissot, a fellow native of Lorraine. See Pomeau *et al.*, *Ecraser l'infâme*, p.87. In a letter to Voltaire dated 30 July 1760, his friend Thieriot portrays Choiseul as an opponent of the philosophes. D9100.
15. There are 44 extant letters sent by Voltaire to Tabareau between December 1766 and

receiving quantities of unsolicited mail, Voltaire – always the shrewd businessman – also asked him to make sure that his employees stop charging 'simple' letters (written on one sheet of paper) as if they were double, a mistake that cost him four *sous* for each letter. A week later he petitioned Tabareau to save him six *sous* per simple letter by seeing to it that correspondence addressed to Gex would be sent directly to Versoix (on French soil), where a post office had been opened in 1768, rather than to Geneva.[16] He had less success with the postmaster in Versoix. For despite the many services Voltaire performed for him, the *philosophe* could not dissuade this gentleman from attempting to tax packages for Lyon at prohibitive rates.[17]

Voltaire's agent Dalloz bore primary responsibility for carrying a vast range of postal materials back and forth between Ferney and the French post offices in Geneva and Versoix (from 1768 to 1774). Early in the morning he rode the five miles to Geneva six times a week, even in the rudest of winters, assisted at times by Voltaire's *pourvoyeur* (purveyor of meat, poultry, etc.), bearing the sundry products of Voltaire's previous work day:[18]

> [M]emoranda and requests, outlines of new plays, drafts and copies, corrections and proofs, actors' roles, legal mumbo jumbo, dozens of letters and notes, and also often, at safe times, those little 'scraps' or 'blots' fresh off the presses of Cramer or Grasset, pamphlets and opuscules folded tight to look like letters. *Les Car, Les Quand*, the *Lettre à Charles Gouju* – all this without counting the dispatch of locally made watches, for which Voltaire obtained a franking privilege in 1771.[19]

While in Geneva performing his duties, poor Dalloz was occasionally made the object of vulgar Francophobic insults, some of which 'Va te faire foutre, va grater ton cu avec celui du Résident, tu as du pain dans tes poches pour les grimauds, tu viens de la part de ces bougres de Français de Ferney, etc. etc. etc.' (Bugger off, go scratch your ass with the Resident's, you've got dough for pedants, you're coming on behalf of

---

January 1776, as well as seven letters addressed to Vasselier; only one of Tabareau's letters to Voltaire has survived. Jean-Joseph Vasselier (1735-1798) is best known as the author of satires and saucy tales. See Anne-Marie Chouillet, Pierre Crépel, 'Un voyage en Italie manqué ou trois encyclopédistes réunis (D'Alembert et Condorcet chez Voltaire)', *Recherches sur Diderot et l'Encyclopédie* 17 (1994), p.34.

16. Voltaire to Jean François René Tabareau, 14 April 1770, D16291. He goes on to ask Tabareau to give notice of this policy; he also promises to have the same notice published in the *Mercure de France* and *La Gazette*, which according to Besterman he never did. On the question of French post offices on foreign soil, see Chapter 1, p.46, 50.
17. Voltaire to Jean Rigoley, baron d'Ogny, 5 June 1772, D16715.
18. Voltaire and Marie Louise Denis to Pierre Michel Hennin, 29 January 1767, D12997.
19. Magnan, 'Postes'. *Les Car* and *Les Quand* were some of the 'monosyllables' aimed at the anti-philosophical academician Le Franc de Pompignan in 1760-1761.

those French buggers from Ferney, etc. etc. etc.) Voltaire reported verbatim to Pierre Michel Hennin, the French Resident in Geneva.[20]

Voltaire also enlisted the aid of allies in high places in order to gain access to franking privileges and signature stamps (*contreseings*), in order to spare his correspondents the expense of paying for postage while also protecting his letters from surveillance and censorship ('[E]lle déroutera les curieux').[21] Some of these allies occupied positions of power: François-Claude Louis Marin was a royal censor and general secretary of the book police; Villemorien was a tax farmer. Other allies, such as Chennevrières at the War Office and Voltaire's friend Damilaville, a minor tax administrator in the royal finance office, themselves had neither power nor wealth, but were able to give him access to the franking privileges of their ministers. For the same reason, Voltaire would occasionally advise his correspondents not to address letters directly to him, but to send them to an intermediary with a franking privilege. On several occasions he instructs his correspondents to address their mail to Marin, so that the royal censor could then forward it with his countersignature to Voltaire. Thus on 15 (?) January 1773 he warns d'Alembert against the imprudence of addressing him letters directly, rather than in a countersigned envelope:

> Je vous trouve bien hardi de m'écrire par la poste en droiture. Est ce que vous ne savez pas que toutes les lettres sont ouvertes, et qu'on connaît votre écriture comme votre style? Que n'envoyez vous vos lettres à Marin? Il les ferait passer sous un contre-seing que la poste respecte.[22]

> I find you quite bold to write to me directly by post. Do you not know that all my letters are opened, and that your handwriting and your style are known? Why do you not send your letters to Marin? He would pass them along under a countersignature that the post respects.

Postal farmers also had franking privileges, but Voltaire had to be careful not to abuse the privilege, since every untaxed letter represented a net loss of income for them:

20. 'Ce sont là, Monsieur, les propres mots de la Philippique prononcée aujourd'hui 16 du mois de la jeunesse, contre Dalloz, commissionnaire de Ferney, porteur, non de pain pour les grimauds, mais d'une petite Truite pour nôtre souper. Ces galanteries arrivent fort souvent. Nous en régalerons M. le Duc De Choiseul, à qui nous devons d'ailleurs des remerciements pour avoir fait acheter et paier par le roi nos montres de grimauds. Je n'ai point vu le cu de Dalloz, je ne crois pas qu'il soit digne de grater le vôtre.' Voltaire to Pierre Michel Hennin, 16 June 1770, D15406. I have translated *grimaud* as 'pedant,' since that is the sense in which Jean-Jacques Rousseau (and before him, Ronsard, in the *Odes*) uses the term in his *Lettre à Christophe Beaumont*. I would like to thank Pierre Frantz and Nicolas Ducimetière for their lexicological advice.
21. Voltaire to the count and countess d'Argental, 22 May 1765, 112 D12612. I also discuss surveillance of Voltaire's mail in Chapter 3, p.104, 107-108.
22. Voltaire to Jean Le Rond d'Alembert (?), 15 January 1773, D18137.

> J'imagine que les fermiers généraux des postes ne veulent pas contresigner de petites Lettres dont le port doit entrer dans la masse commune. Ils veulent bien contresigner les gros paquets, parce que sans celà on ne s'aviserait pas de les envoier par la poste, et qu'ils n'y gagneraient rien. Mais en les priant d'affranchir les Lettres, c'est les prier de donner vingt ou trente sous de leur poche, ce qui étant trop multiplié, fait à la longue une diminution dans la ferme.[23]

> I imagine that the farmers general of the post do not want to countersign little letters whose postage should make up part of the common mass. They are willing to countersign large packages, because otherwise no one would take it into his head to send them by post, and they would thereby derive no profit. But by begging them to frank letters, one is begging them to give twenty or thirty sous from their pocket, which when overly multiplied eventually amounts to a decrease in the farm.

On 11 October 1760, he begs Chennevrières not to make excessive use of the Secretary of War's signature stamp:

> Je vous supplie d'envoyer ce mémoire, non contresigné, à melle Clairon. Il ne faut pas je crois provigner[24] le contreseing Belisle. Mrs de la poste n'en seraient pas contents. D'ailleurs les comédiens sont en état de payer des ports de lettres, mes pièces ne les appauvrissent pas, et je leur abandonne le profit des représentations et de l'impression.[25]

> I pray you to send this memorandum to Mlle Clairon, without countersignature: I should rather not squander the the Belisle countersignature. It would not make the gentlemen of the post happy. Besides the actors [of the Comédie-Française] are quite capable of paying for postage, my plays are not impoverishing them, and I let them have the profits from the performances and the printing.

Yet even when a packet was franked by a man who held the prestigious title of *conseiller d'Etat*, the tax farmers could still decide to tax it, as Voltaire tells his friends the d'Argentals:

> Votre paquet adressé à mr Camp et contresigné Chauvelin, arriva en son temps à Lyon à l'adresse de mr Camp. Les fermiers généraux des postes l'avaient arrêté et contresigné à Paris d'une autre façon en mettant en gros caractères sur l'enveloppe et avec une encre rouge *paquet suspect*. Mr Camp est toujours malade, m. Tronchin qui est à Lyon fut étonné du *suspect* en lettres rouges, il ouvrit le paquet. Les directeurs des postes disputèrent, ils exigèrent je crois un Louis: enfin le paquet qui portait une sous enveloppe à l'adresse de Vagnieres chez Souchay à Geneve m'a été rendu aujourd'hui. La même chose à peu près m'était arrivée à peu près au sujet d'un très petit paquet, aussi contresigné Chauvelin que vous m'aviez adressé il y a environ

23. Voltaire to Thieriot, 29 August 1760, D8419. As I explained in Chapter 2 (p.67), it cost much less to put several letters in a packet than to post them individually.
24. Voltaire to François de Chennevières, 11 October 1760, D8537. According to Besterman's textual note b), this verb has been '[a]ltered in the editions to *prodiguer* but Voltaire may well have used the agricultural *provigner*'.
25. Voltaire to François de Chennevières, 11 October 1760, D8537.

trois semaines. Ainsi vous voyez que les fermiers préfèrent le port aux conseillers d'état intendants des finances.[26]

Your packet addressed to Mr Camp and countersigned Chauvelin eventually arrived at Mr Camp's address. The farmers general of the post had stopped it and countersigned it differently, putting the words *suspicious package* on the envelope in big letters with red ink. Mr Camp is still ill and M. Tronchin, who is in Lyons, was astonished by the *suspicious* in red letters and opened the packet. The directors of the post objected, they asked for a louis, I think: finally the packet, which contained another envelope addressed to Vagnières [Voltaire's secretary] *chez* Souchay in Geneva, was delivered to me today. More or less the same thing had happened to a very small packet, also countersigned Chauvelin, that you had sent me about three weeks ago. So you see that the farmers would rather have postage than defer to Councillors of State intendants of finances.

Suspicious thoughts

The previous passage also serves to recall that by gaining access to the signature stamp of powerful individuals and cultivating his relations with postal administrators, Voltaire was not simply trying to save money and avoid delays, but also looking for ways to give cover to thoughts that could get him and his correspondents into serious trouble. 'La pluspart des lettres sont ouvertes à la poste, he tells d'Alembert, 'Les vôtres l'ont été depuis longtemps.'[27] (Most letters are opened at the post. Yours have been for a long time.) Voltaire knew that his own letters were also being opened, as Sir James Marriott confirmed in a letter of 5 November 1766:

P. S. Il faut que je vous avertisse qu'on fait ouvrir vos Lettres au Bureau du poste en France. La dernière dont vous m'avez honoré étoit rompue et l'on avoit scellé encore avec du cire ordinaire et les fleurs de Lys au dessus de Vos Armes: pour cette raison J'ai prié My Lord Shelburn premier secrétaire d'Etat de se charger de faire venir cette Lettre à vos mains par son canal, et vous pourriez vous adresser à moi par[le] le même.[28]

P.S. I must warn you that your letters are being opened at the post office in France. The last one with which you honored me was broken open and had been resealed with ordinary wax and the fleur-de-lis above your arms: for this reason I begged My Lord Shelburn, First Secretary of State, to see to it that this letter be put in your hands by his channel, and you may address me by the same route.

Moreover the 'vultures' at the post office, as d'Alembert called them, would often simply discard suspicious letters and packets at the post

26. Voltaire to the count and countess d'Argental, 6 July 1765, D11935. In terms of etiquette, *conseillers d'Etat* ranked just below the princes of the blood, cardinals, dukes and peers. François Claude Bernard Louis de Chauvelin (1716-1773), marquis de Chauvelin, was also a career soldier and diplomat. He should not be confused with Germain Louis Chauvelin (1685-1762), who was Louis XV's minister of foreign affairs from 1727-1837.
27. Voltaire to Jean Le Rond d'Alembert, 8 July 1765, D11937.
28. Sir James Marriott to Voltaire, 5 November 1766, D13654.

office.[29] One tactic Voltaire used in the 1760s to protect his mail from prying eyes was have his correspondents address their letters and packages to Souchay and his companion Lefort in Geneva, often care of Voltaire's secretary Wagnières.[30] By writing 'PAQUET SUSPECT' in large red letters on these packages, did the Paris postmasters (who were employed by the tax farmers) mean to bring them to the attention of the Black Cabinet or just simply provide their colleagues in Lyon with a good excuse for collecting extra postage fees?

At times, Voltaire coyly protested the innocence and complete respectability of his thoughts, as in the following passage from a letter of August 1760 nominally addressed to Marmontel, but doubtless also meant to be read by those in the post office who were in the habit of opening and delaying his correspondence. Here he earnestly protests that he is such a model citizen and loyal subject that there is no need to inspect his letters:

> Nous avions été un peu allarmés, Monsieur, de certaines terreurs paniques que Messrs les directeurs de la poste avaient conçües, jamais crainte n'a été plus mal fondée; Monsieur le Duc de Choiseuil et madame de Pompadour, connaissent la façon de penser de l'oncle et de la nièce; on peut tout nous envoier sans risque; on sçait que nous aimons le Roy et l'Etat; ce n'est pas chez nous que des Damiens ont entendu des discours séditieux; on ne prétend point chez nous que l'état doive périr, faute de subsides; nous n'avons point de convulsionaires dans nos terres; je déssèche des marais, je bâtis une Eglise, et je fais des vœux pour le Roy; nous défions tous les jansénistes et tous les molinistes, d'être plus attachez à l'Etat que nous le sommes.[31]

> We had been somewhat alarmed, Sir, by certain panic terrors entertained by the directors of the post; never has a fear been less justified; the Duke de Choiseul and Mme de Pompadour are familiar with the opinions of the uncle and the niece; one can send us anything without risk; it is common knowledge that we love the king and the state; no Damien has ever heard seditious discourse in our home; here no one argues that the state should perish for lack of subsidies; we have no convulsionaries on our lands; I

29. 'J'espère que mr Galatin échappera aux griffes des *vautours*, et que je pourrai lire enfin cette Tolerance, dont nosseigneurs de la rue Platriere, qui ont presque autant d'esprit que nosseigneurs du Parlement, me privent avec une cruauté si intolérable.' Jean Le Rond d'Alembert to Voltaire, 15 January 1764, D11644, emphasis added. The postal administration was located on rue Platrières. See 'Avez vous reçu un paquet du 9 juillet par mr Chauvelin? Quelquefois mrs des postes ouvrent et mettent au rebut'. Voltaire to Charles Augustin Feriol, comte d'Argental, Sunday, 13 July 1760, D8309; '[D]epuis l'équipée de Jean Jaques, on met souvent à Paris au rebut les Lettres qui portent le timbre de Genêve, et dans lesquelles on soupçonne qu'il y a des imprimés.' Voltaire to Ami Camp, 28 September 1763, D10611.
30. Among other examples of this tactic: Voltaire to Paul-Claude Moultou, 17 February 1763, D10205; Voltaire to Gabriel Cramer, *c.*December 1763, D11566.
31. Voltaire to Jean-François Marmontel, 13 August 1760, D8385.

drain swamps, I build a church and make wishes for the king; we defy the Jansenists and the Molinists to be more attached to the state than we are.

He had taken a diametrically opposite view some months earlier in a letter to the marquise Du Deffand, when he claimed that his true thoughts were so daring that he could not possibly confide them to the post: 'En vérité, Madame, il n'y a pas moyen, tant je suis devenu hardi avec l'âge; je ne peux plus écrire que ce que je pense, et je pense si librement qu'il n'y a guères d'aparence d'envoyer mes idées par la poste.[32] (Truthfully, Madame, there is no way, so bold have I become with age; I can no longer write what I think, and I think so freely that it is quite impossible for me to send my ideas by post.) It is not known whether Voltaire sent this letter to Mme Du Deffand by messenger or in an envelope addressed to a third party, though he might even have tempted fate by sending it directly by post. In addition to striking poses of injured innocence and unabashed guilt, Voltaire also affected a third, and more typical posture toward his most controversial books by simply denying authorship and either praising or condemning the work from the perspective of a disinterested third party. The best examples of this tactic can be found in the letters he wrote in the months following the clandestine publication by Grasset in Geneva of the *Philosophical dictionary* in July 1764. In response to the marquise Du Deffand's request for a copy, Voltaire avers that he would rather never have been born than be accused of having written this book and have to endure persecution by spiteful fanatics. He praises the many virtues of a book that he supposedly has not read, much less written, and claims that has not been able to get his hands on a copy:

> Je serais homme à souhaiter de n'être point né si on m'accusait d'avoir fait le dictionaire philos. car quoyque cet ouvrage me paraisse aussi vrai que hardi, quoy qu'il respire la morale la plus pure, les hommes sont si sots et si méchants, les dévots sont si fanatiques que je serais sûrement persécuté. Cet ouvrage que je crois très utile ne sera jamais de moy. Je n'en ay envoyé à personne. J'ay même de la peine à en faire venir quelques exemplaires pour moy même. Dès que j'en aurai, je vous en ferai parvenir. Mais par quelle voye? Je n'en sçais rien. Tous les gros paquets sont saisis à la poste, les ministres n'aiment pas qu'on envoie sous leur nom des choses dont on peut leur faire des reproches. Il faut attendre l'occasion de quelque voiageur.[33]

32. Voltaire to Marie Anne de Vichy de Chamrond, marquise Du Deffand, 17 September 1759, D7757.

33. Voltaire to Marie Anne de Vichy de Chamrond, marquise Du Deffand, 21 September 1764 D12095. A few days later he offers to have a few copies of this satanic book procured in Geneva for Mme d'Epinay. Voltaire to to Louise Florence Pétronille La Live, marquise d'Epinay, 25 September 1764, D12102.

> I should be a man who wished he had not been born if I were accused of having made the philos. dictionary for although this work seems to me as true as it is bold, although it radiates the purest moral standards, men are so foolish and wicked, the pious are so fanatical that I would surely be persecuted. This seemingly very useful work will never be by me. I have not sent any to anyone. I even have difficulty obtaining a few copies for myself. As soon as I have some, I will send you a few. But by what means? I have no idea. All large packages are being seized at the post, the ministers do not like having things sent in their name for which they could be criticized. I shall have to wait for some voyager to stop by.

Instead of simply denying that he wrote the book, Voltaire prefers to say that 'this work will never be by me': that is, he wrote it but will never explicitly admit the fact. In the summer and fall of 1764 Voltaire made a game of sprinkling his correspondence with variants on ironical condemnations of the satanic book, while attributing its authorship to other (usually fictive) persons. As René Pomeau has pointed out, these letters provided a way of disavowing the book and advertising it at the same time.[34]

During the 1760s there were times when Voltaire's mail was kept under particularly close surveillance, most notably in 1766 at the time of the Clèves project, which was conceived in reaction to the hideous punishment for blasphemy inflicted upon the chevalier de La Barre at Abbeville on 1 July of that year.[35] But long before that, his anti-clerical writings had led the Black Cabinet to keep close watch on Voltaire's correspondence. Since he and his correspondents could not trust the security of countersigned letters or packets, they were forced to engage in an endless game of cat and mouse with agents of the royal post. In Voltaire's ecclesiastical metaphor, 'Les pauvres philosophes sont obligés de faire mille tours de passe-passe pour faire parvenir à leurs frères leurs épîtres canoniques'.[36] (Poor philosophers are forced to perform thousands of tricks in order to get their canonical epistles to their brothers.) During the 1760s Voltaire would use one person's countersignature until he realized that these letters (or those of his correspondents) were being opened, at which point he would try a different one, and so on. An interesting variant of this game is played out in the spring of 1765. Voltaire tells his 'dear brother' Damilaville to stop sending him letters under the countersignature of the tax official Gaudet (head of the *vingtième*)[37] and address them instead to Ami Camp; but it then comes

34. Pomeau, *et al.*, *Ecraser l'infâme*, p.203.
35. Horrified and frightened by this event, the seventy-one-year-old Voltaire launched the idea of establishing a philosophical colony in Kleve (Clèves in French) under the protection of Frederick II. He dreamed of Clèves as a 'truth workshop' (*manufacture de la vérité*), where he and other *philosophes* could publish the truth without worrying about censorship. See André Magnan's 'Clèves' in the *Inventaire Voltaire*.
36. Voltaire to Jean Le Rond d'Alembert, 13 December 1763, D10718.
37. The *vingtième* (so-called because it amounted to five percent or one-twentieth of a

to his attention that the letter containing this advice has *itself* been opened, and that Damilaville will therefore need to have recourse to yet another tactic:

> [Mon frère] doit être instruit du juste sujet de mes inquiétudes; il doit savoir qu'un gros paquet envoyé à m. Gaudet a été intercepté.
>
> Il est à croire qu'une lettre, envoyée depuis sous le couvert de m. Gaudet, a été interceptée encore. Dans cette lettre, on avertissait mon cher frère que des gens malintentionnés avaient été alarmés de son commerce avec Genève; qu'on avait ouvert ses lettres depuis plus de six semaines. On donnait l'adresse de m. Camp, banquier à Lyon. Mais comme il y a beaucoup d'apparence que si mon frère a reçu cette lettre, elle a été ouverte, et que si elle ne lui est pas parvenue, on ouvrira toutes les lettres adressées à m. Camp, il faudra prendre d'autres mesures. Je supplie donc mon cher frère de m'instruire de tout ce qui se passe, de me mander quelles lettres il a reçues de moi depuis plus de quinze jours, et d'adresser son paquet à mademoiselle Sainton, à Lyon. Il faudra, sous l'enveloppe de mademoiselle Sainton, écrire simplement à madame Racle à Genève. Les lettres qui arriveront pour madame Racle me seront rendues.[38]

> [My brother] should be informed of the justifiable reasons for my anxiety; he should know that a large packet sent to M. Gaudet has been intercepted.
>
> It would appear that a letter sent afterwards under the authority of Mr Gaudet was intercepted again. In this letter my dear brother was warned that malicious persons had been alarmed by his communications with Geneva; that his letters had been opened for more than six weeks. It gave him the name of Mr Camp, banker in Lyons. But since there is every reason to believe that if my brother received this letter, it had been opened, and that if it did not reach him, all letters sent to Mr Camp will be opened, it will be necessary to take other measures. I beg my dear brother to inform me of what is happening, to let me know what letters he has received from me over the past two weeks, and to send his packet to Mademoiselle Sainton in Lyons. In the packet addressed to Mademoiselle Sainton, he need only write to Madame Racle in Geneva. Letters that arrive for Madame Racle will be forwarded to me.

In a letter dated 9 June 1762 to Fyot de la Marche (who had been a fellow student at the Collège Louis-le-Grand and in 1711-1712 the recipient of five letters that open his correspondence) Voltaire advises the Dijon magistrate not arouse the suspicions of postal employees by putting his seal on packages he might wish to send him:

> [V]ous devez être averti que Mrs des postes ont décachetez plusieurs paquets adressez à m^{r} Dargental sous l'envelope de m^{r} de Courteille.[39] Si vous

---

taxpayer's income) was a direct tax, instituted in 1749 by *Contrôleur général des finances* Marchaut d'Arnouville as a replacement for the *dixième*. Unlike the *dixième*, it applied to the entire population and therefore was met with stiff and effective resistance.

38. Voltaire to Etienne Noël Damilaville, 31 May 1765, D11778. Gaudet was director of the *vingtième* office in Paris. In 1763 Voltaire asks d'Alembert to find someone willing to protect his books with a countersignature. Voltaire to Jean Le Rond d'Alembert, 13 December 1763, D10718.

39. Courteille was Fyot de la Marche's son-in-law.

m'adressez quelque chose par cette voye, ne mettez point de cachet au paquet qui m'est destiné. C'est ce cachet senti par les mains funestes des commis qui autorize leur insolence. Il faut donc passer sa vie à se précautionner contre des ennemis! [40]

[Y]ou should be warned that the gentlemen of the post have unsealed several packets sent to Mr. Dargental in Mr de Courteille's packet. If you address something to me by this means, do not put a seal on the packet meant for me. It is this seal, when sensed by the baneful hands of the postal employees that authorizes their insolence. So one's life has to be spent taking precautions against enemies!

As we noted in Chapter 3, the seal on a letter simultaneously authenticated a document for its addressee and clearly identified its sender to the Black Cabinet. At other times Voltaire would hedge his bets: 'J'écrivis hier à mon cher frère, à son adresse, et je lui envoyai les réponses de m. Tronchin. Je lui écrivis il y a quelques jours un petit billet par m. Héron, et un autre par m. d'Argental.'[41] (I wrote yesterday to my dear brother [Argental] at this address, and I sent him Mr Tronchin's answers. A few days ago I sent him a little note by Mr Héron, and another by Mr d'Argental.) Voltaire would sometimes engage unknown persons as copyists and dictate letters to them or refer to himself under an assumed name, in the hope of outflanking the agents of the Black Cabinet.[42] In a note to his edition (1828-1834) of Voltaire's works, Beuchot remarks that workers in that office admired the style of his letters, which they long believed were written by a certain 'M. Ecrlinf' in Switzerland.[43]

Voltaire also makes frequent mention of delays in postal delivery. He could tolerate delays and devise tactics for evading surveillance, but when his franked letters were lost or even intercepted and confiscated, his patience could be strained to the breaking point. At such times he felt that instead of bringing consolation for the absence of his friends, the post only made that absence more disheartening, acting like a poison rather than a remedy:

Il est bien douloureux que la poste soit infidèle, et que le commerce de l'amitié, la consolation de l'absense soient empoisonez par un brigandage digne des houzards. C'est répandre trop d'amertume sur la vie. Je me sers cette fois cy de la voye de M. Dargental sous l'enveloppe de monsieur de Courteilles.[44]

40. Voltaire to Claude Philippe Fyot de La Marche, 9 June 1762, D9687.
41. Voltaire to Damilaville, 31 May 1765, D11778.
42. Magnan, 'Poste'.
43. *Œuvres de Voltaire* (Paris, 1833), vol.64, *Correspondance* XIV (1768), p.545-46.
44. Voltaire to Damilaville, 11 May 1763, D10385. See 'Est il possible que la plus grande consolation de ma vie, celle d'envoyer des contes par la poste, soit interdite aux pauvres humains? Cela fait *saigner* le cœur.' Voltaire to the count and countess d'Argental, 18 January 1764, D1081. Emphasis added.

It is painful indeed that the post should be unfaithful, and that friendly intercourse, the consolation for absence, be poisoned by a brigandage worthy of hussars. This is to spread too much bitterness on life. This time I am writing by way of Mr Dargental in Mr de Courteille's packet.

Voltaire's depiction of the post as distressingly unfaithful stands in contrast to a passage in the 'Postes' entry of the *Questions sur l'Encyclopédie* (see Chapter 1, p.10-15), where he playfully claimed that the post is more faithful than the mistress who posts her letters to you. In a letter to Marmontel dated 19 June 1763, he blames Rousseau's controversial *Lettre à M. de Beaumont* (1762) for another instance of postal infidelity:

[L]e droit des gens s'accomode peu de l'infidélité de la poste. On saisit un livre, passe encor, mais saisir la lettre qui l'accompagne! se rendre maitre du secret des particuliers, comme si nous étions dans une guerre civile! cela n'est pas dans *l'esprit des loix*. Voilà encor une fois ce que nous a valu Jean Jacques, avec sa lettre à Christophe. Ce polisson insolent gâte le métier. Il semble qu'on ne cherche qu'à rendre la philosophie ridicule.[45]

[T]he law of nations cannot accept the infidelity of the post. To seize a book is one thing, but to seize the letter that accompanies it! to make onself master of individuals' secret thought, as if we were in a civil war! this is not in *the spirit of the laws*. This is one more worry that has been brought us by Jean Jacques with his letter to Christophe. That little devil spoils our job. It seems that one is simply trying to make philosophy look ridiculous.

Voltaire alleges that it is also Rousseau's fault that employees of the post office in Paris have been discarding letters postmarked in Geneva, on the grounds that these probably contain printed matter.[46] It was perhaps only to be expected that two years later Rousseau would in turn hold Voltaire ('the Inquisitor') responsible when his *Lettres écrites de la montagne* were publicly burned in The Hague.[47]

During this period the postal authorities frequently opened Voltaire's packets and letters, but they could also simply refuse to deliver large parcels, books or other printed matter, when these were posted by him or another 'suspicious' person.[48] On occasion it was simply bound

45. Voltaire to Jean-François Marmontel, 19 June 1763, D10450.
46. Voltaire to Ami Camp, 28 September 1763, D10611.
47. 'Je ne doute point, Monsieur, qu'hier jour de Deux-Cent on n'ait brulé mon Livre à Genève; du moins toutes les mesures étoient prises pour cela. Vous aurez Su qu'il fut brulé le 22 à la Haye. Rey me marque que l'Inquisiteur a écrit dans ce pays-là beaucoup de Lettres, et que le Ministre Chais de Genève S'est donné de grands mouvemens.' Jean-Jacques Rousseau to Pierre-Alexandre Du Peyrou, 7 February 1765, *CC*, vol.23, p.310 (3992).
48. 'Il y a eu madame de la réforme dans les postes. Les gros paquets ne passent plus.' Voltaire to Marie Anne de Vichy de Chamrond, marquise Du Deffand, 22 December [1760], D8717. See 'Si vous voyez notre diaconisse madame du Deffant, saluez la pour moy en Belzebuth; dittes luy que je sçais plus comment faire pour luy envoier des infamies. Il devient plus difficile que jamais de confier de gros paquets à la poste.' Voltaire to Jean Le Rond d'Alembert, 17 November 1760, D8643.

volumes that they rejected, as he explains to Mme Fontaine in January of 1762:

> Je ne sais ce qu'est devenu un gros paquet d'amusements de campagne que j'avais envoyé à Ornoi, et que j'avais adressé à un intendant des postes. Il y avait un petit livre relié avec une lettre pour vous, une pour un frère, et quelques manuscrits. Tout cela était très indifférent, mais apparemment le livre relié fit retenir le paquet. J'ai appris depuis qu'il ne fallait envoyer par la poste aucun livre relié. On apprend toujours quelque chose en ce monde.[49]
>
> I do not know what became of a big package of country amusements that I had sent to Ormoi, and which I had addressed to a postal intendant. There was a small bound book with a letter for you, one for a brother, and a few manuscripts. It was all quite harmless, but the bound book seems to have held back the package. Since then I have learned that one must not send any bound volumes by the post. In this world there is always something to be learned.

This is not the only passage in which Voltaire appears to use the word *paquet* in the modern sense of 'package', rather than in the sense ('one or more letters enclosed in an envelope') attested by contemporary dictionaries. In any case, the prohibition seems to have been primarily aimed at items posted abroad. The authorities were particularly concerned to keep unsanctioned material out of Paris ('On m'apprend, mon cher frère, que nous pouvons recevoir dans les païs étrangers des imprimés de Paris mais que nous ne pouvons pas y en envoyer dans vôtre ville' [My dear brother, I am informed that in foreign countries we may receive printed matter from Paris but that we cannot send any to your city]),[50] but they do not seem to have spared the rest of the country, either. As Voltaire told Gabriel Cramer, 'Il est plus difficile actuellement de faire entrer un bon ouvrage en France, que d'y avoir de bonnes troupes et une bonne marine.'[51] (It is presently more difficult to introduce a good book to France than to have good troops and a good navy.) He makes similar complaints on many other occasions.[52]

Still, there can be little doubt that, despite occasional moments of discouragement, Voltaire enjoyed the challenge of having continually to invent new tactics to outwit his adversaries. Indeed although it became an obsessive preoccupation during the decade of the *Philosophical dictionary* and the various anti-clerical 'affairs', there was nothing new about his

49. Voltaire to Marie Elisabeth de Dompierre de Fontaine, 4 January 1762, D10253. See '[I]l y a un paquet tout prêt pour vous et pour Mr le Président Hainaut, mais on ne sçait comment faire pour dépècher ces paquets par la poste.' Voltaire to Marie de Vichy de Chamrond, marquise Du Deffand, 10 October 1760, D8535; Voltaire to Claude Adrien Helvetius, 12 December 1760, D8691.
50. Voltaire to Damilaville, 27 May 1763, D11233.
51. Voltaire to Gabriel Cramer, 21 May 1765, D12611.
52. See Voltaire to the count and countess d'Argental, 19 May 1763, D10394; Voltaire to Damilaville, 23 May 1763, D10405.

desire to exploit the post in order to get the better of those who might restrict his movements or cast a censorious eye on his letters. It had been discernible as early as 1713, when François-Marie Arouet was nineteen years old and forced to return to Paris from the Netherlands after his father had foiled his scandalous attempt to elope with a French Protestant refugee named Olympe du Noyer. Writing 'from the bottom [*fond*] of a yacht' (his obsession with persecution and isolation is already perceptible here) on the way back to France, he of course tells 'Pimpette' how much he misses her, but he also instructs her to include in her response a second letter that can provide him with cover for the first:

> Que je suis heureux que l'honneur se trouve d'accord avec l'amour; écrivez moi à Paris à mon adresse tous les ordinaires; mandez moi les moindres particularités qui vous regarderont, ne manquez pas à m'envoyer dans la première lettre que vous m'écrirez, une autre lettre s'adressant à moi, dans laquelle vous me parlerez comme à un ami, et non comme à un amant, vous y ferez succinctement la peinture de tous vos malheurs: que votre vertu y paraisse dans tout son jour sans affectation; enfin servez[-]vous de tout votre esprit pour m'écrire une lettre que je puisse montrer à ceux à qui je serai obligé de parler de vous, que notre tendresse cependant ne perde rien à tout cela; et si dans cette lettre dont je vous parle vous ne me parlez que d'estime, marquez moi dans l'autre tout l'amour que le mien mérite.[53]

> How happy I am that honor happens to agree with love; write to me in Paris by every ordinary post; tell me about the slightest details in your life, do not fail to include in the first letter you send me another letter addressed to me, in which you speak to me as if to a friend, and not a lover, in it you will paint a succinct portrait of your misfortunes; let your virtue appear in full light without affectation; in other words use all your wit to write me a letter that I can show to those with whom I shall be obliged to talk about you, but without any loss of tenderness; if in the letter I am talking to you about you speak only of esteem, put in the other one all the love that my love deserves.

If Mlle du Noyer's response to this letter had survived, it could provide us with an invaluable case study of the ways in which letter writers are always making choices regarding what can and cannot be said. In the absence of this response, it can only be said that, although Voltaire shared with most letter-writers of his time a conception of the post as a medium 'through [which] the absent become ... present' and 'the consolation of life', what marks this relationship to the post as distinctively Voltairean is a playful inclination to use letters as a way to get the better of those who had the power to threaten his liberty of movement and thought.

53. Voltaire to Catherine Olympe Petit du Noyer, 19 December 1713, D18.

5. Rousseau: *vox clamantis*

> La poste me trahit et ne sauroit me servir [...] Présence ou rien.[1] (The post betrays me and cannot possibly serve me... Presence or nothing.)
>
> Rousseau to Pierre-Alexandre Du Peyrou

> Je me ris des machines qu'ils entassent sans cesse autour de moi. Elles S'écrouleront par leur propre masse, et le cri de la vérité percera le Ciel tôt ou tard.[2] (I laugh at the machines they pile up around me. They will collapse under their own weight, and the cry of truth will sooner or later break through to Heaven.)
>
> Rousseau to Charles-Henri Jules de Clermont Tonnerre

Persecution

The post may have been a 'fine invention' in the eyes of Mme de Sévigné and the 'consolation of life' for Voltaire, but Jean-Jacques Rousseau saw it as one of his most relentless and fiendish tormentors. While taking refuge from religious persecution on the continent at Richard Davenport's mansion at Wootton in Staffordshire, Rousseau told a friend from Geneva that 'The post betrays me and cannot possibly serve me'. Although he made this claim in the spring of 1767, at a time when he was about to give way to full-blown persecution delirium, it may not have been completely unjustified. Rousseau knew that his erstwhile friend David Hume had been opening all of his incoming and outgoing mail, and perhaps not always with the best of intentions.[3] In his experience,

1. Rousseau to Pierre Alexandre Du Peyrou, 4 April 1767, *CC*, vol.32, p.8 (5811). Original spelling and punctuation retained, here and elsewhere.
2. Rousseau to Charles Henri Jules, comte de Clermont-Tonnerre, 18 September 1768, *CC*, vol.36, p.106 (6434).
3. '[T]o save Rousseau expense, Hume was in the habit of opening all letters addressed to him and returning to the sender any that he judged unimportant.' Leopold Damrosch, *Jean-Jacques Rousseau: restless genius* (Boston, MA, 2005), p.419. Hume's account of the affair is contained in *A Concise and genuine account of the dispute between Mr Hume and Mr Rousseau with the letters that passed between them* (London, T. Becket & P. A. De Hondt, 1766). For discussion of the relationship between Hume and Rousseau, see Robert Zaretsky and John T. Scott, *The Philosophers' quarrel: Rousseau, Hume and the limits of human understanding* (New Haven, CT, 2009); Benoît Mély, *Jean-Jacques Rousseau: un intellectuel en rupture* (Paris, 1985).

either the post would lay siege to his precious solitude by raining a tempest of unwanted letters upon him – costing him money he could ill afford to spend and making excessive demands upon his time – or, when he needed to receive vital news, it would leave him desperately alone. As he put it, 'Les lettres me pleuvent quand elles ne Sont pas necessaires, et dans les momens critiques tout se tait'.[4] (Letters rain down upon me when they are not necessary, and at critical moments, everything falls silent.) Here, too, he was only slightly exaggerating the truth, as was often the case when he grumbled about his enemies.[5] For in the wake of the phenomenal success of his epistolary novel, *Julie, or The New Heloise* (1761) perhaps the best-selling book of the eighteenth century, letters from impassioned readers had begun raining furiously upon him.[6] Unlike Voltaire and perhaps by his own choice, Rousseau was poor, and it was therefore to be expected that the cost of the packages and letters he received should prey on his mind.

His growing exasperation with this costly deluge of unsolicited mail was already evident in a letter to his Amsterdam publisher Marc-Michel Rey, dated 4 February 1762:

> Si vous pouviez m'envoyer les épreuves du *Contrat social* deux à deux cela feroit quelque économie, car pour chaque épreuve le pacquet me coûte quarante sols de port, et il ne me coûte qu'un écu quand il y en a deux. Croiriez-vous qu'il m'en coûte cinq cent francs par an en ports de lettres. Tous les désœuvrés de France et de l'Europe m'écrivent par la poste, et qui pis est exigent des réponses; tous les petits Auteurs de Paris m'envoyent de même leurs misérables brochures, me font payer 40 à 50^s^ de port d'un présent que je ne payerois pas 10^s^ chez le libraire et dont je ne donnerois pas un liard, et par dessus le marché il leur faut un remercîment.[7]

> If you could send me the proofs of *The Social contract* two at a time, that would save me some money, since for each proof the packet costs me forty *sols* in postage, and it only costs me an *écu* when there are two of them. Would you believe that postage for letters costs me five hundred francs a year. All the idle people in France and Europe write to me by the post, and worse still they expect responses; all the little Authors in Paris also send

---

Dena Goodman offers a detailed and temperate account of the factors that led *philosophes* and the public to take sides in 'The Hume-Rousseau affair: from private *querelle* to public *procès*', *Eighteenth-century studies* 25:2 (Winter 1991-1992), p.171-201, see David Edmonds and John Eidinow, *Rousseau's dog: two great thinkers at war in the Age of Enlightenment* (London, 2001), as well as the same authors' 'Enlightened enemies,' *The Guardian*, Friday 28 April 2006.

4. Rousseau to François Henri d'Ivernois, Saturday, 15 December 1764, *CC*, vol.22, p.237 (3741).
5. As Damrosch remarks, 'Rousseau was the only important writer in Europe who had been systematically expelled from one country after another and denounced by former friends and associates as well as by governments and churches', *Rousseau*, p.418.
6. See Darnton, *The Great cat massacre*, p.242; and Damrosch, *Rousseau*, p.324-25.
7. Rousseau to Jean-Michel Rey, 4 February 1762, *CC*, vol.10, p.83 (1664).

me their miserable pamphlets, make me pay 40 to 50s of postage for a gift that wouldn't cost me 10s at the bookseller's and that I wouldn't give a farthing for, and on top of all that they expect me to thank them.

If Rousseau did indeed pay that much for postage in that year, his annoyance would certainly have been justified, since five hundred francs would probably have represented close to half of his total income for the year.[8] It is difficult, if not impossible, to confirm his estimate of his expenses for postage during that year, but this may not be far from the truth. As we saw in Chapter 2 (p.64ff), postage rates for letters were based on the number of sheets, whether or not the sheets were wrapped in an 'envelope', the delivery speed (ordinary or extraordinary), and the destination (or distance to the destination) itself. For packages containing proofs, weight would have been another significant consideration. The *Correspondance complète* contains over 230 letters sent to Rousseau between February 1761 and January 1762, some of which were attached to proofs or books. Only about ten percent of the extant letters were addressed to Rousseau by persons apparently unknown to him; however he must have refused to accept a great many more, since he more than once justified his failure to respond to a letter by referring to an established habit of rejecting letters whose handwriting was not familiar. After his traumatic experiences of the mid-1760s with the post in England (to which I shall return), when such a letter arrived with an English postmark, he could violently 'repulse' it, as he explains in a letter to his friend Isabelle Guyenet:

> Après avoir longtems hésité, chére Isabelle, je prends le parti le plus simple et le plus franc de vous dire fidellement ce qui m'est arrivé au sujet de votre derniére lettre. Je suis depuis longtems dans l'usage de *rebuter* toutes celles dont je ne connois pas l'écriture, et le nombre de celles que je reçois se réduit à bien peu de chose. J'ai eu beaucoup de peine à engager mes voisins officieux à n'en point recevoir pour moi. Un d'entre eux, plus obstiné que les autres en retira une en notre absence tymbrée d'Angleterre qu'il m'apporta fort obligeamment en trés mauvais état après l'avoir gardée deux jours. Je vis qu'après avoir satisfait sa curiosité il vouloit être remboursé du port; je le lui remboursai donc, mais en même tems voyant le tymbre d'Angleterre où je n'ai ni ne veux avoir de correspondant dont l'écriture me soit inconnue et ne faisant pas attention à la votre, dans le prémier mouvement de mon depit je déchirai devant lui la lettre sans l'ouvrir et j'en jettai les pièces par la fenêtre. Un moment après ma femme étant rentrée ramassa quelques lambeaux volés dans la chambre; et jugez avec quel regret je reconnus en regardant l'écriture de ma chére Isabelle, connoissance dans laquelle quelques mots

8. At this point in his life, Rousseau was not exactly poor, but his modest income came primarily from the sale of his manuscripts to publishers, who then pocketed the profits on book sales. In addition to the income from manuscript sales, he would later receive an annual income of 600 livres/francs from his patron Lord Keith.

saisis ça et là me confirmérent. La plupart des piéces étoient tombées dans l'égout d'un toit qui est sous ma fenêtre; nous y jettames de l'eau pour tâcher de les faire couler pour les ravoir, mais inutilement. Voila, chère Isabelle, l'histoire de mon étourderie et de mon Malheur.[9]

After much hesitation, dear Isabelle, I am resolving to do the simplest and most honest thing by faithfully telling you what happened to me in regard to your last letter. I have long been in the habit of *repulsing* all letters whose handwriting I am not acquainted with, and the number I receive does not amount to much. I have had great difficulty persuading my helpful neighbors not to receive any letters for me. During our absence one of them, who is more stubborn than the others, accepted a letter that was stamped in England and which he most obligingly brought to me in a very poor state after having kept it for two days. I could see that after having satisfied his curiosity he wanted to be reimbursed for the postage, and so I reimbursed him; but when I also saw the postmark from England where I neither have nor wish to have any correspondents whose handwriting is unknown to me and without paying attention to yours, I was at first moved by spite to tear up the letter in front of him without opening it and throw the pieces out the window; imagine with what regret I then recognized the handwriting of my dear Isabelle, knowledge that was confirmed when I looked at a few words here and there. Most of the pieces had fallen into the gutter of the roof that is beneath my window; we threw water on them to try to make them float down and then retrieve them, but in vain. That, dear Isabelle, is the story of my careless mistake and my misfortune.

Some of the extant letters were sent to Rousseau by correspondents (such as Malesherbes and the duke of Luxemburg) with franking privileges; but for the vast majority he had to pay postage. When the postage paid is indicated on these letters, it usually ranges between 6 and 10 *sous*; a few cost only 4 *sous*, and he paid 35 *sous* for a letter that contained proofs from Rey.[10]

However much he had been paying for postage, by early March 1762 Rousseau could no longer bear the onslaught of mail and (as Voltaire had done the previous year)[11] finally resorted to having a public notice published, in the *Mercure de France*:

Jean Jacques Rousseau, Citoyen de Gen[è]ve, prie MM. les Auteurs de ne plus lui envoyer leurs Ouvrages, surtout par la poste, et Messieurs les Beaux-Esprits de ne plus lui écrire des Lettres de compliment, même

9. Rousseau to Isabelle Guyenet, 14 August 1772, *CC*, vol.39, p.110 (6960). Emphasis added. In a letter dated 22 October 1773, he explains to the duchess of Portland that a letter she sent him was inadvertently refused because 'la quantité de sotes lettres qui me venoient de toutes parts par la poste me force à rebuter toutes celles dont l'écriture ne m'est pas connue'. *CC*, vol.39, p.203 (7015).

10. Information about postage paid for Rousseau's correspondence can be found in the critical apparatus of Leigh's *Correspondance complète* under 'Envelope.' However what Leigh means by the 'envelope' is the information (address, postmark and endorsements) inscribed on the exposed section of a letter, whereas in seventeenth- and eighteenth-century France, an *enveloppe* was the extra sheet of paper that was occasionally wrapped and sealed around a letter. When correspondents of this period used envelopes, they wrote the address on both the envelope and the letter within. See Chapter 2, p.57-60 for a fuller discussion of folding and envelopes.

11. See Chapter 4, p.127.

affranchies; n'étant pas en état de payer tant de ports, ni de répondre à tant de Lettres.[12]

Jean-Jacques Rousseau, citizen of Geneva, begs Milords the authors send him their works no longer, especially by the post, and Milords the fine wits to quit sending him even their franked letters of compliment; he is not in a fit state to pay for so much postage or to respond to so many letters.

Few of his admirers seem to have read the *Mercure de France*, for this announcement had little effect. In fact, R. A. Leigh's superb edition of the correspondence suggests that the number of letters Rousseau accepted after publishing this notice actually *increased* considerably: after having risen from 58 letters in 1760 to 208 in 1761, this number grew to 329 in 1762 and finally reached a maximum of 471 letters in 1765, after which it steadily declined. Nevertheless his perception of letters as a personal assault lasted until at least as late as 1770 – a year for which the *Correspondance complète* contains only 23 letters received (accepted) – he instructed a correspondent not to give his address to anyone, 'afin qu on ne m'accable pas de lettres' (so that I not be overburdened by letters).[13] In September 1765, during the year when the number of letters he accepted reached its highest point, Rousseau sought protection from the spate of expensive and annoying letters by returning to the Ile Saint-Pierre on the Lac de Bienne (Bielersee/Lake Biel) in western Switzerland, where he had spent ten idyllic days in July of that year. As his fate would have it, not only did the deluge of unsolicited letters continue, but because the island was not served by the post, letters for Rousseau had to be delivered at great cost by hired boatmen.[14] On September 15, 1765, he pleaded with his friend Du Peyrou to find a way of saving him from these ruinous expenses:

Si vous n'avez pas la bonté de faire entendre à M. le Major qu'à moins de cas trés pressans il ne faut pas envoyer des bateaux exprès, je ferai des fraix effroyables en lettres inutiles et d'autant plus onéreux que je ne pourrai pas refuser mes lettres comme je faisois par la poste. J'espérois avoir dans cette isle l'avantage que les lettres me parviendroient difficilement, et au contraire, j'en suis accablé de toutes parts avec cette différence qu'il faut payer les bateliers qui les portent dix fois plus que par la poste.[15]

12. Rousseau aux auteurs et aux beaux esprits, early March 1762, *CC*, vol.10, p.134 (1698). According to the obituary of Leonard Nimoy by Steve Chawkins of the *Los Angeles times* (7 February, 2015), Nimoy 'was disquieted by mountains of fan mail addressed not to Leonard Nimoy, but to 'Mr Spock, Hollywood, Calif.'. All the same, this celebrity did not have to pay the postage on his fan mail, unlike Voltaire and Rousseau.
13. This in a postscript to Rousseau to Marc-Antoine Louis Claret de la Tourrette, 4 July 1770, *CC*, vol.38, p.53 (6742).
14. In a letter to his publisher Duchesne, Rousseau also laments his fatal relationship with the post: 'Il semble qu'il y ait à tout ce que vous m'envoyez une fatalité qui fait que rien ne me peut parvenir.' Rousseau to Nicolas-Bonaventure Duchesne, 5 April 1763, *CC*, vol.16, p.31 (2597).
15. Rousseau to Pierre-Alexandre Du Peyrou, 15 September 1765, *CC*, vol.27, p.17-18 (4665).

> If you are not good enough to explain to the major that except for very urgent cases express boats must not be sent, I shall incur frightful expenses for letters that are useless and all the more onerous because I shall not be able to refuse my letters as I did by post. I hoped that on this island I would have the advantage that letters would not reach me easily, and on the contrary, I am overwhelmed by letters from all over except that the boatmen who bring them have to be paid ten times more than by post.

By mid-October, the Petty Council of Berne had solved the problem by expelling Rousseau from its territory. Shortly thereafter, David Hume would offer him asylum in England, thereby opening an even more eventful chapter in Jean-Jacques Rousseau's troubled relationship with the post.

Ambiguity

More than any other writer of the eighteenth century, Rousseau was conscious of what Vincent Kaufmann has called *l'équivoque épistolaire* (epistolary ambiguity): the fact that although letters seemingly bring correspondents closer together, they can also keep them at a distance, thereby favoring the insurmountable distance between writer and reader that defines modern literature. As we have seen, in his correspondence Rousseau views the post negatively, as a medium that betrays his thoughts, persecutes and impoverishes him, and as a technology that cruelly isolates and separates him from his interlocutors. 'Presence... or nothing', he exclaims. However in his novel *Julie ou La Nouvelle Héloïse* epistolary distance plays a more complex role, both for the characters and for Rousseau.

His characters use epistolary distance to write what they cannot or dare not say in person. A man of humble birth, St Preux has fallen in love with Julie d'Etange. In this circumstance, social convention requires him to keep silent about it and leave: 'Il faut vous fuir, mademoiselle, je le sens bien: j'aurais dû moins attendre; ou plutôt il fallait ne plus vous voir jamais.' ('I must flee you Mademoiselle, that I can see: I should not have waited nearly so long, or rather it were better never to have laid eyes on you.')[16] What he should do or have done (*Il faut, il fallait*) was to sacrifice his feelings, to 'flee' Julie, avoid her and never see her again. By declaring himself, St Preux fails to respect that convention, even though he does not brazenly defy it either (he does not go down on his knees in front of her). Instead, even though they both live under the same roof, he declares his love to Julie in a letter. Thanks to the ambiguous status of a letter, he can overcome the contradiction between making a declaration and

16. Rousseau, *Julie ou La Nouvelle Héloïse*, *Œuvres complètes* (henceforth *OC*) vol.2 (Paris, 1964), p.31. Translation from *Julie, or, The new Heloise: letters of two lovers who live in a small town at the foot of the Alps*, translated by Philip Stewart and Jean Vaché (Hanover, MD, 1997).

keeping silent; he can avoid having to choose between the requirements of social convention and the urgings of the heart. This contradiction will inhabit the entire novel. The reason he gives for this choice is that his humble social position forbids him from making such a declaration in Julie's presence ('J'espère que je ne m'oublierai jamais jusqu'à vous tenir des discours qu'il ne vous convient pas d'entendre.'). Still, by writing his declaration instead of trying to make it orally, St Preux also prevents Julie from interrupting him, and thereby gives himself the time needed to develop various exculpatory arguments, as well as the distance necessary to protect both himself and Julie from the immediate consequences of whatever words they would be led to speak: while she reads the letter, there can be no dialogue. This opening gambit will be reiterated throughout the novel, as the lovers repeatedly choose to distance themselves from each other. It is always in letters and from a distance that St Preux and Julie will seek to overcome the physical and social distance that separates them, and in letters that they will best succeed at conveying their very being to each other more forcefully than 'live' communication (which in Rousseau's experience always left something to be desired) would allow.

Costs

> Que j'ai souffert en la recevant, cette lettre souhaitée avec tant d'ardeur!
>
> *Julie ou la Nouvelle Héloïse*, Part I, letter 21

Like many of his contemporaries, Rousseau often refers to the high cost of postage, as well as the lack of security and unreliability of the mail. Yet although he would complain loudly and often about the cost of postage to both himself and his more needy correspondents, this subject does not appear in his correspondence until after the appearance of the *Second discourse* in 1754 (when he was 42 years old), three years after the controversial *Discourse on the sciences and the arts* had begun to turn Rousseau into a celebrity, and yet 'not only famous, but famous for not wanting to be famous'.[17] He would prove himself a genius at self-promotion, repeatedly drawing the attention of the public by taking highly controversial positions in his published work and then making a public spectacle of himself, only to resent the loss of privacy that he had himself provoked. As we shall see, his ambivalence toward his own

17. Antoine Lilti, *Figures publiques: l'invention de la célébrité 1750-1850* (Paris, 2014), p.158. Lilti grants a central position to Rousseau in his recent study of the emergence of celebrity. 'In the middle of the 1760s Rousseau is, with Voltaire, doubtless the most celebrated writer of his time.' *Figures publiques*, p.155.

celebrity is linked to his ambivalent attitude toward the post. Although he repeatedly fretted about the interception and suppression of his correspondence by the post and devoted much energy to inventing tactics for evading surveillance and censorship, it was also not until *Julie ou La Nouvelle Héloïse* (1761) became a best-seller that these topics began appearing in his letters. Rousseau's epistolary novel touched the hearts of innumerable readers, who believed so passionately in the reality of its characters that they swamped him with demands for news of them. The author fled their countless letters of gratitude like the plague.[18]

Before the cost of postage and security of mail became explicit issues for Rousseau, he also shared with many of his contemporaries an awareness of the unreliability of the post: due to poor roads, foul weather and the incompetence of postal employees, correspondence was often delayed. He also tried to beware of what he called his own *bêtise.*[19] Finally, there was always the possibility that even when his letters reached their destination in good time, the addressee (like the reader of his published works) would misunderstand what he said (or at least what he thought he had said), with occasionally dramatic consequences.[20] Despite all of these drawbacks, Rousseau still considered the post to be the promptest and most secure method of delivery for manuscripts and proofs. As he says to Marc-Michel Rey, 'J'approuve que vous m'adressiez les épreuves directement par la *poste*; c'est la voye la plus prompte et la plus sure'[21] (I approve of your sending me the proofs directly by post, it is the most prompt and secure means). However on at least one occasion his concern with security led him to seek a messenger for delivery of a manuscript. Since he knew that *Lettre sur les spectacles* (1758) would arouse a great deal of hostility (particularly among the Encyclopedists), he did not

18. Darnton, *The Great cat massacre*, p.242-49.
19. On the other hand, there was also a strange moment in 1768 when one of his letters had not reached its destination and Rousseau implausibly claimed that it was the first time this had happened in the thirty years he had been using the French post. Rousseau to Pierre-Alexandre Du Peyrou, 14 January 1768, *CC*, vol.35, p.27 (6199). He often complained about mistreatment at the hands of the Geneva post (for example, in Rousseau to Isaac Ami Marcet de Mézières, 20 August 1762, *CC*, vol.12, p.212 [2092]), but on one occasion expressed confidence in the 'fidelity' of the Swiss post. Rousseau to Professeur Usteri, 27 January 1765, *CC*, vol.23, p.205 (393). Yet as he had told Madame de Warens over thirty years before the above letter to Du Peyrou, he also needed to beware of his own tendency to do or say foolish things (that is, his unconscious): 'Que voulez-vous, Madame, que je vous dise; quand j'agis, je crois faire les plus belles choses du monde, et puis, il se trouve au bout que ce ne sont que sottises: je le reconnois parfaitement bien moi-même. *Il faudra tâcher de se roidir contre sa bêtise à l'avenir*, et faire plus d'attention sur sa conduite.' Rousseau to Françoise Louise Eléonore de La Tour, baronne de Warens, 23 October 1737, *CC*, vol.1, p.54 (18). Emphasis added. Cf. Whyman, *The Pen and the people*, p.55ff.
20. For example, in Rousseau to Pierre-Alexandre Du Peyrou, 8 January 1767, *CC*, vol.32, p.33-34 (5667bis).
21. Rousseau to Marc-Michel Rey, 29 November 1761, *CC*, vol.9, p.284 (1568).

want to rely upon the post to carry the manuscript safely from Montmorency to Paris and onward to Amsterdam. Rousseau therefore told Rey that if a totally reliable agent (by which he meant neither his erstwhile friends Diderot and Deleyre nor indeed anyone who was French) was not available to fetch the manuscript at Montmorency, then he himself would carry it to Rey's agent in Paris:

> Mon Manuscrit est prét; vous le ferez retirer quand il vous plaira, ou s'il le faut absolument, je tâcherai de le porter à Paris. Je vous prie seulement dans l'un et l'autre cas de m'avertir quelques jours à l'avance, afin que je le relise avant de le donner... Je vous repéte qu'il sera remis cacheté à vôtre Correspondant sans avoir été vû que de moi seul, je souhaiterois même que ce correspondant fut sûr et ne fut pas françois; j'exclud surtout nommêment Mrs Diderot et De Leyre. Ne m'écrivez plus, non plus, sous le pli de ce dernier.[22]

> My manuscript is ready; you will have it fetched when you wish, or if it is absolutely necessary, I shall attempt to take it to Paris. In either case I beg you just to notify me a few days in advance, so that I can reread it before submitting it... Let me repeat that it will be delivered to your representative sealed, having been seen by me alone, I should even wish that this representative be reliable and not French; I explicitly exclude Messrs Diderot and De Leyre. Do not write to me any more either in an envelope bearing the latter's name.

Yet on occasion even a reliable private messenger was of no use to him, such as when he was bent upon sending the second part of *Julie* by messenger to Mme d'Houdetot; he feared that customs inspectors at the gates of Paris would desecrate the precious manuscript notebooks:

> En voulant remettre le pacquet à vôtre Messager il n'a jamais pu le faire entrer dans sa poche. D'ailleurs il m'a dit qu'on le fouilloit toujours à la barriére avec le plus grand soin. Il arrivera de là que les cahiers seront visités salis, et peut-être dépareillés. Cet inconvenient me fait une peine mortelle, et en vérité malgré la repugnance que j'ai de vous faire encore attendre je ne puis me résoudre à exposer ma pauvre Julie à passer par les mains de ces gens là.[23]

> When I tried to deliver the packet to your messenger he could not manage to fit it in his pocket. Moreover he told me that he was always very carefully searched at the tollgate. This will mean that the notebooks will be examined, dirtied and pages may even be lost. This risk causes me mortal pain, and in truth despite how repugnant it is for me to make you wait I cannot bring myself to expose my poor Julie to those people's hands.

This fear that contact with postal workers might sully 'his Julie' (that is, the novel, its heroine and maybe even Mme d'Houdetot, with whom he was madly in love at the time) suggests that, like so many of his admiring

22. Rousseau to Marc-Michel Rey, 15 April 1758, *CC*, vol.5, p.70-71 (638).
23. Rousseau to Elisabeth Françoise Sophie La Live de Bellegarde, comtesse d'Houdetot, 13 February 1758, *CC*, vol.6, p.30 (614).

readers, Rousseau could not always distinguish between reality and the characters in the sentimental novel that he himself had written. It also testifies to Rousseau's belief that everything that originated in a pure heart was destined to be corrupted as soon as it took material form.

A strange and troubling example of this latter phenomenon occurs in a series of letters toward the end of Part II of *Julie ou La Nouvelle Héloïse* (1761), most of which concern a portrait of Julie that she sends from her rural village near Lake Geneva to her plebeian lover St Preux in Paris.[24] Although the portrait is not mentioned in three of these letters (xxi, in which St Preux responds to Julie's request for a verbal portrait of Parisian women; xxiii, on the Paris Opera; xxvi, on St Preux's visit to a bordello), all seven letters constitute a coherent sequence devoted to the effects of art on women and their beholders. In II, xxii, when St Preux first beholds the portrait (or 'talisman' of love), he is overcome by desire because he takes it for the living presence of Julie herself; however he quickly realizes that it is only an artistic illusion, and begins to suffer from Julie's absence as intensely as he had been excited by the illusion of her presence. Upon further reflection (II, xxv), he notes the discrepancies between the portrait and its living model: it fails to reproduce either the inimitable perfections of Julie or her few but charming imperfections (*défauts*), and – worse still – it lacks sexual modesty. St Preux therefore hires another artist to correct the errors in the portrait and cover up Julie's décolleté. As he explains, 'C'est pour mieux te voir tout entière que je t'habille avec tant de soin'. In the last letter of the sequence (II, xxvi), St Preux confesses to Julie that a few of his compatriots have since taken him to what he eventually discovered to be a house of ill repute, where he involuntarily drank to excess and guiltily awakened the next morning in the arms of a prostitute. In effect, St Preux who, while in Paris had only an impeccably pure mental image of Julie, is punished/punishes himself for having desired a material image of her, even though it was she who ordered the portrait and sent it to him in the first place. Taken as a sequence, these letters provide an eloquent example of the damage that in Rousseau's mind could be inflicted by the materialization of a purely ideal object. After this long epistolary novel had attained unprecedented public success, Rousseau would refuse to respond to letters from impassioned readers who were eager to learn what had become of his characters or if Julie had really existed. By rebuffing their queries, he reiterated St Preux's tactic of having Julie's breasts covered in order better to keep them for himself, in his imagination. Like St Preux, Rousseau wanted to preserve 'his poor Julie' from contamination by the public.

24. *Julie*, *OC*, vol.2, letters xx-xxvi.

For letters Rousseau generally preferred to use a messenger. When scheduled messenger service was available, it cost no more than the post and (as he tells Mme d'Houdetot) it could even provide faster service:

> Je vous écris... par le Messager de Montmorenci qui va trois fois la semaine à Paris faire les commissions et porter les Lettres du tiers et du quart, et qu'on préfére à la poste, parce qu'il n'en coûte pas plus pour les ports de Lettre et qu'on a la reponse le même jour.[25]

> I am writing to you... by the Montmorency messenger service, which goes to Paris three times a week to do errands and carry letters for others, and which is preferable to the post, because it is no more expensive and one has a reply on the same day.

Sometimes an obliging friend would carry letters for him, thereby also protecting them from interception by agents of the postal service.[26] If neither a scheduled service nor a friend was available, Rousseau could engage a special messenger; although he had to pay more for the service, it also provided the means of obtaining a prompt response from the receiver. On the other hand, although he usually preferred to send mail by messenger, Rousseau sometimes recommended the post as a rapid and convenient means of delivery, and on one occasion he even reproached a correspondent for *not* having used it.[27] Moreover there was one aspect of private messenger service that he disliked: when a letter arrived by messenger, he felt pressured to compose a response on the spot, since otherwise he would eventually have to pay postage to another messenger. Indeed whereas many users of the post experienced scheduled collection and delivery times as a constraint upon their liberty, postal schedules provided Rousseau with a convenient excuse for not responding to letters as promptly as his correspondents might have wished.[28]

25. Rousseau to Elisabeth Françoise Sophie de La Live de Bellegarde, comtesse d'Houdetot, 17 November 1757, *CC*, vol.5, p.363 (577). In 1762 he would tell Moultou, 'Je vous envoie ce billet par le Messager, plustot que par la poste, afin que si vous avez quelque chose à m'envoyer vous en ayez la comodité'. Rousseau to Paul-Claude Moultou, 19 December 1762, *CC*, vol.14, p.21 (2396). For more details on messenger services, see Chapter 2, p.75-79.
26. 'Sachant bien que toutes mes lettres étoient ouvertes à la poste, à profiter du retour de M. Pepin de Belleisle qui m'étant venu voir la veille, m'accabloit des plus pressantes offres de Service, et je lui remis le matin une lettre pour Mad^e^ de Brionne qui en contenoit une autre pour M. le Prince de Conti, l'une et l'autre écrites si à la hâte qu'ayant été contraint d'en transcrire une, j'envoyai le brouillon au lieu de la copie.' Rousseau to Chrétien Guillaume de Lamoignon de Malesherbes, Friday, 23 November 1770, *CC*, vol.37, p.142 (6812).
27. Rousseau to Louise-Florence-Pétronille Lalive d'Epinay, 25 November, 1756, *CC*, vol.4, p.128 (453); Rousseau to Toussaint-Pierre Lenieps, Februry 1757, *CC*, vol.4, p.156 (473); Rousseau to Daniel Roguin, 28 March 1763, *CC*, vol.15, p.330 (2572). The last of these letters has been lost, but its content is confirmed by Roguin's response of 2 April 1763, *CC*, vol.16, p.16 (2588).
28. See Rousseau to Madeline-Catherine Delessert, née Boy de la Tour, 26 March 1770, *CC*, vol.37, p.348 (6698).

While Rousseau's complaints about communication by post are justified to a certain extent, they are also symptoms of a more fundamental anxiety about epistolary communication, and about communication in general. He worried much more about this problem than most other users of the post, and certainly more than circumstances justified. It was vitally important for Rousseau to receive letters and books and, perhaps even more so, for him to transmit the impassioned dispatches that constitute his *œuvre*. In the letter where he condemns the post as essentially treacherous, he implicitly concedes that this treachery is built into all forms of communication at a distance, since even a private messenger cannot ensure that an absent interlocutor will understand his meaning: 'The post betrays me and cannot possibly serve me. In my position only the sight of a man can be of use to me. Presence or nothing.'[29] This anxiety can perhaps be understood in terms of Rousseau's well-known distrust of mediation in all of its forms and his corresponding desire for transparent communication, themes that have been amply documented by Jean Starobinski and others.[30] All the same, because Jean-Jacques Rousseau spent so much of his life on the move, in flight from real or imaginary enemies and in search of solitude, the only way he could call out to distant friends, acquaintances or publishers was by letter. Although this great social theorist was singularly averse to human society and naturally inclined to solitude (to *se circonscrire* [encircle himself], as he said in the fifth *Promenade*),[31] he also needed to correspond freely with the outside world. Reliable messengers were not often available to him; so that despite all its drawbacks – its expense and lack of security, its unreliability and opacity – the post provided Rousseau with the most convenient means of communicating with absent publishers, allies and friends. However as we shall see, there were times when the drawbacks of the post outweighed its convenience.

Just checking

Symptoms of this anxiety about postal communication appear in the very first (extant) letter in which Rousseau mentions the post. In the fall of 1737, he found himself in Montpellier, having tried his hand at various kinds of labor (lackey, secretary, interpreter, music teacher) since he had run away from Geneva in 1728. On 23 October 1737, Rousseau, who was

29. Rousseau to Pierre-Alexandre Du Peyrou, 4 April 1767, *CC*, vol.33, p.7-8 (5811).
30. Jean Starobinski, *La Transparence et l'obstacle* (Paris, 1957). See Paul de Man, *Allegories of reading: figural language in Rousseau, Nietzsche, Rilke and Proust* (New Haven, CT, 1979); Thomas M. Kavanagh, *Writing the truth: authority and desire in Rousseau* (Berkeley, CA, 1987); Greg Hill, *Rousseau's theory of human communication: transparent and opaque societies* (New York, 2006).
31. Rousseau, *OC*, vol.1, p.1040.

twenty-five years old and still unknown to the wider world, wrote a letter to his former guardian and occasional lover, Mme de Warens ('Maman'). He begins by expressing his concern about her welfare, since he has not heard from her in a month:

> Voici un mois passé de mon arrivée à Montpellier, sans avoir pu recevoir aucune nouvelle de votre part, quoique j'aie écrit plusieurs fois, et par différentes voies. Vous pouvez croire que je ne suis pas fort tranquille, et que ma situation n'est pas des plus gracieuses; je vous proteste cependant, Madame, avec la plus parfaite sincérité, que ma plus grande inquiétude vient de la crainte, qu'il ne vous soit arrivé quelque accident.[32]

> A month has passed now since my arrival in Montpellier, without having received any word from you, although I have written several times, and by different means. You can believe that I am not very easy, and that my situation is not among the most gracious; yet I protest, Madame, with the most perfect sincerity, that my greatest concern comes from the fear that some accident may have befallen you.

The sentiments expressed in these opening sentences are perfectly conventional, although perhaps not entirely sincere, for Rousseau may have been less worried about the well-being of Mme de Warens than he was about the loss of a source of income. However the rest of the letter is almost entirely devoted to discussion of various means of increasing the probability that his message and the response he requires from her will arrive at their destination, and in good time. He explains that he is sending copies of his letter by *three* different routes (two messengers, plus the regular post); and in the postscript, he suggests that she use two different methods for sending him her response. Rousseau even specifies the days of the week when Mme de Warens will need to post her response in order for it to reach him in a timely fashion via Lyon, and provides an address in Montpellier that is even more precise than the one she has presumably been using. Perhaps these precautions also aim to ensure that she can have no plausible reason for later claiming either that she did not receive his letter or that her response was delayed by the post:

> Je vous écris cet ordinaire-ci par trois différentes voies, savoir par Mrs Vépres, M. Micoud, et en droiture; il est impossible, qu'une de ces trois lettres ne vous parvienne; ainsi, j'en attends la réponse dans trois semaines au plus tard, passé ce temps-là, si je n'ai point de nouvelles, je serai contraint de partir dans le dernier désordre, et de me rendre à Chambéry comme je pourrai. Ce soir la poste doit arriver, et il se peut qu'il y aura quelque lettre pour moi; peut-être n'avez vous pas fait mettre les vôtres à la poste, les jours qu'il falloit; car j'aurois réponse depuis quinze jours, si les lettres avoient fait chemin dans leur temps. Vos lettres doivent passer par Lyon pour venir ici; ainsi c'est les Mercredis et Samedis de bon matin qu'elles doivent être mises à

32. Rousseau to Françoise Louise Eléonore de La Tour, baronne de Warens, 23 October 1737, *CC*, vol.1, p.53 (18).

la poste; je vous avois donné précédemment l'adresse de ma pension: il vaudroit peut-être mieux les adresser en droiture où je suis logé, par ce que je suis sûr de les recevoir exactement. C'est chez M. Barcellon, Huissier de la Bourse, en rue Basse, proche du Palais. J'ai l'honneur d'être avec un profond respect, Madame,

JJ Rousseau

Si vous avez quelque chose a m'envoyer par la voie des marchands de Lyon, et que vous écriviez, par exemple, à Mrs Vépres par le même ordinaire qu'à moi; je dois, s'ils sont exacts, recevoir leur lettre en même tems que la vôtre.[33]

I am writing this ordinary to you by three different means, namely, Mssrs Vépres, M. Micoud, and directly by post; it is impossible that one of these three letters should fail to reach you; I shall therefore expect the response in three weeks at the latest, beyond which point, if I have no word, I shall be forced to leave in a state of complete unrest and to go to Chambéry as best I can. This evening the post is scheduled to arrive, and there may be a letter for me; maybe you didn't mail yours on the right days; for I would have had a response for a fortnight, if the letters had made their way on time. Your letters must pass through Lyon to get here; thus they should be posted on Wednesdays and Saturdays early in the morning; I had previously given you the address of my boarding house: it would perhaps be better to address them directly to my lodgings, because I am sure to receive them punctually. It is care of Mr Barcellon, porter at the stock market, on the rue Basse, near the Palace. Madame, with deep respect I have the honor of being

JJ Rousseau

If you have something to send me by way of the Lyon merchants, and you wrote, for example, to Mssrs Vépres by the same ordinary as I, I should (if they are punctual) receive their letter at the same time as yours.

Rousseau's future references to the post would contain many variations on all of these themes, which one might call 'phatic', as they are all related to a need to establish contact: the urgent need to know whether a letter or package has been sent and delivered, the desire to make the delivery of an item more likely by sending it (or having it sent) in duplicate or triplicate, offering precise details about post routes and schedules, informing his correspondents of the delivery method(s) he is using (post or messenger), confirming or further specifying his address, announcing (or threatening) future action if he does not receive a response in timely fashion.[34] All of these concerns are based on his assumption (contrary to the proverb) that no news is bad news or, as Rousseau puts it,

33. Rousseau to Françoise Louise Eléonore de La Tour, baronne de Warens, 23 October 1737, *CC*, vol.1, p.53 (18).

34. Rousseau to François Joseph de Conzié, comte des Charmettes, 21 September 1743, *CC*, vol.1 , p.194 (59); Rousseau to Elisabeth Françoise Sophie La Live de Bellegarde, comtesse d'Houdetot, 17 September 1757, *CC*, vol.4, p.363 (577); Rousseau to Elisabeth Françoise Sophie La Live de Bellegarde, comtesse d'Houdetot, 15 January 1758, *CC*, vol.5, p.19-21 (609); Rousseau to Marc-Michel Rey, 14 May 1758, *CC*, vol.5, p.119 (645); Rousseau to Marc-Michel Rey, 20 July 1758, *CC*, vol.5, p.19-19 (673); Rousseau to Marc-Michel Rey, 10 August 1758, *CC*, vol.5, p.125-26 (677); Rousseau to Marc-Michel Rey, 22 June 1760, *CC*, vol.7, p.146-47 (1027); Rousseau to Marc-Michel Rey, 5 October 1760, *CC*, vol.7, p.246 (1113); Rousseau to Marc-Michel Rey, 1 October 1762, *CC*, vol.14, p.146-47 (2358); Pierre

'La pire de toutes les nouvelles pour moi, c'est de n'en recevoir aucune'.[35] (The worst of all news for me is not to receive any.)

This assumption governs St Preux's behavior during his first prolonged separation from Julie. When he arrives in the Valais, he immediately posts a letter to her, but five days later he has not yet received a response and is seized by hysterical anxiety:

> Je commence à être fort inquiet du sort de ma première lettre; elle fut écrite et mise à la poste en arrivant: l'adresse en est fidèlement copiée sur celle que vous m'envoyâtes: je vous ai envoyé la mienne avec le même soin, et si vous aviez fait exactement réponse, elle aurait déjà dû me parvenir. Cette réponse pourtant ne vient point, et il n'y a nulle cause possible et funeste de son retard que mon esprit troublé ne se figure. O ma Julie! que d'imprévues catastrophes peuvent en huit jours rompre à jamais les plus doux liens du monde![36]

> I am beginning to worry considerably about the fate of my first letter; it was written and posted on my arrival; the address was faithfully copied from the one you sent me; I sent you mine with equal care, and if you had replied punctually, it should already have reached me. Yet this reply does not come, and there is no possible dire reason for its delay that my troubled spirit does not imagine. O my Julie, in one week how many unforeseen catastrophes can break forever the world's sweetest bonds!

In her response, Julie chides him for letting his imagination get the best of him and brings him back to postal realities:

> Pensâtes-vous, en arrivant à Sion, qu'un courrier tout prêt n'attendait pour partir que votre lettre, que cette lettre me serait remise en arrivant ici, et que les occasions ne favoriseraient pas ma réponse?... Vos deux lettres me sont parvenues à la fois, parce que le courrier, qui ne passe qu'une fois la semaine* n'est parti qu'avec la seconde. Il faut un certain temps pour distribuer les lettres ; il en faut à mon commissionnaire pour me rendre la mienne en secret, et le courrier ne retourne pas d'ici le lendemain du jour qu'il est arrivé. Ainsi, tout bien calculé, il nous faut huit jours, quand celui du courrier est bien choisi, pour recevoir réponse d'un de l'autre; ce que je vous explique afin de calmer une fois pour toutes votre impatiente vivacité.
>
> * Il passe à présent deux fois.[37]

> Did you imagine that when you reached Sion a ready Courier would be awaiting only your letter for his departure, that the letter would be delivered to me the moment it arrived here, and that circumstances would no less favor my reply? Such is not the way things work, my fine friend. Your two letters reached me at the same time, because the Courier, who comes only once a week,* set out only with the second. It takes a certain

---

Guy to Rousseau, 25 March 1763, *CC*, vol.15, p.528 (2565); Rousseau to Captain Hyacinthe-Antoine d'Astier de Commessière, 22 April 1764, *CC*, vol.19, p.316 (3232); Rousseau to François Coindet, 25 August 1767, *CC*, vol.34, p.53 (6037) ; Rousseau to Isabelle Guyenet, 22 October 1772, *CC*, vol.39, p.117 (6969).

35. Rousseau to François Joseph de Conzié, comte des Charmettes, 21 September 1743, *CC*, vol.1, p.154 (59).
36. Rousseau, *Julie*, *OC*, vol.1, xix. Translations from Stewart, Vaché, *Julie, or, The New Heloise* (p. 146).
37. Rousseau, *Julie*, *OC*, vol.1, xx.

amount of time to deliver letters; it takes more for my agent to bring me mine in secret, and the Courier does not return from here the day after his arrival. Thus all told, we need eight days, when the Courier's day is well chosen, to receive replies from each other; I explain this in order to calm once and for all your impatient petulance. [...]
* By now he comes twice.

Like Rousseau's other editorial footnotes to *Julie*, this last line fosters the illusion that the correspondence is not a fiction. Like the rest of Julie's reply, it testifies to the attention Rousseau paid to postal arrangements and the extensive knowledge of the practical workings of the post that his anxiety about postal communication had forced him to acquire.

In a letter to the French draper Jean Antoine Charbonnel, dated 4 November 1737, he magnifies the self-pitying tone of the letter to Mme de Warens cited above (written ten days earlier) while rehearsing many of the same themes: his correspondent is guilty of not having responded in two whole months to any of the many letters that Rousseau claims to have sent him by various means, Rousseau is friendless and alone in Montpellier, and (here the request for charity becomes explicit) he is so poor that he may have to sell some of his furniture to pay for his medicine. In another attempt to have a message delivered in duplicate, he then asks Charbonnel to repeat this information 'To Whom it May Concern,' that is, to Mme de Warens. He also resorted to duplicate messages in 1758, when he was corresponding with Marc-Michel Rey in Amsterdam about the proofs of the *Lettre à M. d'Alembert* and had good reason to fear that his correspondence would be suppressed; he would again have recourse to duplicates in late 1760, when he was correcting the proofs of *La Nouvelle Héloïse*, as well as in 1762.[38] Many of Rousseau's contemporaries made copies of their outgoing letters, but Rousseau was so obsessed by the possibility that his letters might go astray that, when he sent several letters in a *paquet*, he also kept a record of each letter it contained. In April 1763, during the hubbub over the *Lettre à Christophe de Beaumont*, Rousseau sent his Parisian publisher Duchesne a letter in which he summarized the contents of a *paquet* that he feared had been lost.[39] This turns out to have been a sensible precaution, since there is no record of this package's having reached its destination. Moreover it is important to note that, in other contexts at least, every one of these precautions was a perfectly reasonable and common way of dealing with the difficulties of postal communication.[40]

38. Rousseau to Marc-Michel Rey, 14 May 1758, *CC*, vol.5, p.78 (645); Rousseau to Marc-Michel Rey, 5 October 1760, *CC*, vol.7, p.246 (1113); Rousseau to Marc-Michel Rey, 1 December 1762, *CC*, vol.14, p.146-47 (2358).
39. Rousseau to Nicolas-Bonaventure Duchesne, 28 April 1763, *CC*, vol.16, p.119-19 (2654).
40. For example, as Bannet indicates, in the context of transatlantic communication. *Empire of letters*, p.258ff.

In 1758, at the height of Rousseau's unrequited passion for Sophie d'Houdetot, his phatic anxiety took a poignant and perverse form when he begged the countess just to mail him a blank piece of paper once a week. He knows that she doesn't love him, he bitterly concedes, but if he can recognize her handwriting or seal on the outside of the folded sheet, he will be free to imagine that the inside says whatever his heart desires:

> Parlons sincèrement, je ne pense pas que l'empressement d'avoir de mes nouvelles vous empêche de dormir. Pour me tranquilliser sur les vôtres, faites mettre tous les huit jours une feuille blanche à la poste, pourvù que je voye vôtre écriture sur l'adresse, où [ou] seulement vôtre cachet, je serai content et me dirai tout ce qui ne sera pas dans la Lettre.[41]

> Let us speak sincerely; I do not think that your eagerness to have news from me keeps you from sleeping. To put my mind at rest about your news, once a week have a blank sheet posted to me, and as long as I see your handwriting on the address or only your seal, I shall be content and will tell myself everything that is not in the letter.

Here Rousseau conceives an epistolary version of what the linguist Roman Jakobson called the 'zero sign': a term that (like *thingamajig* or *whatchamacallit*), has no specific meaning but has the capacity to signify anything and everything.[42] As her next (extant) letter to him makes no reference to this strange proposal, Madame d'Houdetot does not seem to have encouraged Rousseau's fantasy, which would also have provided him with a convenient way of accumulating a collection of fetishes.[43]

In 1760, while Rousseau was in the process of correcting the proofs of *La Nouvelle Héloïse*, which his Amsterdam printer, Marc-Michel Rey, was mailing to him at Montmorency, he devised an elaborate strategy for finding out whether any of the packages they mailed to each other had got lost so that, if necessary, they could attempt to compensate for the loss:

> Voici je crois ce qu'il faut que nous fassions desormais l'un et l'autre; c'est jusqu'à la fin de l'impression, soit qu'il y ait des envois soit qu'il n'y en ait pas 1° d'écrire un mot à chaque ordinaire sans jamais y manquer. Car de cette maniére quand l'un ou l'autre ne recevra rien, il en pourra conclurre qu'il y a surement lettre ou pacquet égaré ou retardé; 2° de mettre nos lettres ou pacquets à la poste nous-mêmes ou de ne les y faire mettre que par des gens surs. Pour vous épargner quelque partie du port j'ai quelquefois envoyé vos pacquets à la poste de Paris par occasion. Je ne le ferai plus; mais tous mes pacquets seront mis à la poste de Montmorenci par moimême ou par Mlle Le Vasseur. 3° il faut tenir par devers soi note de ce que contient chaque pacquet qu'on envoye, afin que s'il est égaré, on sache d'abord ce qui doit

41. Rousseau to Elisabeth Françoise Sophie La Live de Bellegarde, comtesse d'Houdetot, 15 January 1758, *CC*, vol.5, p.21 (609).
42. See Roman Jakobson, 'Sign zero,' in *Selected writings*, vol.II (The Hague, 1971), p.4; Roland Barthes, *Writing degree zero and Elements of semiology* (Boston, MA, 1970).
43. Elisabeth Françoise Sophie de La Live de Bellegarde, comtesse d'Houdetot to Rousseau, 28 January 1758, *CC*, vol.5, 25 (612).

être renvoyé par duplicata. Si ces précautions ne suffisent pas, je ne sais qu'y faire autre.[44]

Here is how I think we need to proceed henceforth: until the printing is complete, whether or not there are mailings, 1. write a note at each ordinary without fail. For this way when one or the other does not receive anything, he will be able to conclude that a letter or a packet has definitely gone astray or been delayed; 2. take our letters or packets to the post ourselves or have them posted by reliable people. To spare you part of the postage I have occasionally sent your packets to the Paris post. I shall no longer do this; but all my packets will be posted at Montmorency by myself or Mlle Le Vasseur. 3. we must keep notes on the contents of every packet that we send, so that if it has gone astray, we immediately know what must be resent in duplicate. If these precautions do not suffice, I do not know what to do.

It would have been difficult to imagine a more painstaking, tiresome and ultimately futile strategy. Certainly neither party ever tried to adopt it. At some level even Rousseau must have realized that no matter how many duplicates (and duplicates of duplicates, *ad infinitum*) he and Rey could have made of their correspondence or how carefully they might have tried to keep notes on everything that was contained in every mailing, there would still have been no foolproof procedure for ensuring that their letters and packages did not go astray; just as there would have been no absolutely certain method of avoiding mistakes in their notes on the contents of their packages. Like his curious proposal to Mme d'Houdetot, this was one more fantasy of lossless communication. It was the first of many elaborate and completely impractical plans that Rousseau imagined in the hope of overcoming postal 'treachery' in all its forms.

Cost control

References to the high cost of postage do not appear in Rousseau's correspondence until the end of 1754, when he started asking his Amsterdam publisher Marc-Michel Rey (also a Genevan) to look for less expensive ways of sending material to him, and (in 1758) not to waste money mailing materials that were not urgent.[45] Writing from Montmorency on 15 December 1759, he expresses the fear that postage

44. Rousseau to Marc-Michel Rey, 22 June 1760, *CC*, vol.7, p146-47 (1027).

45. Rousseau to Marc-Michel Rey, 12 October 1754, *CC*, vol.3, p.69 (261); Rousseau to Marc-Michel Rey, 24 January 1755, *CC*, vol.3, p.95 (274); Rousseau to Marc-Michel Rey, 6 March 1755, *CC*, vol.5, p.105 (280); Rousseau to Marc-Michel Rey, 8 July 1758, *CC*, vol.5, p.110-11 (667); Rousseau to Jean-François Deluc, 20 October 1762, *CC*, vol.18, p.56 (2980). On at least one occasion, he avoids having to pay postage by returning an unopened package to its sender. Rousseau to Pierre Clappier, 26 May 1769, *CC*, vol.37, p.93 (6573). In Book Ten of the *Confessions*, Rousseau cites the habit that rich Parisian women had of having messengers carry letters to him at the Hermitage or Montmorency – the messengers would arrive in a sweat and he feel obliged to give them a generous tip – as one of many examples of the fact that relationships between people who are not equal always make the weaker party suffer. *OC*, vol.1, p.514.

for the proofs of *La Nouvelle Héloïse* could cost him more than he was receiving for writing the novel. He therefore suggests two ways that Rey might spare him that burden: either Rey could agree to pay Rousseau in books rather than money (but this would require Rousseau to negotiate a reduction in postage fees) or he could ask for permission to use the franking privilege of Malesherbes (director of royal censorship and supporter of the Encyclopedists).[46] In fact, as Rousseau remarks in the *Confessions*, Malesherbes did assist him in precisely this way during correction of the proofs of the novel's first edition.[47] Nevertheless when a second edition of the novel was being prepared in late 1761, we find Rousseau once again asking Rey to avoid mailing the proofs directly to him.[48] Nor was he indifferent to the cost of postage to his correspondents: on at least one occasion he uses a messenger in order to spare Rey the postage fees; he apologizes to the Huguenot pastor Paul Claude Moultou for making him pay so much for postage; and at one point he even asks Moultou to wait until he has recopied the manuscript of the *Profession de foi d'un vicaire Savoyard* in smaller characters, so that there will be fewer sheets in the package.[49]

Rousseau tends to see the cost of postage as an insult added to the injury inflicted by the worthless material that people send him. For example, he sends a small package to the Swiss academic Leonhard Usteri, along with the comment that it will cost the Swiss academic 'plus que ne valent l'ouvrage et l'Auteur'[50] (more than the work and the author are worth). During this same period, two of his acquaintances committed the offense of mailing him a copy of Voltaire's burlesque poem *La Guerre civile de Genève,* after which they received the following caustic response:

> Si je vous ai coûté sept francs de port pour des épreuves vous me l'avez bien rendu, car ce pacquet m'en a coûté quinze. Quinze francs de port pour des vers françois, c'est beaucoup. Quand vous voudrez desormais me faire des présens à ce prix, que ce ne soit plus des vers, je vous en prie [...] Je n'ai point oui parler du Livre de Botanique, il me feroit pourtant plus de plaisir que des vers françois, pourvu qu'il ne vint pas par la poste.[51]

46. Rousseau to Marc-Michel Rey, 15 December 1759, *CC*, vol.6, p.234-35 (908).
47. Rousseau, *Confessions*, vol.X, p.511. See Damrosch, *Jean-Jacques Rousseau*, p.324.
48. 'Il faudra penser d'avance au moyen de me faire parvenir les épreuves [of the corrected *Julie*]; car directement par la poste les fraix en sont excessifs.' Rousseau to Marc-Michel Rey, 7 November 1761, *CC*, vol.9, p.221 (1534). Rousseau could also worry about what postage on the proofs would cost Rey. 'Ma préface en forme d'entretien [to *Julie*] est imprimée et publique depuis deux jours; je suppose que Duchesne vous l'aura envoyée; c'est pourquoi je ne l'envoye pas par la *poste* à cause des fraix.' Rousseau to Marc-Michel Rey, 18 February 1761, *CC*, vol.8, p.128 (1300).
49. Rousseau to Paul Claude Moultou, 18 January 1762, *CC*, vol.10, p.41 (1641).
50. Rousseau to Leonhard Usteri, 11 April 1763, *CC*, vol.16, p.51 (2610).
51. Rousseau to Pierre Guy de la Roche and Henri Laliaud, 15 November 1766, *CC*, vol.16, p.158 (5549). Voltaire had quite a different idea of the value of French verse: 'On m'a

If I cost you seven francs for the postage of proofs you returned the favor, for this packet cost me fifteen. Fifteen francs of postage for French verse is a great deal. From now on when you wish to give me presents at this price, let it not be verse, I pray you [...] I have not heard anything about the botany book, yet it would give me more pleasure than French verse, provided it did not come by post.

Back in France a year later, Rousseau sharply rebukes his Genevan friend d'Ivernois for imposing upon him the monetary and psychic cost of receiving yet another work by Voltaire, a mistake for which he has compensated by treating himself to the pleasure of tossing the book into the fire:

Quoique je fusse accoutumé, mon bon ami, à recevoir de vous des pacquets fréquens et couteux, j'ai été vivement allarmé à la vue du dernier, taxé et payé six livres quatre sols de port. J'ai cru d'abord qu'il S'agissoit de quelque nouveau trouble dans votre Ville dont vous m'envoyiez à la hâte l'important et cruel détail, mais à peine en ai-je parcouru cinq ou six lignes que je me suis tranquillisé voyant de quoi il S'agissoit, et de peur d'être tenté d'en lire davantage je me suis pressé de jetter mes six Livres quatre sols au feu, Surpris je l'avoue, que mon ami Monsieur d'Ivernois m'envoyât de pareils paquets de si loin par la poste, et bien plus Surpris encore qu'il m'osât conseiller d'y répondre. Mes conseils, mon bon ami, me paroissent meilleurs que les votres, et ne méritoient assurément pas un pareil retour de votre part.[52]

Although I was accustomed, my dear friend, to receiving frequent and costly packets from you, I was seriously alarmed by the sight of the most recent one, which cost six *livres* four *sols* for postage. At first I thought it was about some new disturbance in your city that you hastened to report to me in great and cruel detail, but I had skimmed barely five or six lines when I was relieved to see what it was about, and for fear of being tempted to read any more I hastened to throw my six *livres* four *sols* into the fire. surprised, I admit, that my friend Mister d'Ivernois should send me such packets from so far away by post, and even more surprised that he should dare advise me to compose a response. My advice, my dear friend, always seems better to me than yours, and assuredly did not deserve this kind of repayment.

False address

Rousseau went to such great lengths to provoke the most powerful persons in Europe with the expression of his radical opinions in matters of religion and politics that eventually he had even better reasons than Voltaire to worry about the interception and suppression of his writings, whether they were meant for publication or not. For this reason, he took various precautions in the hope of keeping his letters and packages safe from censorship and suppression. It was not until late 1759, when his

envoyé par la poste cette tragédie d'Edouard de Gresset, et il m'en a coûté une pistole de port que je regreterois baucoup s'il n'y avoit pas quelques baux vers dans la pièce.' Voltaire to Bonaventure Moussinot, 26 March 1740, D2189.

52. Rousseau to François Henri d'Ivernois, 26 April 1768, *CC*, vol.35, p.264 (6337).

publisher Rey was preparing to send him proofs of *La Nouvelle Héloïse* that Rousseau began fearing for the interception or suppression of his correspondence. In a letter dated 15 December 1759 he gives Rey detailed instructions on how to send him the proofs without alerting the authorities:

> 1. Faire tous vos pacquets petits et chacun d'une feuille seulement, ou de deux tout au plus.
> 2. Enveloper le pacquet d'un simple fil cacheté ou de deux bandes de papier, sans que mon nom y paroisse, puis plier le tout dans une seule envelope à l'adresse indiquée. Le pacquet me parviendra quoique mon nom n'y soit pas: cela est convenu d'avance.
> 3. Si vous joignez un billet au pacquet, faites en sorte que ce billet ne contienne rien d'où l'on puisse inférer que le pacquet n'est pas pour la personne à laquelle il est addressé. Quand vous serez obligé d'ecrire quelque particularité qui me désigne, écrivez à part et directement à mon addresse.
> 4. Servez vous alternativement des deux adresses et n'employez pas la même deux fois de suite. Il seroit même à desirer que le cachet ne fut pas le même, ni l'écriture de la même main.
>
> Voilà, mon cher Rey, bien des soins pour un home aussi vif que vous. Si vous n'en oubliez que le quart, je n'aurai pas trop à me plaindre.[53]

> 1. Make all your packets small and each one of one, or at most two, sheets.
> 2. Wrap the packet in a simple sealed thread or in one or two strips of paper; without showing my name, then send it all in a single envelope to the address indicated. The packet will reach me even though my name does not appear: that has already been arranged.
> 3. If you put a note in the packet, make sure that the note contains nothing that would justify the inference that the packet is not for the person to whom it is addressed. When you are obliged to write some detail concerning me, write separately and directly to my address.
> 4. Use the two addresses alternately and do not use the same one twice in a row. It would even be desirable to use a different seal and writing by a different hand.
>
> My dear Rey, these are a great many worries for a man as quick-tempered as you. If you only forget a quarter of them, I shall not have much subject for complaint.

Before that time the only semblance of a precaution he took was in a letter to Mme de Francueil dated 20 April 1751. It was written in what Leigh calls a charmingly simple code, in order to disguise the confession that he had indeed abandoned all five of his children by Thérèse Levasseur at the Foundling Hospital (*Hôpital des Enfants-trouvés*).[54] But starting in early 1762, he repeatedly mentions the fact that his letters are being opened, deliberately delayed or even preventing from reaching

53. Rousseau to Marc-Michel Rey, 15 December 1759, *CC*, vol.6, p.234-36 (908).

54. A = 1, B = 2, etc. Leigh's textual note *a*. Rousseau to Suzanne Dupin de Francueil, 20 April 1751, *CC*, vol.2, p.144 (157).

their destination; he advises his correspondents to avoid sending confidential information by post; and he urges them to address his letters to a pseudonym ('Renou' or 'Mme Renou') or a third party, not to include his name in the address, etc.[55] Several years later, during his stay in England, when he discovered that his incoming and outgoing letters were being opened somewhere between Wootton and London, Rousseau formulated increasingly complex but equally fruitless plans for using codes to foil the post. At the time, he was preparing a draft of his *Confessions* and horribly afraid that before he died the preparatory materials would fall into the hands of his enemies. On 8 January 1767, after chiding Du Peyrou for misremembering the contents of the letter in which he broke off relations with Hume, Rousseau announced his intention of sending him a code for use in their future correspondence. To discourage his enemies from opening the letter containing the key, it would have a tamper-evident seal, in the form of an 'Arabesque talisman'.[56] Unfortunately for Rousseau, the precaution proved futile: the letter arrived with no special seal, having clearly been opened – just as he had guessed it would be – and sloppily resealed.[57] Whether the persons intercepting Rousseau's mail did not care to hide the fact or were simply incompetent, the code had been compromised. In England, where he did not speak the language, Rousseau was now feeling increasingly isolated and alarmed. Because he had received no mail from his friend and patron Lord Keith in Potsdam since November of the previous year, he imagined that Keith had somehow been turned against him by Hume; Davenport, who was a friend of Hume, continued to do favors for Rousseau, but when he responded with English restraint to the latter's outpourings of sentiment (his *épanchements*), Rousseau found him suspiciously remote. Finally, Du Peyrou had suggested that, in case of

55. These themes appear in, among other letters: Rousseau to Nicolas Bonaventure Duchêne, 17 May 1762, *CC*, vol.10, p.245-46 (1775); Rousseau to Paul Claude Moultou, 9 September 1762, *CC*, vol.13, p.291 (2144); Rousseau to Marc-Michel Rey, 19 February 1762, *CC*, vol.15, p.203 (2492); Rousseau to Jean-Baptiste Junet, 20 February 1763, *CC*, vol.15, p.216 (2500); Rousseau to Marie-Madeleine de Brémond d'Ars, marquise de Verdelin, 30 April 1763, *CC*, vol.16, p,128 (2663). In 1764 Rousseau sends a correspondent a manuscript of the *Lettres de la montagne* in short installments, rather than all at once, in order to reduce the chance of the entire work's being lost. Rousseau to captain Hyacinthe-Antoine d'Astier de Commessière, 22 April 1764, *CC*, vol.19, p.316 (3232).

56. Rousseau to Pierre-Alexandre Du Peyrou, 8 January 1767, *CC*, vol.32. p.28-30, 32-34 (5667, 5667bis). For Rousseau's letter to Hume, see David Hume, *The Letters of David Hume*, ed. J. Y. T. Greig (Oxford, 1932), vol.2, p.385-401.

57. In a letter to Du Peyrou dated 2 March 1767 (*CC*, vol.32, p.199 (5762)), Rousseau expresses his suspicion that the letter containing the code (28 February 1767, *CC*, vol.32, p.188 (5753): this letter has been lost) would not reach its receiver intact. Du Peyrou soon confirms that suspicion. Pierre-Alexandre Du Peyrou to Rousseau, 16 March 1767, *CC*, vol.32, p.220 (5778).

need, he might address himself to Jean-François Maximilien de Cerjat, a Swiss aristocrat living in Lincolnshire. Rousseau posted the appeal but received no response, probably because his letter was misdirected; but for him this meant that his enemies had completely succeeded in cutting him off from the world.[58]

In the mistaken belief that Rousseau's correspondence was being intercepted in Paris rather than London, Du Peyrou then asked relatives in Amsterdam to forward his next letter to Rousseau in England. Unfortunately for Rousseau, either because the postal gods were intent on persecuting Rousseau or (more probably) because the letter bore an incorrect address, the message was initially delivered in London to his cousin Jean Rousseau, whom Jean-Jacques considered as Hume's henchman ('l'âme dannée du bon David'). When the letter finally arrived in Wootton, he fell into deep despair; for he had no doubt that the letter had been opened. As he told Du Peyrou, 'Your letter has certainly been opened'. Far from the presence of his French-speaking friends and at the mercy of people he did not trust, he now believed that even private messengers were no more reliable than the post. In the opening words of the posthumous *Reveries*, Rousseau would proclaim that he was 'alone on earth'. In this response to Du Peyrou, he declares that he is 'de tous côtés sous le piège' (surrounded by snares on all sides), completely alone in a hostile universe and powerless to extricate himself from entanglement in a web of treacherous letters. Since the people intercepting his mail are keeping all possible interlocutors at an inaccessible distance, how can he possibly address himself to Cerjat? He might as well be trying to write to a man on the moon:

> Mon cher Hote, je suis de tous côtés sous le piege... Les gens qui portent et rapportent mes lettres, ceux de la poste, tout m'est egalement suspect, je suis dans les mains de tout le monde sans qu'il me soit possible de faire un seul mouvement pour me dégager. Vous me faites rire par le sang-froid avec lequel vous me marquez, *addressez-vous à celui-ci, ou à celui-là*; c'est comme si vous me disiez adressez-vous à un habitant de la lune. S'adresser est un mot bientôt dit, mais il faut savoir comment. Il n'y a que la face d'un ami qui puisse me tirer d'affaire, toutes les lettres ne font que me trahir et m'embourber. Celles que je reçois et que j'écris sont toutes vues par mes ennemis, ce n'est pas le moyen de me tirer de leur main.[59]

58. Rousseau to Jean-François-Maximilien Cerjat, 18 January 1767, *CC*, vol.32, p.32 (5679, 5679bis); Rousseau to Pierre-Alexandre Du Peyrou, 14 February 1767, *CC*, vol.32, p.140 (5727). In a letter to Bernard Granville (who lived at Calwich Abbey, near Wootton), Rousseau already expresses doubts about whether the letter to Cerjat has been properly routed. Rousseau to Bernard Granville, 16 January 1767, *CC*, vol.32, p.49-50 (5676)

59. Rousseau to Pierre-Alexandre Du Peyrou, 2 April 1767, *CC*, vol.33, p.4-5 (5809). Original emphasis.

> My dear Host, I am surrounded by snares on all sides... The people from who carry my letters back and forth, the people at the post, everything is equally suspicious to me, and I am in everyone's hands without being able to make a single move to free myself. You make me laugh when you coolly tell me, *address yourself to this man or that*; it is as if you told me address yourself to an inhabitant of the moon. To address oneself is an expression that is easily said, but one has to know how. Only a friendly face can deliver me, all letters only betray me and bog me down. Those I receive and those I write are seen by my enemies, this is not the way to get me out of their grasp.

More than ever, Rousseau's epistolary dilemma had become one of *address*. A mistaken address had doubtless kept Rousseau's letter to Cerjat from reaching its destination and had also caused Du Peyrou's letter to Jean-Jacques to be delivered to Jean Rousseau in London. Now it was the very possibility of address, of *addressing oneself*, or perhaps of *addressing one's self* that had been called into question. 'To address oneself is... easily said, but the thing is to know how.' How can he address himself, he wonders, if there is no one left to address? Indeed if it is true, as Bakhtin has argued, that the nature and very existence of the self depends upon a relationship with another, when Rousseau has no one left to address, he will no longer even *have* a self to address with.[60] Symptoms of persecution delirium are beginning to appear, as he apprehends the moment when his enemies will not only have discredited him, but consigned him to non-existence, when they will finally have completely effaced him. In marked contrast with Voltaire, for whom the post makes 'the absent become... present', Rousseau will not settle for epistolary space, which James How has called 'a space in which it was possible for *something approximating a face-to-face exchange* to take place'.[61] He will accept no approximation of the actual presence of a friendly face. '[T]he post betrays me and cannot possibly serve me. In my position only the sight of a man can be useful to me. Presence or nothing.'[62] In this predicament only a friend's face can deliver him from his enemies and unto himself.

All the same, Rousseau clearly had not given up all hope of deliverance, since in the same letter he explained to Cerjat that, on the remote chance that he had succeeded in establishing a secure communication channel with Cerjat, he has drafted a second code. The instructions for its use are complicated, to say the least:

> Si le ciel veut que ma précédente lettre à M. de C. *Cerjat* ait échappé à mes gardes, qu'il l'ait receue, et qu'il envoye l'exprès, nous sommes forts; car j'ai

60. See Tzvetan Todorov, *Mikhaïl Bakhtine: le principe dialogique* (Paris, 1981), p.145ff.
61. How, *Epistolary spaces*, p.7. Emphasis added. See Chapter 6, p.174-76. and my review of this book at http://www.cla.csulb.edu/ebro/epistolary-spaces-english-letter-writing-from-the-foundation-of-the-post-office-to-richardsons-clarissa (last accessed on 3 October 2015).
62. Rousseau to Pierre-Alexandre Du Peyrou, 4 April 1767, *CC*, vol.33, p.32 (5811). For a nuanced discussion of the metaphor of familiar letter-writing as face-to-face conversation, see Brant, *Empire of letters*, p.21.

mon second chiffre tout prêt, je le ferai partir avec cette lettre-ci, et j'espére qu'il ne tombera plus dans les mains de M. Colombiés, ni de mon cher Cousin. S'il m'arrive de me servir du prémier ce sera pour donner le change, n'ajoûtez aucune foi à ce que je vous marquerai de cette maniére, à moins que vous ne lisiez en tête ce mot écrit de ma main, *vrai*.[63]

If heaven has wished my previous letter to M. de C. *Cerjat* to escape my guards, for him to receive it and send it by messenger, our position is strong; for my second cipher is all ready, I will send it with this letter, and I hope that it will not fall into the hands of M. Colombiés Jean Rousseau's employer or my dear cousin. If it should use the first cipher, it will be to allay suspicion, do not believe anything I write to you this way, unless you read at the top this word in my hand, *true*.

Du Peyrou never mentions having received this letter, but he does acknowledge receipt of a nearly identical one, written on 4 April, which arrived two weeks later with no sign of having been opened. On the other hand, in his response Du Peyrou says nothing about having received a code, which leaves open the questions of whether the letter was opened, whether the code had been removed, and whether it ever contained one.[64] Whatever the case may have been, Rousseau tacitly acknowledged the futility of trying to send the key to a code by post, for there are no indications that he ever used either of the codes that were meant for Du Peyrou; nor is there any further reference to codes in his correspondence. Nevertheless for several more weeks Rousseau remained in the throes of delusions of persecution by the agents of the post. In an apparent attempt to reach what he imagined as the safety of Cerjac's home in Lincolnshire, he fled Wootton and somehow ended up one hundred miles to the east in a town called Spalding. Yet although (or perhaps because) Rousseau was obsessed with the notion that it was his fate to be persecuted by the post, he aggravated his 'captivity' by taking lodgings at Spalding with the postmaster himself! Whereupon he appealed to Richard Davenport to let him return to the lesser captivity of Wootton:

Vous devez être offensé, Monsieur; mais vous avez assés d'entrailles pour cesser de l'être quand vous songerez à mon sort. Je préférois la liberté au séjour de votre maison; ce sentiment est bien excusable. Mais je préfère infiniment le séjour de votre maison à toute autre captivité et je préférerois toute autre captivité à celle où je suis, qui est horrible, et qui, quoiqu'il arrive, ne sauroit durer. Si vous voulez bien, Monsieur, me recevoir derechef chez vous, je suis prêt à m'y rendre au cas qu'on m'en laisse la liberté; et quand j'y serois, aprés l'expérience que j'ai faite, difficilement serois-je tenté d'en ressortir pour chercher de nouveaux malheurs. Si ma proposition vous

63. Rousseau to Jean-François-Maximilien Cerjat, 18 January 1767, *CC*, vol.32, p.52-53 (5679, 5679bis).

64. Du Peyrou acknowledges receipt of Rousseau's letter of 4 April 1767 in Pierre-Alexandre Du Peyrou to Rousseau, 26 April 1767, *CC*. vol.33, p.31 (5834).

agrée, tâchez, Monsieur, de me le faire savoir par quelque voye sure, et de faciliter mon retour d'ici chez vous. Si vous ne faites que m'écrire par la poste, vôtre lettre me parviendra d'autant moins que je suis logé chez le maître de poste.[65]

You must be offended, Sir; but you have enough heart to cease being so when you consider my fate. I preferred liberty to dwelling in your house; this sentiment is quite excusable. But I infinitely prefer dwelling in your house to any other form of captivity and I should prefer any other form to the horrible captivity I presently suffer and which, whatever happens, cannot last. If you are willing, Sir, to receive me once again at your home, I am ready to go there if I am allowed to do so; and if I were there, after the experience I have had I would not easily be tempted to leave again to seek new misfortunes. If my proposal suits you, Sir, please try to let me know by some reliable means and to facilitate my return from here to your home. If you must write to me by post, my letter will have even less chance of reaching me as I am staying in the postmaster's house.

Davenport responded by urging Rousseau to leave Spalding ('I have always understood it to be one of the most Cursed disagreeable places in England') and return to Wootton as soon as possible, but by then Rousseau had already made his way to Dover, and from there back to France.

Rousseau would continue to portray himself as an innocent victim of persecution by agents of the post. The surveillance and interception of his correspondence, combined with his distrust of the post and, more generally, of the distance inherent to all forms of communication ('Presence or nothing') – even 'live' communication – made it impossible for him to believe in what Kafka (who shared his distrust of telecommunication in all forms) would call 'the easy possibility of letter writing'. *Vox clamantis*, all Rousseau could do was issue dispatches from the solitude to which his temperament and his actions condemned him: '[I]ls auront beau faire. Je me ris des machines qu'ils entassent sans cesse autour de moi. Elles S'écrouleront par leur propre masse, et le cri de la vérité percera le Ciel tôt ou tard.'[66] ([I]n vain will they try. I laugh at the machines they pile up around me. These will collapse under their own weight, and the cry of truth will sooner or later break through to Heaven.)

65. Rousseau to Richard Davenport, 11 May 1767, *CC*, vol.33, p.54 (5851).

66. Rousseau to Charles Henry Jules de Clermont-Tonnerre, comte de Clermont-Tonnerre, 18 September 1768, *CC*, vol.36, p.106 (6434).

6. A postal world

> [The early modern postal system] was the most advanced communications system ever to have existed. Within a few years of being established, it had begun to influence people's perceptions of space and time, religion and politics.
>
> Wolfgang Behringer[1]

Whether written on papyrus and delivered by messenger or composed on electronic screens and delivered by electrical pulses, the post has always been a product of social relations and material circumstances, just as it has always played a role in the production of those relations and circumstances. The institution of publicly available postal systems transformed the early modern world in many ways: from its sounds and sights, to the 'cultural capital' of its inhabitants and the representation, perception, and control of time and space. In this chapter I shall explore the nature of these complex and far-reaching changes.

Sounds

Starting in the Renaissance, the sound of the post horn became a ubiquitous part of the sonic environment all over Europe. In the words of Wolfgang Behringer, 'By day and by night, the resounding sound of the post horn became the embodiment of speed, the symbol of an entire epoch'.[2] It has been argued that the instrument was first introduced by members of the Butcher post, who blew their horn to announce their arrival to those who had cattle to sell.[3] Whatever the precise origins of the post horn may be, by the fifteenth-century messengers working for the king of Castile had exclusive right to use it, and it was not long before Franz von Taxis had seen to it that the postilions (guards) of the Taxis post, and sometimes the couriers themselves, would herald their coming

1. Behringer, 'Communications revolutions', p.369.
2. Behringer, *Thurn und Taxis*, p.364. As its title suggests, the relationship between commercial imperatives and the speed of postal communications is a major theme of the same author's *Im Zeichen des Merkur*.
3. Zilliacus, *Pillar to post*, p.41; Hiller, *Das große Buch vom Posthorn*, p.10; Roberto Bacheri, 'Il corno di posta: da mezzo di segnalizazione a strumento sinfonico' [catalogue of exhibition at the Institute for the Study of Postal History in Prato], *Quaderni di storia postale* 12 (March 1989). The main source for information on the history and sounds of the post horn is Karl Thieme, 'Zur Geschichte des Posthorns', in *Posthornschule und Posthorn-Taschenliederbuch* (Leipzig, 1908).

with a blast of the post horn.[4] In short order nearly every postal system in Europe would make use of the instrument.[5] For centuries the Taxis Post, Butcher post and other mounted messenger services vied for exclusive use of the post horn over the territories they covered, until the early eighteenth century, when the Emperor granted the Taxis a monopoly over use of the instrument. All other travelers were required to yield the right of way to Taxis couriers; at night cities had to open their gates to Taxis couriers and the latter were exempt from toll fees. In order that the changing stations might receive advance warning, post horn signals were coded to indicate not only the type of mail (express, normal, local, packages), but also arrival, departure and distress, and the number of carriages and horses.[6]

From a rather short natural instrument capable of playing only a fundamental tone and its octave, the post horn gradually became a more flexible, longer and eventually chromatic instrument, which played a significant role in literature and music.[7] The post horn is heard on two occasions in Part II (1615) of *Don Quixote*. In the episode where Quixote and Sancho Panza learn a way of breaking the spell that has supposedly been cast upon Dulcinea, they encounter a demonic postilion who twice produces a 'hoarse and terrifying sound' on a 'huge hollow horn that served him as a bugle'. Later, when Sancho is in his governorship, a *corneta de posta* sounds to announce to him that a letter has arrived from his patron, the Duke.[8]

One can also hear echoes of the post in classical music, notably in

4. Kalmus, *Weltgeschichte der Post*, p.50; Schafer, *The Soundscape*, p.47. In a personal communication, Dr Ernst Popp told Schafer that in Austria post horns were also heard until after the First World War and that even in the late 1970s no one was permitted to carry or sound a post horn, 'thereby enhancing the sentimental symbolism of the instrument' (Article 24 of the Austrian Postal Regulations, 1957)'. *The Soundscape*, p.47. Behringer notes the presence of the post horn during the early modern period in *Im Zeichen des Merkur*, p.60, 63, 93, 111, 123ff, 134, 138, 619.
5. According to Hiller (*Das große Buch vom Posthorn*, p.47), whose source is presumably Karl Thieme, post horns were occasionally used in France in the first half of the nineteenth century. He also mentions that in the Paris Conservatory there is a post horn, dated 1820, made by Courtois *frères*. In Elizabethan England, post riders were required to sound the post horn whenever they met company, within towns, and 'at least thrice every mile'. *Reports of the Royal Commission on Historical Manuscripts*, cited in Robinson, *The British Post Office*, p.15.
6. Zilliacus, *Pillar to post*, p.52; Hiller, *Das große Buch vom Posthorn*, p.13. That code was not uniform throughout Europe.
7. Early post horns were about 50-70 cm long, whereas the tube of a natural baroque trumpet was about 230 cm long. Hiller, *Das große Buch vom Posthorn*, p.14. Hiller provides numerous examples of post horn signals and melodies. Zilliacus (*Pillar to post*, p.94) also reproduces several examples of postal horn signals.
8. Miguel de Cervantes, *Don Quixote* (New York, 1949), part 2, ch.34, p.738-39; ch.47, p.810. I would like to thank my colleague James Maraniss for the second reference.

Mozart's *Posthorn serenade* (K320) and Mahler's *Third Symphony*. In addition, eight composers, the most famous of whom is Franz Schubert, have set to music the text of Wilhelm Müller's poem 'Von der Straße her ein Posthorn klingt' (From the street below a post horn sounds).[9] In Schubert's setting, the song (now entitled 'Die Post') opens the second half of the late (1827) 24-song cycle *Winterreise* (*Winter journey*).[10] Like *Die schöne Müllerin*, Schubert's other great song cycle, *Winterreise* is a long dramatic monologue that recounts the sufferings caused by a young man's unrequited love. Both the song's original key of E-flat major (for tenor) and the alternate key of C major (for baritone) are traditional post horn keys. (Two other well-known imitations of postal sounds can be heard at the beginning and the end of Beethoven's Piano Sonata op.81a, *Les Adieux* [1809], which is also in E-flat major.) In the first two measures of the piano introduction, eighth-note arpeggios played by the left hand in moderately fast (*etwas geschwind*) 6/8 time capture the steady clip of the post horse's hooves, while in the next two measures broken arpeggios and dotted figures in the right hand mimic the post horn signal for the arrival of a courier. Schubert's music imitates the sounds of the post horn, the horses' hoofs, as well as the rapid beating of the lover's heart: both an external reality that anyone can hear and an internal reality of which only the unrequited lover is aware. In E-flat major, the sprightly tones of the introduction, first and third stanzas suggest a perfect coincidence between the spirited sounds that the lover hears and the elation that he feels at the arrival of the post:

> [1]
> Von der Strasse her ein Posthorn klingt.
> Was hat es, dass es so hoch aufspringt,
> Mein Herz?
>
> From the street below a posthorn sounds.
> Why is it that it leaps so high,
> My heart?

However it quickly becomes clear that this happy coincidence is only apparent. For even though the young man cannot keep his heart from leaping with anticipation of a letter from his beloved, he knows that the letter is not coming and never will. This painful reality makes itself felt at the beginning of the second and fourth stanzas, when the song conveys the lover's deep sorrow by passing briefly into the minor mode, a

9. Hiller, *Das große Buch vom Posthorn*, p.75.

10. In the full text of Müller's *Winterreise*, this poem is the sixth (rather than the thirteenth) in the 24-poem sequence. On the possible meaning of the ordering of these poems see Richard Kramer's *Distant cycles: Schubert and the conceiving of song* (Chicago, IL, 1994), p.172-73.

contrast that Schubert beautifully exploits throughout the song cycle. Here the alternation between major (stanzas 1 and 3) and minor (stanzas 2 and 4) modes expresses the young man's helpless shifts from hope to despair:

> [2]
> Die Post bringt keinen Brief für dich.
> Was drängst du denn so wunderlich,
> Mein Herz?
> [3]
> Nun ja, die Post kommt aus der Stadt
> Wo ich ein liebes Liebchen hatt,
> Mein Herz!
> [4]
> Willst wohl einmal hinübersehn
> Und fragen, wie es dort mag geh'n,
> Mein Herz?
> (Wilhelm Müller [1794-1827])
>
> The Post brings no letter for you.
> So why do you pound so marvelously,
> My heart?
>
> Ah yes, the post comes from the town
> Where I once had a dear love,
> My heart!
>
> Perhaps you'd like to take a look there
> And ask how things are going there,
> My heart?

As Charles Rosen remarked in *The Romantic generation*, 'It was Schubert's genius to find a way to represent both past and present in a single motif'.[11] In this song the sounds of the post horn and the post horses' hoofs ultimately represent the sounds of daily life, moving forward on schedule, indifferent to the melancholy in which the young man's heart remains sunk.

In France the sonic environment was enhanced by the crack of a whip, rather than the sound of a post horn. French postilions used the whip not only to spur on the horses, but – as with the post horn in the Hapsburg territories and Britain – to announce their arrival and send other coded messages, such as the fact that they would be needing the services of the local blacksmith.[12] In Paris, the urban soundscape was also modified in 1760 by the successful introduction of the *petite poste*: its nearly 200 carriers went about the city in their blue uniforms, shaking a clapper to

11. Charles Rosen, *The Romantic generation* (Cambridge, MA, 1995), p.123. Kramer discusses Schubert's use of harmony to evoke distance in 'Die Post' in *Distant cycles*, p.173-75.
12. Marchand, *Le Maître de poste*, p.264.

announce their arrival.[13] The post filled English towns with the sounds of both the post horn and bells, which from 1702 to 1846 announced the arrival of letter collectors.[14]

'Letteracy' as cultural capital

Eve Tavor Bannet has coined the term 'letteracy' to describe 'the collection of different skills, values, and kinds of knowledge beyond mere literacy that were involved in achieving competency in the writing, reading and interpreting of letters'.[15] Although she does not refer to Pierre Bourdieu, I would like to suggest that what Bannet terms 'letteracy' is a form of what he calls 'embodied cultural capital'. The concept of cultural capital refers to the non-financial assets (competencies, skills, qualifications) that enable people to mobilize cultural authority and promote their social mobility. Embodied cultural capital consists of one's consciously acquired properties, in addition to the properties one has acquired through socialization, culture and traditions; it is a means of communication and self-presentation acquired from one's surrounding culture.[16] Wolfgang Behringer has argued that the early modern post was part of a communications revolution that was 'the motor that enabled the construction of the infrastructure of the modern world'.[17] Each of these communications revolutions has demanded the acquisition of a new kind of embodied cultural capital.[18] In the rest of this chapter I contend that the post also fashioned new dispositions toward space and time, some of which would be augmented by later forms of information technology.

13. *Le Maître de poste*, p.115. As mentioned in Chapter 1, p.42, in the previous century Renouard de Villayer had attempted to establish a *petite poste* in Paris, but without success.
14. The practice was initiated by an entrepreneur named Charles Povey, in connection with his attempt to set up a 'Halfpenny Carriage' (town post) in 1709. Although a lawsuit brought by the Post Office quickly put an end to this venture, 'the Post Office adopted his use of bell ringers for collecting letters'. Robinson, *The British Post Office*, p.87-88. This practice was further extended in the early nineteenth century, until it was discontinued in 1846. *The British Post Office*, p.205, 333.
15. *Empire of letters*, p.xvii. She adds: 'Under letteracy, I include associated cultural information, such as common conceptions of letter-writing, awareness of current epistolary practices, basic knowledge about where letter-writing was taught and about how it was taught or to be learned, even how to "read" and use a letter manual.'
16. Cultural capital is one of the three forms of capital (economic, social, cultural) that Bourdieu identifies in 'The forms of capital', in John G. Richardson (ed.), *Handbook of theory and research for the sociology of education* (New York, 1986), p.241-58. He distinguishes among three types of cultural capital: embodied, objectified and institutionalized.
17. 'Communications revolutions', p.374.
18. Michael Emmison and John Frow first proposed to think about 'Information technology as cultural capital', *Australian universities review* 1 (1998), p.41-45.

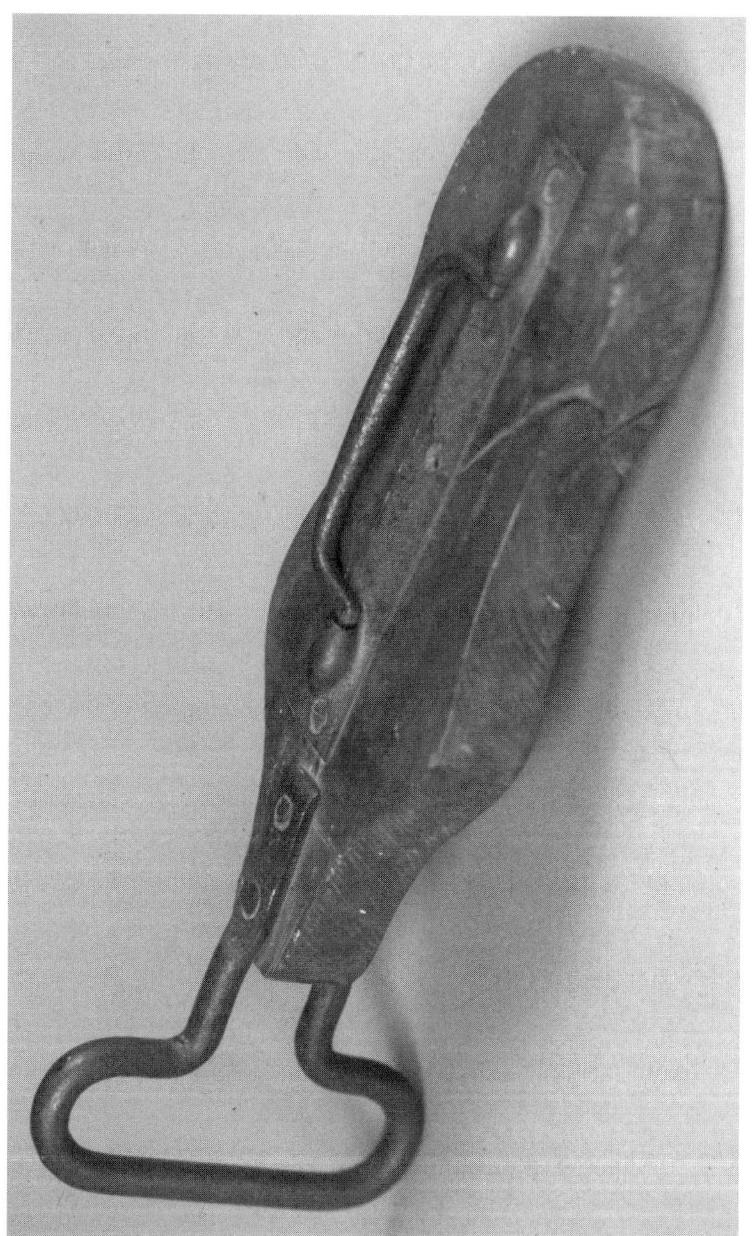

Figure 8: *Claquoir de facteur* XVIIIe / A clapper announced the arrival of *petite poste* mail carriers.

Space

> [S]ocial relationships themselves, the nature of space and of political relations... are transformed by the viscosity or the speed of correspondence.[19]

Changes in the perception of space had already begun in the Renaissance, with such sociocultural developments as the discovery of perspective in art.[20] The institution of publicly available postal services and improvement in the quality of roads made places (such as central France or Wales) that had seemed distant appear closer, and it also created new representational spaces.[21] In the early seventeenth century maps began to appear – first in France and later in the rest of Europe – that showed European cities linked by postal routes rather than roads.[22] These representational spaces were 'part of a wider movement to assert human control over space and time'.[23] Once the expectation of postal 'connectedness' had been established, it would become a token of civilization for Europeans traveling in 'barbarous' regions of the world. Consider the testimony of a certain Mr Du Mont, who in 1699 lamented the absence of postal (and other civic) services in Turkey:

> There are no regular postal services, neither for travelers nor for letters. If you wish to write to some fairly distant place – which is neither Constantinople, Alep nor Cairo – you must wait for the opportunity: sometimes a year, and even from Smyrna to Constantinople, we have only Arabs who go on foot and who often do not leave for more than a month. From this you can imagine how many places there are where news takes a year to arrive.[24]

As Dena Goodman has pointed out, epistolary networks occupied an ambiguous space that overlapped the ill-defined boundaries of the public and private spheres.[25] The role of postal services in defining a

19. Daniel Roche, 'Avant-propos' to Pierre-Yves Beaurepaire (ed.), *La Plume et la toile: pouvoirs et réseaux de correspondance dans l'Europe des Lumières* (Artois, 2002), p.8. My own translation.
20. In 'Communications revolutions', 366-67, Behringer considers some of the explanations that have been proposed for this change.
21. Dohrn-van Rossum, *History of the hour*, p.344.
22. Behringer cites the *Carte géographique des postes qui traversent la France* (Paris, 1632, Melchior Tavernier) of Nicholas Sanson d'Abbéville as the earliest example of this sort of map. 'Communications revolutions', p.360.
23. Whyman, *The Pen and the people*, p.47.
24. *Voyages de Mr Du Mont en France, en Italie, en Allemagne, à Malthe, et en Turquie* (The Hague, Etienne Foulque and François Honoré, 1699), p.113. My own translation.
25. 'Between the immediacy of conversation and the publicity of print, lay the epistolary networks that embody the ambiguity of a public sphere made up of private persons. [...] [L]etters and correspondences crossed the ill-defined boundaries between private and public spheres in the eighteenth century and thereby raised fundamental questions about

space that was neither entirely public nor completely private has also been described by James How in *Epistolary spaces*, a study of English letter-writing between the founding of the Post Office and the publication of Richardson's *Clarissa*. How compares the opening of postal spaces in the early modern period to the opening of new and seemingly unlimited cyberspaces in our own era. 'Unlike private messenger services', he remarks, 'the national Post Office provided regular, permanent and "public" spaces within which supposedly "private" writings travel.' Correspondents could therefore imagine themselves connected to each other on a permanent basis, although not without the permanent and justifiable apprehension that their letters might be intercepted by agents of the state.[26] The notion of 'epistolary spaces' is based on an analogy with Henri Lefebvre's idea of 'social space'.[27] In opposition to what he saw as the idealist excesses of so-called structuralist thought, Lefebvre insisted that social space is 'real space', the space of 'social practice', which he distinguishes from ideal (mental) space.[28] James How defines epistolary spaces as institutionalized 'spaces of connection, providing permanent and seemingly unbreakable links between people and places'. Yet he recognizes that epistolary spaces exist not only in physical and social ('real') space, but in the imagination, too.[29]

On a methodological level, it is important to distinguish between these two kinds of epistolary spaces: those that are representations (Lefebvre's 'representational spaces')[30] and those that are physical (infrastructure, persons) and social. One cannot physically inhabit representations of epistolary space (although they can inhabit us), but one can inhabit or regulate such epistolary 'spaces of connection' as post offices, postal vehicles and postal routes. During the early modern period, the 'Republic of Letters' was another such epistolary space: infinite, eternal and universal in the imagination of its members, but in reality European,

---

relationships between individuals, and between the individual and the state.' Goodman, 'Epistolary property', p.340.

26. How, *Epistolary spaces*, p.1, 5.
27. Lefebvre, *The Production of space* (Oxford, 1991 [1st French edn, 1974]). Lefebvre's book is part of his extended polemic with the 'structuralist' and 'post-structuralist' thinkers who dominated the French intellectual scene in the 1960s and 1970s.
28. Lefebvre, *The Production of space*, p.14.
29. '[E]pistolary spaces are "public" spaces within which supposedly "private" writings travel – at once imaginary and real: imaginary, because you can't really inhabit them as you can other social spaces – all meetings and incidents there are only metaphorical: real, because they were policed by a government ever more keen to monitor the letters that passed along the national postal routes.' How, *Epistolary spaces*, p.5.
30. Representational spaces are: 'space as directly *lived* through its associated images and symbols,' Lefebvre, *The Production of Space*, p.39ff.

mutable and highly particularized.[31] Keeping these two spaces separate for methodological purposes does not prevent one from observing that in practice they interact and interfere with each other in many ways. For example, until the advent of electronic mail, the letter itself contained the most significant physical traces (handwriting, ink, drawings, smudges, tears, scents and so on) of human presence in 'epistolary space', every one of which affected the way that these spaces were imagined.[32] Likewise the fact that one's 'private' writings were, could be or were even meant to be read by a third party, irrevocably transformed the representation of epistolary space.

Before the advent of postal arrangements accessible to the public in England, France and the Hapsburg Empire, one could picture a letter as a way of making a temporary connection between two isolated points, but state-sponsored postal services made it possible to imagine that by sending a letter one was entering a preexisting network.[33] Due to the rapid growth of London in the seventeenth and eighteenth centuries, the city became the center of that network in England and a particular object of fascination; it was 'a vortex at the heart of epistolary space to which all letters and the thoughts of all their writers and readers gravitated'.[34] In Renaissance France, the center of gravity of the postal system was in the Loire Valley, before moving to Lyon in the middle of the seventeenth century, and in the latter half of the century finally – due to the establishment of the court at Versailles and Louis XIV's annexation of several provinces in the north and east – to Paris.[35] In the eighteenth century Paris became the center, not only of epistolary space, but of a postal, commercial and fashion system, what Goodman calls a 'mediated' community (in contrast to the 'natural' community of village or province).[36] As Behringer and How have remarked, epistolary spaces opened up new avenues and forms of behavior, allowing women and men of lowly social position to act in ways that would previously have been inconceivable.[37] The easy availability of postal connections also meant that letters were no longer primarily devoted to business or

31. Françoise Waquet, 'L'espace de la République des Lettres', in *Commercium litterarium: la communication dans la République des Lettres* (Amsterdam and Maarssen, 1994), p.175-89.
32. See Chapter 2.
33. On the 'network' metaphor, see Roche, 'Avant-propos', in Beaurepaire, *La Plume et la toile*, p.10. On the historical significance of networks and networking, see Behringer, *Im Zeichen des Merkur*, p.672ff.
34. How, *Epistolary spaces*, p.8. However, as Whyman notes, 'The dominance of London as a hub for all mail was broken' by the new system of bye and cross routes that Ralph Allen created from 1720-1764. *The Pen and the people*, p.57.
35. Bretagnolle and Verdier, 'Images d'un réseau en évolution'.
36. Goodman, *Becoming a woman*, p.9.
37. Behringer, 'Communications revolutions', p.362-63; How, *Epistolary spaces*, p.5, 78ff, 144ff.

emergency messages and could begin to resemble conversation. Although conversation is in some ways different from letter-writing, the trope of letter-writing as conversation quickly became commonplace.[38] The post office, as Susan Whyman has argued, played an important role in the rise of the public sphere by creating 'a public space for private conversations of people ranging from paupers to professionals'.[39] Finally, the fact that state-sponsored epistolary space was under continual surveillance also spurred marginalized groups, such as Quakers, Jews and French Protestants, to create secret message delivery systems not unlike the one imagined by Thomas Pynchon in *The Crying of lot 49*.[40] In the course of her investigations of the latter system, Pynchon's heroine Oedipa Maas discovers that it has been underground ever since its defeat by the Thurn and Taxis post in the eighteenth century. I shall discuss the importance of Pynchon's imaginary post at the end of this chapter.

Time 1 (posthaste)

In an age of email and text messaging, letters written on paper and carried by post have become known in contemporary slang as 'snail mail', and 'a postal service minute' means a length of time that is 50 percent longer than it should be (as in 'Place in the microwave for 1 minute 30, or a postal service minute').[41] In contrast, throughout the early modern period, the post was the fastest means of communication and transport.

38. For discussion of the trope of the letter as conversation, see Brant, *Eighteenth-century letters*, p.21-24, and Roger Duchêne, *Comme une lettre à la poste: les progrès de l'écriture personnelle sous Louis XIV* (Paris, 2006), p.195ff. How notes that '[T]he ability to exchange messages frequently and almost casually gave the impression of a space in which it was possible for something approximating a face-to-face exchange to take place.' *Epistolary spaces*, p.7:
39. Whyman, *The Pen and the people*, p.71. As Whyman states here, and as Behringer has argued in 'Communications revolutions' (p.354, 369, 373), it was not just in coffee houses and salons that a critical public sphere (Habermas's *Öffentlichkeit*) was formed. Behringer argues (*pace* Habermas) that long before the eighteenth century 'the public availability of the communication system was the most important precondition for the emergence of a critical public sphere'. *Im Zeichen des Merkur*, p.472.
40. According to James How, Liza Picard (*Restoration London*, p.72) has speculated 'that the Society of Friends must have had an effective and yet secret postal system of its own. She reasons that the Post Office had perfected its techniques for intercepting letters to such a degree that if the Friends had tried to arrange their illegal meetings by means of letters sent by the regular post, then they would surely have been discovered. And yet the meetings went ahead'. How, *Epistolary spaces*, p.57-58. See Pynchon, *The Crying of lot 49*. This tradition still lives in the United States: see Jason Boog, 'Thomas Pynchon's Trystero spreads around the world', *Galley cat* (15 June 2012) http://www.mediabistro.com/galleycat/thomas-pynchon-trystero_b53106 (last accessed 10 August 2015); and 'Pynchon Wiki' http://cl49.pynchonwiki.com/wiki/index.php?title=Main_Page (last accessed 10 August 2015).
41. According to one contributor to the online *Urban dictionary* (http://urbandictionary.com; last accessed 10 August 2015).

As we have already noted, the post horn would become the symbol of an epoch focused on increasing the speed of communications and transportation. In everyday speech, the word 'post' was associated with the greatest possible speed that man could attain.[42] Both the *Oxford English dictionary* and the *Dictionnaire littré* attest sixteenth-century examples of 'in post' or *en poste* in the sense of 'with haste, at full speed', while 'posthaste' and 'post-wise' meant 'great expedition in traveling', 'with all possible haste and expedition'. With typical self-deprecation, Montaigne remarks in the first book of his *Essais* that 'J'escris mes lettres tousjours en poste'[43] (I always write my letters posthaste). In Shakespeare's *Richard II*, the king's servant Bushy informs him that:

> Old John of Gaunt is grievous sick, my lord,
> Suddenly taken, and hath sent *posthaste*
> To entreat your majesty to visit him. (I, iv, 54-56; emphasis added)

In the seventeenth century, Corneille's comedy *La Suite du menteur* (1645), opens with a scene in which we learn that after the mendacious hero had abandoned his fiancée, the young lady married his father, leading to the latter's premature death:

> Voilà donc le bonhomme enfin à sa seconde
> C'est à dire qu'il prend la poste de l'autre monde;
> Un peu moins de deux mois le met dans le cercueil.[44]
>
> The old fool found himself with a lovely young wife
> That is, he took the post for the afterlife
> In barely two months she put him in a coffin

And according to Furetière's 1690 *Dictionnaire universel*:

> POSTE refers to the journey and the diligence shown by the courier, or to the courier himself, and to the packets that come by this means [...] In this sense one says that a bad doctor sends people *by post* to the other world, to say that he makes them die quickly. One also speaks of delivering a message *in post*, to mean promptly, although one does it by foot.[45] (Emphasis added)

Likewise the expression *con la celerità de la stapheta* (as fast as a mounted courier) designated the fastest possible form of conveyance.[46]

The association between the post and rapid conveyance of messages

42. Christophe Studeny, 'L'éveil de la vitesse: la France au galop de la malle-poste', *Revue de la Bibliothèque nationale* 40 (Summer 1991), p.44.
43. Montaigne, *Essais* vol.I, xl, in *Œuvres complètes* (Paris, 1962), p.247; or *Les Essais*, Villey-Saulnier edn (Paris, 1978-), vol.I, p.253.
44. Corneille, *Le Menteur*, I, i, 67-69. In *Théâtre complet* (Paris, 1960), vol.2. My translation.
45. Antoine Furetière, *Dictionnaire universel, contenant généralement tous les mots françois, tant vieux que modernes, & les Termes de toutes les sciences et des arts* (The Hague and Rotterdam, A. and R. Leers, 1690).
46. Behringer, 'Communications revolutions', p.339.

and passengers was forged during the period of economic and demographic changes that Fernand Braudel called the 'long sixteenth century' (1450-1650).[47] Toward the beginning of that period, greater speed in transport and communications links may not have mattered in ordinary business practices, but it was crucial for mercantile speculation and in the military sphere.[48] In the fifteenth century, it became possible to measure time in hours, rather than days and thereby to create new methods of time control, first in the military-political sphere and then in commerce and the postal services.[49] Joint pressure from all of these sectors turned speed into a measurable variable, which was 'the prime objective of communication'.[50] By the end of the century, nascent continental postal services used regulations on the speed of messenger traffic, as well as hour passes (the ancestors of postmarks), and thereby 'combined methods of transport and time control into permanent and large-scale organizations'.[51]

It has been argued that the transformation of post roads that began to take shape in the late fifteenth century guaranteed technical and organizational innovations and contributed to a change in the perception of time and space.[52] In England the post had become a government-sponsored service early in the reign of Henry VIII (perhaps as early as 1516), but by the latter half of the sixteenth century there was much complaint about its slowness. As Robinson suggests, 'This may mean... a growing sense of the need for haste in sending and receiving important dispatches'.[53] Such pressure is probably linked to the tendency of emerging capitalist societies to place a greater value on the efficient use of time, a topic to which I shall return below.[54] In any event, as soon

47. See Chapter 1, p.24.
48. 'News about harvest sizes and prices, about cargoes and shipwrecks were as prized and – figuratively speaking – highly traded among merchants as reports about the actions of the enemy among generals, for whom a quick shifting of troops could decide the outcome of a campaign. In both cases there existed an ardent interest in the fastest possible and exclusive conveyance of information.' Dorhn-van Rossum, *History of the hour*, p.331.
49. *History of the hour*, p.108ff.
50. Behringer, 'Communications revolutions', p.342.
51. 'Communications revolutions', p.333-35. Marco Polo's travel account suggests that in late thirteenth-century China the arrival and departure time of postal messengers was already being controlled. See Dorhn-van Rossum, *History of the hour*, p.331-32.
52. These innovations affected 'not just the speed, but above all the regularity of the post, through regularly scheduled departures of messengers, and the organization of stages, inns or stables'. Plebani, 'La correspondenza nell'antico regime', p.46.
53. Robinson, *The British Post Office*, p.7, p.14.
54. On the emergence and internalization of 'work time,' see the classic articles by Edward. P. Thompson ('Time, work-discipline and industrial capitalism', *Past and present* 38 (1967), p.56-97) and Jacques Le Goff, 'Merchant's time and church's time in the Middle Ages', in Jacques Le Goff, *Time, work and culture in the Middle Ages*, trans. Arthur Goldhammer

as postal service was made available to the public, its users called for improvements, began to expect a quick response from their correspondents and started excusing themselves for not responding sooner. At the beginning of the sixteenth century, the Thurn and Taxis post had begun to promote increases in the speed and efficiency of its couriers by attaching dockets to the correspondence they carried. Moreover there is ample evidence that these increases actually did occur, in France and Germany, throughout the entire premodern period.[55] In the last decades of the seventeenth century the British Post Office sought to increase the speed of postal communication by requiring that letters be stamped with the date and time of arrival at the post office ('so that no Letter Carryer may dare to detayne a letter from post to post, which before was usual'), attempting to prepare maps of the stage towns and the mileage between them and systematizing the use of post labels ('stating the hour of arrival and dispatch of each mail') by each postmaster on the road.[56] However, as we noted in Chapter 1, another reason for progress in the speed, regularity and efficiency of communications during this period was the general improvement of post roads and postal vehicles. These infrastructural improvements heightened the effect of earlier increases in the quality of postal organization (such as the establishment of postal routes with relays placed at regular intervals, periodicity and the growing density of the postal networks) which Behringer considers to have been 'the pioneering factor in [the] development of greater regularity and speed' in communication.[57]

When new postal services were created to satisfy the demands of merchants and others for speedier and more regular delivery of news from distant places, those places began to appear less distant. Mail coaches began to alter the perception of time and space, as maps of mail routes made space measurable and previously remote places look accessible.[58] Senders and recipients of mail acquired a new sense of urgency about delivery times, and they began to measure time and organize their daily lives around the schedule of mail deliveries. In mid-seventeenth-century Paris, Renouard de Villayer's short-lived *petite poste* catered to a desire for speedier communications and induced some people to organize their lives around the schedule of the post.[59] And as

(Chicago, IL, 1980), p.29-42; as well as Dohrn-von Rossum, *History of the hour*, p.289ff. See also Whyman, *The Pen and the people*, p.59.

55. Behringer, 'Communications revolutions', p.343-45.
56. Robinson, *The British Post Office*, p.58-59.
57. Behringer, 'Communications revolutions', p.346.
58. 'Communications revolutions', p.363.
59. DeJean makes this point in her discussion of the correspondence of Madeleine de Scudéry and Paul Pélisson, *How Paris became Paris*, p.124-25.

we shall see below, in the last decades of the seventeenth century the correspondence of Mme de Sévigné would offer even more eloquent testimony to the ordering (if not the subordination) of a life to postal imperatives. By the time of the Enlightenment (the 'Century of Letters')[60] the development of European postal systems had turned the rhythm of postal service into a social institution of the cultured elite. It is known that in Germany, for example, correspondents were acutely aware of this rhythm.[61] Behringer observes that it was no coincidence that Goethe's father's house was located in the immediate vicinity of the Taxis palace in Frankfurt.

News

At first the public post provided a way for businesses and individuals to exchange reports of recent occurrences in distant places, but soon letters, both public and private, became synonymous with 'news'.[62] Indeed the earliest 'news papers' (originally two separate words) were produced by postmasters.[63] The publication schedule of the earliest newspapers was set to the weekly rhythm of postal deliveries, as well as the topicality, universality and accessibility of the post.[64] To trumpet the newness of their information these newspapers used names associated with the post – such as Courier, Postilion, Post, Post-Dispatch, Messenger, etc. In modern English, the association between the post and the timely delivery of news survives in such expressions as 'to keep (someone) posted' and 'to post a message'.

In Restoration England, the deputy to the secretary of state continued the practice, adopted under Cromwell, of using the Royal Post as a means of surveillance and then used the government's official newspaper, *The London gazette* (1666-1688), to circulate what he wished.[65] And in the 1670s

60. Georg Steinhausen, *Geschichte des Deutschen Briefes* (Berlin, 1889-1991), vol.II, p.245; cited by Behringer, 'Communications revolutions', p.365.
61. '[They] sat down at their desks at the appointed time and rushed to make the deadline at the post office. The great literary figures of the time, from Lessing to Goethe and Schiller, had one thing in common: one wrote on every post day [*posttäglich*], that is, as often as the post was operated.' 'Communications revolutions', p.116.
62. Habermas, *The Structural transformation of the public sphere*, p.16-17.
63. See Behringer, *Im Zeichen des Merkur*, p.304-310. See also Zilliacus, *Pillar to post*, p.89. In North America, Benjamin Franklin served as the publisher of the *Pennsylvania gazette* and as the first Postmaster General under the Continental Congress. See also: Behringer, 'Communications revolutions', p.365; Eugène Vaillé, 'La poste et la presse sous l'ancien régime', *Bulletin d'information, de documentation et de statistique du Ministère des P.T.T.* 9 (1936), p.33-68. Bannet, *Empire of letters*, p.10-11.
64. Behringer discusses the relationship between the periodicity of postal riders and the 'media revolution' in 'Communications revolutions', p.349ff. See Plebani, 'La correspondenza nell'antico regime', p.46.
65. Whyman, *The Pen and the people*, p.49-50.

he gave the Six Clerks of the Road the privilege of sending newspapers postage-free.[66] In his dramatic poem *Samson Agonistes* (1671), Milton associates the speediness of postal delivery with the spread of bad news by having the Hebrew chorus proclaim that '[E]vil news rides post, while good news baits [*pauses to rest*]'.[67]

Time 2: measurement and discipline

> The Communications Revolution did more than any other change to replace a world of the miraculous with a world of the measurable.[68]

As early as the fourteenth century postal couriers in the duchy of Milan had to know how to use mechanical clocks in order to record precisely when they received letters and transported goods at the post office.[69] Innovations in chronometry would eventually transform the temporal dimension of the 'social and cultural milieu' created by the post.[70] Recent studies have shown some of the ways in which advances in chronometry in seventeenth- and eighteenth-century England and seventeenth-century France affected the organization and representation of time. In *Telling time*, Stuart Sherman recounts how Christiaan Huyghens's application of the pendulum (invented by Galileo) as a regulator for clock mechanisms (1657) made it possible to break time down, to analyze it into units as small as minutes and seconds. Huyghens's invention of the spiral spring in 1675 'miniaturized the regular oscillations of the pendulum and thus rendered possible an unprecedented degree of accuracy in watches'.[71] Sherman observes that by attending to the minutes and seconds of their daily schedules, owners of watches increasingly came to inhabit a private realm of experience, in which they defined and tracked themselves in chronological terms.[72] A concern with precision in the making of pocket watches equipped with separate second hands developed at the same time that coaches of the nobility, which had been characterized by a surfeit of decoration, were

66. Whyman argues that this measure 'had a profound impact on the spread of news'. *The Pen and the people*, p.52. On postal surveillance under Cromwell, see my Chapter 3, p.108-109.
67. *Samson agonistes* (1538), in *The Portable Milton*, edited and introduced by Douglas Bush (New York, 1977).
68. Behringer, 'Communications revolutions', p.372.
69. Behringer, 'Communications revolutions', p.339.
70. Livet, 'La route royale et la civilisation française', p.71.
71. Stuart Sherman, *Telling time: clocks, diaries, and English diurnal form, 1600-1785* (Chicago, IL, 1985), p.5.
72. 'Huygensian precision conduces to privacy. It has to do with the status in the late seventeenth century of the minute as a unit of measurement, and with its consequent eligibility as a means of self-definition, a tool for self-tracking.' Sherman, *Telling time*, p.87.

replaced by better sprung, faster, more functional vehicles.[73] In *Time and ways of knowing under Louis XIV*, Roland Racevskis builds on Sherman's work to show how the emphasis on the productive and efficient use of time in Louvois's reform of the French postal system caused its employees to rely upon the new timepieces to track themselves at work. 'Under Louvois', he notes, 'postal administrators continued watching the clock, around the clock'.[74] French government regulations required that postmasters be ready to receive messengers at all hours, and that town governors keep their gates open at night to receive postal messengers. Under threat of sanctions, French postmasters were required to empty mailboxes precisely at noon and to accept no unofficial mail after that time, in order to allow time for preparing the *melons* (mail packets) for departure at exactly 2:00 p.m.; similarly, once they had begun their journeys, messengers were prohibited from stopping along the way, for any reason.[75] In Denmark the salary of postmen and mail carriers depended on how rapidly they could perform their service.

Subject to time

If the unreliability of mail service during this period gave all users of the post good reason to worry about the fate of their letters, the material conditions of postal exchange often affected the very nature of their correspondence. With the advent of national postal services, offering the ability to send and receive letters quickly and regularly, the writing of letters became less of a special occasion (with letters written in Latin in a highly ornate style), and more of an expeditious activity.[76] Consider the case of Mme de Sévigné's (1626-1696) letters to her daughter, Mme de Grignan. As the Sévigné specialist Roger Duchêne has observed, unlike more scholarly or decorous correspondents of the period, the marquise and her daughter did not write letters to each other with the knowledge or expectation that they would be read aloud and eventually published, but simply to continue exchanging their thoughts and feelings when circumstances kept them apart. For this reason their letters were less carefully composed than scholarly letters and more subject to the circumstances of their composition.[77] Sévigné expressed her gratitude

73. 'Separate second hands began to appear on more functional watches, while there was a rapid acceleration in the rapidity of cabriolets and mail coaches, a harbinger of all our technology of speed.' Studeny, 'L'éveil de la vitesse', p.54. In ch.1003 ('Chaise de poste') of the *Tableau de Paris* Mercier remarks that 'Le goût a banni des voitures actuelles l'or et l'argent, il a prononcé plus hautement qu'une loi somptuaire.'
74. Racevskis, *Time and ways of knowing*, p.98.
75. *Time and ways of knowing*, p.97ff.
76. How, *Epistolary spaces*, p.7.
77. 'Especially in the case of Mme de Sévigné, these were letters written only for their

for the existence of the post when she famously exclaimed, 'C'est une belle invention que la poste', already proverbial words that would be echoed a century later in Voltaire's article on the posts.[78] However, as Werner Sombart notes, 'This innovation was more than a "*belle invention*", an invention very pleasant for the individual: it completely revolutionized the whole of cultural life'.[79] As Duchêne has shown, far from writing these letters spontaneously, Mme de Sévigné organized her life around the departures and (especially) the arrivals of the 'ordinary' post.[80] To a certain extent the same was true in England, where '[p]eople of all ranks wrote at particular hours on specific days, so as to make optimal use of the post'.[81] In fact, since neither Mme de Sévigné nor Mme de Grignan could afford a regular private messenger service, it was thanks to Louvois's reform of the French postal system that they were even capable of engaging in regular semiweekly correspondence. Fortunately for Mme de Sévigné, the year before her daughter first left for Provence (1671) a second day was added to what had been the weekly service on the route between her country home in Vitré, in Brittany, and Paris, whence her letters were forwarded to Aix-en-Provence via Burgundy; moreover, in 1670, a new post office had been created in Montélimar, where the letters for Grignan arrived.[82] Responses from

addressee, without a thought for the secondary audience to whom this person could possibly be induced to show them, either when the letters were received or later, and with even less consideration of the possibility that they could eventually be published.' Duchêne, *Comme une lettre à la poste*, p.119.

78. The quasi-proverbial status of the expression is attested by the first edition of the *Dictionnaire de l'Académie française* in 1694 (Paris, J. B. Coignard), in which the definition of 'Poste' contains this example: *la poste est une belle invention*. This expression occurs in a letter by Madame de Sévigné to her daughter dated 12 July 1671, as part of an illustration of a remark by Pascal about greed. Mme de Sévigné to Mme de Grignan, *Correspondance*, vol.1, p.294. In the 'Postes' article of the *Questions sur l'Encyclopédie*, Voltaire (who was a great admirer of Mme de Sévigné's 'natural' style) maintains that 'La France, où cette *belle invention* fut renouvelée dans nos temps barbares, a rendu ce service à toute l'Europe'. *OCV*, vol.42B, p.471, emphasis added.

79. Werner Sombart, *Der moderne Kapitalismus. Historisch-systematische Darstellung des gesamteuropäischen Wirtschaftslebens von seinen Anfängen bis zur Gegenwart*, 3 vols (Munich and Leipzig, 1916-1927; new edn Munich, 1987), vol.II:1, p.372. Cited by Behringer, in 'Communications revolutions', p.371.

80. Duchêne, *Comme une lettre à la poste*, p.206ff. Diderot tells Sophie Volland: 'Je ne serais pas assez aimé, si les jours de poste n'étaient pas pour et pour moi des jours de fête, et je n'aimerais pas assez.' Diderot to Sophie Volland, 31 August 1760, *Correspondance*, vol.3, p.44.

81. Whyman, *The Pen and the people*, 59.

82. Duchêne, *Comme une lettre à la poste*, p.206-207. The correspondence between Mme de Sévigné and Mme de Grignan covers a total of eight and a half years, composed of nine separations between 1671 and 1690. In what follows I am summarizing Duchêne, *Comme une lettre à la poste*, p.205ff.

Mme de Grignan were subject to the same schedule, and to the same hazards – letters delayed or gone astray – of the post. A half a century earlier there had been very few post offices in Provence, and letters did not even leave Paris for Provence until there were enough of them to justify the departure of a courier.[83] When Mme de Sévigné was staying in Paris, she initially (February 1671) had her letters posted on Wednesdays and Fridays; when she was sojourning in Brittany, she had them delivered on Sundays and Wednesdays to the post office in Vitré, where the same semiweekly schedule remained in effect throughout the duration of her correspondence. In fair weather, it would then take two days for a letter written in Vitré to reach Paris, and five or six days (or occasionally four) for it to arrive in Grignan or Aix.

The semiweekly arrivals of the couriers from Provence influenced the composition, the length and even the content of Sévigné's letters to her daughter. The marquise makes this relationship explicit in a letter written in Paris on 11 March 1672:

> [J]e reçois le lundi une de vos lettres; j'y fais un commencement de réponse à la chaude. Le mardi, s'il y a quelque affaire ou quelque nouvelle, je reprends ma lettre et je vous mande ce que j'en sais. Le mercredi, je reçois encore une lettre de vous; j'y fais réponse, et je finis par là.[84]

> On Monday I receive one of your letters. I straightway compose the beginning of a response. On Tuesday, if there is something important to discuss or some news, I take up my letter again and tell you what I know about it. On Wednesday I receive another letter from you; I answer it and end there.

As Duchêne points out, the letters she wrote in Paris on Fridays have a different tone ('centered on herself and her circle') than the ones written on Wednesdays ('invaded by the world of her correspondent').[85] Starting in 1685, thanks to a further improvement in the postal system, letters left Paris for the South three times a week (Mondays, Wednesdays and Fridays); from that point on, the average number of pages Sévigné wrote each week from Paris to Mme de Grignan increased.[86] Mme de Sévigné's letters to her daughter illustrate how improvements in postal services transformed the nature of all regular and intimate correspondence.[87]

The delivery schedule of the post affected not only the length and nature of private correspondence, but also gave the post a new role in the emotional lives of early modern people. We have already noted that

83. *Comme une lettre à la poste*, p.206.
84. Mme de Sévigné to Mme de Grignan, 11 March 1672, vol.1, p.457. Sévigné uses almost the same words in her letter to Mme de Grignan of 19 August 1676, *Correspondance*, vol.2, p.372.
85. *Comme une lettre à la poste*, p.210.
86. *Comme une lettre à la poste*, p.207.
87. *Comme une lettre à la poste*, p.211-12.

in the early modern period the very possibility of relying on the post for rapid and (more or less) reliable news led the public to desire even speedier and more frequent mail deliveries. Now the same forces (the demand for more rapid exchange of information and more efficient use of time, etc.) that had led to improvements in the speed, regularity and reliability of the post and disposed individuals to inhabit a private realm of experience also organized that private realm in accordance with schedules and time constraints. During periods of separation from Mme de Grignan, Mme de Sévigné organized her daily life around the anticipation of letters from her daughter in Provence. According to the rhythm of mail deliveries, her mood alternated between joy and sorrow: 'Quand les lettres de Provence arrivent, c'est une joie parmi tous ceux qui m'aiment, comme c'est une tristesse quand je suis longtemps sans en avoir.'[88] (When the letters from Provence arrive, they bring joy to those who love me, just as they bring sadness when it has been a long time since I have received one.) Every time a letter from Grignan arrived, the marquise could imagine that she was actually listening to her daughter; and then, while she composed a response (often in several stages, in order to make the pleasure last) she would have the impression of prolonging the conversation. Her perception of time, like her mood, oscillated according to the rhythm of mail deliveries. While she was reading a new letter from Mme de Grignan, time raced by; but when she was waiting for a letter to arrive, it ground to a halt: 'Je trouve comme vous, ma bonne, et *peut-être plus que vous*, qu'il y a loin d'un ordinaire à l'autre. Ce temps, qui me fâche quelque fois de courir si vite, s'arrête tout court, comme vous dites.'[89] (Like you, my dear, and maybe even more than you, I find that it is a long time from one ordinary to the next. Time, which sometimes distresses me by passing so quickly, stops short as you say.) Presence and absence are often represented or experienced in spatial terms, but Sévigné's comments on the post remind us that they also have a temporal dimension; absence entails not just distance but also delay.

Impatience

This private subjection to a rational economy of time made possible a new emotional state: the impatience caused by delay. In a letter dated 25 November, 1671, Mme de Sévigné tells her daughter: 'J'attends vendredi de vos lettres avec mon impatience *ordinaire*.' (I await one of your letters on Friday with my *ordinary* impatience.) (Emphasis added) As Racevskis

88. Mme de Sévigné to Mme de Grignan, 18 March 1671, *Correspondance*, vol.1, p.189.
89. Mme de Sévigne to Mme de Grignan, 19 June 1675. *Correspondance*, vol.1, p.736, emphasis added.

observes, Sévigné is playing here on the word *ordinaire*, which refers to both her 'ordinary' impatience and the 'ordinary' (regularly-scheduled) mail delivery.[90] Before the Renaissance, 'patience' had signified 'The suffering or enduring (of pain, trouble, or evil) with calmness and composure' (*OED*) and 'impatience' the failure to do so. However in the sixteenth century impatience (*Ungeduld*, etc.) began to lose its etymological relationship to suffering and to acquire the additional meaning of 'intolerance of delay; restlessness of desire or expectation; restless longing or eagerness', which has since become the most common sense of the word.[91] Sévigné is impatient in this historically recent sense: she cannot bear to wait for the next letter from her daughter. Needless to say, this is not yet the impatience of a society that stresses efficiency, where 'time is money' (as Benjamin Franklin famously put it): Mme de Sévigné does not feel impatient because she thinks that her time is being wasted.

Paradoxically, it was only because Louvois's postal system had given her a reason to anticipate the regular arrival of letters that Mme de Sévigné could feel such impatience. Indeed as soon as it became possible for a letter to make her daughter seem present two and even three times a week, the marquise also grew impatient with the very intervals that separated one arrival of the post from the next: 'Dès que j'ai reçu une lettre, j'en voudrais tout à l'heure une autre; je ne respire que pour en recevoir.' (As soon as I have received a letter, I would like another one very soon; I breathe only to receive one.)[92] If there had been no postal system with regular mail deliveries, Mme de Sévigné might still have been anxious to receive news from her daughter, and she certainly would have found ways to suggest that Mme de Grignan didn't love her enough ('I find [...], *maybe even more than you*, that is a long time from one ordinary to another'); but she would not have expected the next letter to arrive on a specific day and would therefore not have been impatient to receive it. Prior to the existence of publicly available and reliable postal service, the prolonged absence of Mme de Grignan was something that the marquise would simply have had to endure, patiently or not.

In his treatise on education, *Emile* (1762), Rousseau attributes this

90. Duchêne, *Comme une lettre à la poste*, p.107. In a similar vein, Sévigné writes that 'Si on pouvait avoir un peu de patience, on épargnerait bien du chagrin; le temps en ôte autant qu'il en donne'. Mme de Sévigné to Mme de Grignan, 24 November 1675, *Correspondance*, vol.2, p.169.

91. The earliest example of impatience at delay cited by the *Oxford English Dictionary* is dated 1581: 'Impacience, which can abide no tarying' (Richard Mulcaster, *Positions, wherein those primitive circumstances be examined, which are necessarie for the training up of children* [1581]). In 1596, Shakespeare's Juliet uses the word in a similar way: 'So tedious is this day/As is the night before some festival/To an impatient child that hath new robes/And may not wear them' (*Romeo and Juliet*, III, ii, 28-31).

92. February 18, 1671 *Correspondance*, vol.1, p.161.

impatience to the incapacity of his contemporaries to enjoy the present moment. He draws a contrast between the abstracted life of a man who travels by post – he only cares about getting somewhere as fast as possible – and the mindfulness of the man who travels on foot. The post traveler 'court pour cou[r]rir, et vient en poste sans autre objet que de retourner de même' (runs for the sake of running, and comes by post for no other reason than to return the same way); he subjects himself to a schedule and a fixed itinerary, while the walker enjoys every moment of his life because he is free to stop and go where and when he pleases. Rousseau concludes that: 'Quand on ne veut qu'arriver on peut cou[r]rir en chaise de poste; mais quand on veut voyager, il faut aller à pied.' (When all one wants is to arrive, one can run in a post chaise; but if one wants to travel, one must go on foot.)[93] In addition, without knowledge of the days when letters were scheduled to arrive and depart, Mme de Sévigné would not have anticipated the arrival of a letter or set aside time to respond to it. The early modern post made it possible to conceive of correspondence as a regular exchange between two people.

Deliverance time

> If the tower is everywhere and the knight of deliverance no proof against its magic, what else?
>
> *The Crying of lot 49*[94]

Mme de Sévigné's letters to her daughter provide an early example of a syndrome that one might call affective dependence on mail (ADM).[95] Susan Whyman, who cites examples of this dependence among both middle-class and working-class correspondents, does not hesitate to call the condition an 'addiction'.[96] In a letter to his French colleague Jérôme Lalande (1732-1807), the Austro-Hungarian astronomer Franz Xaver von Zach (1754-1832) describes the symptoms of a particularly acute case of this intense craving, in which the erotic element is made explicit:

93. Rousseau, *OC*, vol.4, p.771, 773. Despite his pride in having carried out all his observations of Paris on foot, Mercier differs from Rousseau on this point: 'Voyager à pied, c'est voyager comme Thalès et Rousseau, mais de nos jours cela devient impraticable: la chaise de poste s'arrête à volonté, et franchit rapidement ce qui ne mérite pas d'être vu.' *Tableau de Paris*, ch.1003, p.1451-52.
94. Pynchon, *The Crying of lot 49*, p.22.
95. Racevskis, *Time and ways of knowing*, p.107. Like Voltaire (and doubtless others who were dependent on mail), Mme de Sévigné also cultivated the acquaintance of postal employees who would be able to expedite the delivery of her letters to and from Provence. She also had the habit of writing *de provision*, that is, without the immediate intention or capability of sending a letter. *Time and ways of knowing*, p.111-12, 127.
96. Whyman, *The Pen and the people*, p.59.

Very dear friend, illustrious colleague

We are like two lovers who court each other. Reading our letters one would say that these two people are very much in love and very passionate. You long to receive my letters, you count the pages and you devour them. It is not the same for me, but worse, for when your letters seem not to arrive, it makes me uneasy and puts me in the foulest of humors, I am like a languishing mistress; but as soon as I catch sight of the handwriting and address of your letter, I am a changed man. I do not, like you, count the pages of your letters, but I count the lines and the words; I do not devour them either, but I savor them slowly and in long draughts, so as to prolong the pleasure. I am an Epicurean in this way, and I read and reread your letters and end up translating them and adding commentaries and notes. It is a text that I work on *con amore*.[97]

Sévigné's and Zach's expressions of amorous impatience with the post underline an obvious difference between the early modern post and all the other things in this world that could make one impatient: it is a dialogic vehicle. As Mme de Sévigné wrote to her daughter, 'Nos lettres sont des conversations; je vous parle, et vous me répondez' (Our letters are conversations; I speak to you, and you answer me).[98] Before the creation of the modern post, private messengers carried letters whenever they were needed, along whatever route was most convenient. These services were 'personal' in that they were accessible only to specific persons, but in the modern sense of 'having a relationship to a person's intimate affairs' the letters they delivered usually had nothing personal about them. On the other hand, although the early modern post was an impersonal collection and delivery agency, it carried vast quantities of intimate, personal correspondence.[99] Voltaire put it best when he wrote that 'through [the post] the absent become present; it is the consolation of life'.

The early modern post arose from the need of European merchants to manage their widespread business interests and rapidly became the most efficient way of receiving 'news' from distant places, while also enabling intellectuals to exchange ideas at great distances. It offered the hope of bringing alive people from whom one had been separated by the growth of the capitalist mode of production, the development of an integrated 'world economy': that is, by the same conditions that made publicly

97. Franz Xaver von Sachs to Jérôme Lalande, 21 April 1796. Cited by Simone Dumont, in *Un Astronome des Lumières: Jérôme Lalande* (Paris, 2007), p.259.

98. Madame de Sévigné to Madame de Grignan, 7 August 1675, *Correspondance*, vol.2, p.39.

99. 'In the context of letter-writing, "personal" is useful in that it recognizes the significance of letters to individuals and to relationships. It is preferable to "private", a term that is simply inaccurate for many eighteenth-century familiar letters, which were composed in company, voluntarily circulated beyond the addressee and frequently found their way into print.' Brant, *Empire of letters*, p.5.

available postal systems possible and necessary. Within that society an emphasis on the productive and efficient use of time has left moderns increasingly confined within a private realm of experience; but many have found in the post a way – literature is another – of trying to communicate that experience (or the impossibility of communicating it) with the absent. To Mme de Sévigné, Voltaire, Zach and countless others, the post raised the possibility of making absent friends and loved ones seem present.[100] Although there was nothing that Jean-Jacques Rousseau could have wanted more ('Presence or nothing', he told his friend Du Peyrou), he was so acutely aware of what one might call the evasion of presence – the infinite capacity of presence to elude one's grasp – that he could not share other people's confidence in communication, by letter or in general.

Postmodern

> Now recks no lord but the stilleto's Thorn,
> And Tacit lies the gold once-knotted horn.
> No hallowed skein of stars can ward, I trow,
> Who's once been set his tryst with Trystero
>
> *The Courier's tragedy*, Act IV

Jean-Jacques Rousseau anticipated Kafka in entertaining what has become a typically modern suspicion about the possibility of postal communication. That same suspicion permeates Thomas Pynchon's brilliant novel *The Crying of lot 49*, where a muted post horn symbolizes the underground Trystero (sometimes spelled Tristero) postal system, whose supporters, 'whoever they were, [aimed] to mute the Thurn and Taxis post horn'.[101]

The muted post horn is also related to the 'mute stamps' (mute because they cannot voice their meaning) in the collection of the late Pierce Inverarity, the enigmatic former lover of Oedipa Maas, who on the opening page of the novel receives a letter informing her that she has been designated to administer his vast and tangled estate. This letter sets her off on a journey to southern California that will turn into a fruitless

100. In her study of subjectivity in Diderot's correspondence, Geneviève Cammagre concludes that: '[I]n the Diderot who writes the letters to Sophie, a desiring being is expressed who seeks to "stretch out his arms" to reach the absent woman, so that the suffering of temporary absences might cease and, more silently, the endless suffering caused by the incapacity, whatever his writing strategies and his will for fusion may be, to annex the Other.' *Roman et histoire de soi: la notion de sujet dans la Correspondance de Diderot* (Paris, 2000), p.229. My own translation.

101. Pynchon, *The Crying of lot 49*, p.97. An extensive bibliography of the literature on this novel can be found in J. Kerry Grant, *A Companion to The Crying of lot 49* (Athens, GA, and London, 2008).

quest for understanding of herself and her world. In the stamp collection is a set of not quite authentic American stamps that composes Lot 49 of Inverarity's estate and which at the end of the story is about to be 'cried' (publicly offered for sale). Each of these stamps bears a subtle but sinister alteration (such as 'The deep violet 3¢ regular issue of 1954 had a faint, menacing smile on the face of the Statue of Liberty') seemingly made by allies of Trystero, in the slender hope of striking fear in the hearts of the United States Postal Service and its accomplices and reducing them to silence.[102] The muted post horn also points to all the messages that Trystero and his faithful apparently want to keep secret, and to his name, which they want to suppress entirely. Oedipa attends a performance of a parodic Jacobean revenge drama called *The Courier's tragedy*, during which the actor (who is also the director of the play) playing Gennaro reveals that name by uttering a variant line (of unknown origin): 'Who once has set his tryst with Trystero'. A few days after the performance, the man inexplicably commits suicide.

The watchword of the Trystero post is WASTE, an acronym for 'We Await Silent Tristero's Empire'. It apparently is a promise to faithfully await the coming of a reign of silence and to hasten that day by muting (canceling, weakening, erasing, distorting) the import of all attempts at postal communication. In this respect, the letters in *The Crying of lot 49* participate in the nature of all its texts and signs: they promise a significance ('[I]t seemed that a pattern was beginning to emerge, having to do with the mail and how it was delivered') on which they never deliver.[103] Usually the anticipated meaning is simply weakened. For example, the letters that Oedipa Maas receives from her husband are always frustratingly trivial ('The letter itself had nothing much to say'), just as those received by Mike Fallopian and other users of a secret mail system continually disappoint them ('That's how it is', Fallopian confessed bitterly, 'most of the time').[104]

An apparent exception to this rule occurs in Act IV of *The Courier's tragedy*, whose twisted and silly plot is summarized by the narrator. Here the text of a letter is not only canceled, but also miraculously rewritten by unknown forces so as to say exactly the opposite of what was in the original letter. The evil duke Angelo of Squamuglia, having murdered the duke of the neighboring duchy of Faggio and had him replaced by the legitimate heir's equally evil half brother, learns that a coup d'état has taken place in Faggio and various armies are now preparing to invade Squamuglia. Niccolò, rightful heir to the duchy of Faggio, has so far

102. Pynchon, *The Crying of lot 49*, p.45, 174.
103. *The Crying of lot 49*, p.89.
104. *The Crying of lot 49*, p.45, 53.

escaped assassination by disguising himself as a special courier of the Thurn and Taxis post. In an effort to forestall the invasion, the evil duke decides to write a deceitful letter to Gennaro, the interim head of state in Faggio, in which he assures him of his good intentions. He entrusts it to Niccolò, the eponymous courier. Stopping on the way to Faggio, Niccolò opens the letter and, since he is fully aware that it contains 'a pack of lies', sarcastically reads parts of it aloud. However before Niccolò can deliver the letter and accede to the throne of Faggio, duke Angelo discovers the courier's true identity, and shortly thereafter the virtuous Niccolò is killed by grotesque footpads in black.[105] Gennaro's forces come to a halt by the shores of a lake, where one of his men discovers Niccolò's dead body. Whereupon a seemingly miraculous transformation of the letter and its meaning is revealed:

> [A soldier] hands Gennaro a roll of parchment, stained with blood, which was found on the body. From its seal we can see it's the letter from Angelo that Niccolò was carrying. Gennaro glances at it, does a double take, reads it aloud. It is no longer the lying document Niccolò read us excerpts from at all, but now miraculously a long confession by Angelo of all his crimes.[106]

If the mendacious text that Niccolò read had simply been lost or distorted, it could serve as another example of Trystero's sinister muting action. But the text of this letter (written in ink made of charcoal derived from the bones of the Lost Guard of Faggio) has not only been erased, but it has also been replaced by another text, one that tells the truth. Something more, or at least different, from Trystero's mute seems to be at work here. The simplest and maybe also the best explanation for this apparent miracle is that one should not expect consistent ideas from novelists: after all, writers of fiction are less interested in providing a systematic interpretation of the world than in discovering its complexity and magic. One could also view the apparently miraculous transformation of Angelo's letter as the work of those mediating 'specters' [*Gespenster*] by whom Kafka believed that epistolary communication is haunted.[107] However one chooses to interpret this strange occurrence, the fact remains that just as the courier Niccolò fails to deliver the letter entrusted to him, so all letters in *The Crying of lot 49* fail to convey the significance that is expected of them. The meaning they deliver is always more or less than what is expected, but never the same. Perhaps what is significant about these letters is neither the intentions of their authors

105. Paralyzed by a mysterious force, all he can say before being killed is 'T-t-t-t-,' which the narrator remarks 'may be the shortest line ever written in blank verse'. *The Crying of lot 49*, p.73.
106. *The Crying of lot 49*, p.74.
107. See my discussion of Kafka's specters in the Introduction, p.16-18.

nor the expectations of their recipients, but the simple fact that they continue to circulate on a regular basis.[108]

The postal promise

Karen Engle has argued that the letter carrier is 'the promissory figure par excellence':

> In its idealized form, the letter carrier is the postal system's embodied materialization of its social contract. For the system's smooth operation, the mail carrier must be received as the promissory figure par excellence: a paragon of consistency, predictability and trustworthiness traversing the same route day in, day out. Undeviating and reliable; come snow, sleet, rain and apocalypse, your carrier delivers. This promise to deliver includes a promise to transmit meaning; to deliver communication in pure, unsullied form.[109]

The symbol of the muted post horn speaks of the failure of the post to deliver on the promise of stable, lossless communication. Moreover in *The Crying of lot 49* it is not just letters that fail to keep their promises, but all texts and signs. Like the reader, Oedipa Maas never reaches the end of her quest to read meaning into the constellation of portentous signs (the 'hallowed skein of stars') that she sees, or thinks she sees, all around her in the text that is the world she inhabits. Something always comes along to prevent delivery of the message, to trivialize or degrade it. For example, at the beginning of her quest, Oedipa is driving south in her rented Impala. When she catches sight of the southern California town of San Narciso in the valley below and perceives a resemblance between its layout and the printed circuit of a transistor radio, she feels that she is about to receive a revelation:

> Though she knew even less about radios than about Southern Californians, there were to both outward patterns a hieroglyphic sense of concealed meaning, of an intent to communicate. There'd seemed to be no limit to what the printed circuit could have told her (if she had tried to find out); so in her first minute of San Narciso, a revelation also trembled just past the threshold of her understanding.[110]

Likewise, on the last page of the novel she is left in an auction room, wondering what she will do when the mysterious bidder on Lot 49

108. "'It's the principle", Fallopian agreed, sounding defensive. "To keep it up to some kind of reasonable volume, each member has to send at least one letter a week through the Yoyodyne system. If you don't, you get fined."' *The Crying of lot 49*, p.53.

109. Karen Engle, 'The post of the Post', *Journal of political and social thought* 1:4 (2003), http://www.yorku.ca/jspot/4/engle.htm#RETURN3 (last accessed 10 August 2015).

110. *The Crying of lot 49*, p.24. Oedipa also feels impelled toward revelation when reading the map of the Fangoso Lagoons (p.31) and observing 'the incredible network of lines' (p.77) in Randolph Driblette's face.

'reveal[s] himself'. But the promise of revelation is not fulfilled in this place or at any other relay on her voyage of discovery, since any possible illumination is always trivialized or degraded; as later on in this same passage, when the possibility of an epiphany is forestalled successively by a cloud, smog, quotation marks and a burst of colloquial speech: 'She gave it up presently, as if a cloud had approached the sun or the smog thickened, and so broken the "religious instant", whatever it might've been.'[111] In contrast to a high modern classic like Proust's *A La recherche du temps perdu*, where a sign or 'text' like the Martinville steeples, when glimpsed from a moving carriage, seems to promise a revelation that ultimately is disclosed, in Pynchon's 'postmodern' classic the quest for meaning is held in abeyance.[112] Doubtless the insatiability of the desire for presence is one reason why, no matter how many improvements are made in the speed, quality and reliability of telecommunications, these are soon experienced as intolerably, painfully inadequate.[113] Whether 'snail mail' or e-mail, the post is a medium that promises to deliver presence. It makes a promise that, like the promise of deliverance from time, will always await fulfillment.

111. *The Crying of lot 49*, p.25.
112. Frank Kermode makes a similar point when he remarks (following Barthes) that 'deception (in the French sense, "disappointment") [is] an inherent property of narratives.' *The Art of telling: essays on fiction* (Cambridge, MA, 1983), p.82.
113. A thoughtful discussion of the relationship between technology and the experience of speed can be found in Judy Wacjman, *Pressed for time: the acceleration of life in digital capitalism* (Chicago, IL, 2014).

Bibliography

Primary sources

Académie française, *Dictionnaire de l'Académie française*, 1st edn (Paris, J. B. Coignard, 1694).

–, *Dictionnaire de l'Académie française*, 4th edn (Paris, Ve de Bernard Brunet, 1762).

Almanach royal (Paris, Le Breton, 1755).

Archives parlementaires, 1re série, tome VIII, p.284, séance du 27 juillet 1789.

Argenson, *see* Voyer de Paulmy.

Tableau général du goût, des modes et costumes de Paris, par une société d'artistes et de gens de lettres (Paris, An VII), vol.I.

Berthier de Sauvigny, Louis Bénigné-François, *Jugement souverain qui condamne Gilles Breton, facteur du bureau de la poste aux lettres d'Etampes à être mis au carcan et à un bannissement de la généralité de Paris pendant trois ans* (Paris, Imprimerie Royale, 1 April 1746).

Cappart, Hubert, 'La petite poste de Paris', http://e.boonafoux-amvd.chez-alice.fr/jadis/jadis1/cappart.htm (last accessed 29 September 2015).

Cervantes, Miguel de, *Don Quixote* (New York, 1949).

Choderlos de Laclos, Pierre Ambroise François, *Les Liaisons dangereuses*, preface, notes Michel Delon (Paris, 2002).

–, *Les Liaisons dangereuses*, translated and with an introduction by P. W. K. Stone (London, 1961).

Corneille, Pierre, *Théâtre complet* (Paris, 1960).

Cradock, Anna Francesca, *La Vie française à la veille de la Révolution (1783-1786): journal inédit de Madame Cradock, traduit d'après le manuscrit original par Mme O. Delphin-Balleyguier* (Paris, 1911).

Déclaration du Roy en Interprétation de l'Edit de Création de la Charge de Grand Maistre et Sur-Intendant des Postes (Chez la Veuve de François Muguet, Hubert Muguet, Premier Imprimeur du Roy, et Louis Denis de Latour Libraire, rue de la Harpe, aux trois Rois, 28 August 1716).

Diderot, Denis, *Correspondance* (Paris, 1955-1970).

Du Mont, Jean, *Voyages de Mr du Mont en France, en Italie, en Allemagne, à Malthe, et en Turquie* (The Hague, Etienne Foulque and François Honoré, 1699).

Edit du Roy, Portant création de la Charge de grand Maistre & Sur-Intendant général des Postes, Courriers & Relais de France, & d'autres Charges subalternes pour le service des Postes (Chez la Veuve de François Muguet, Hubert Muguet, Premier Imprimeur du Roy, et Louis Denis de Latour Libraire, rue de la Harpe, aux trois Rois, September 1715).

Edit du Roy, Portant Création de Cent mille livres de Rentes viagères assignées sur la Ferme des Postes, pour les Actionnaires de la Loterie, Establie en conséquence de la Déclaration de Sa Majesté du 21 Août 1717 (Paris, Imprimerie Royale, 1717).

*Edit du Roy, Portant suppression de la Charge de Grand-Maître et Surintendant général des Postes et

Relais de France (Paris, Pierre Simon, August 1726).

Edit du Roy, Portant suppression des Offices de Controlleurs Provinciaux des Postes & Relais de France (Paris, Pierre Simon, March 1728).

Edit du Roy, Portant création de six cens mille livres de Rentes sur la Ferme Générale des Postes (Paris, Imprimerie Royale, November 1735).

Edit du Roy, Portant suppression de plusieurs Charges & Offices sur les Postes (Paris, Imprimerie Royale, May 1738).

Edit du Roy, Portant création de six cens mille livres de Rentes sur la Ferme générale des Postes, juin 1742 (Paris, Imprimerie Royale, June 1742).

Edit du Roy, Portant création de cinq cens mille livres de rentes héréditaires au denier vingt, sur la ferme générale des Postes, décembre 1756 (Paris, Imprimerie Royale, December 1746).

Edit du Roy, Portant création de deux millions de livres de rentes viagères sur l'Hôtel de ville de Paris; et de neuf cens mille livres de rentes héréditaires sur la Ferme générale des Postes (Paris, Imprimerie Royale, May 1751).

Encyclopédie ou, Dictionnaire raisonné des sciences, des arts et des métiers par une sociéte de gens de lettres/mis en ordre et publié par M. Diderot; et quant à la partie mathématique, par M. d'Alembert (Paris, Briasson *et al.*, 1751-1765).

Elisabeth Charlotte von der Pfalz, Princess Palatine, *Aus den Briefen der Herzogin an die Kurfürstin Sophie von Hannover: ein Beitrag zur Kulturgeschichte des 17. und 18. Jahrhunderts*, ed. Eduard Bodemann (Hanover, 1891).

Fréminville, Edmé de la Poix de, *Dictionnaire ou Traité de la police générale des villes, bourgs, paroisses, et seigneuries de la campagne. Dans lequel on trouvera tout ce qui est nécessaire de savoir & de pratiquer en cette partie, par un procureur fiscal...* (Paris, chez les associés du privilège des ouvrages de l'auteur, 1778).

Furetière, Antoine, *Dictionnaire universel, contenant généralement tous les mots françois, tant vieux que modernes, & les Termes de toutes les sciences et des arts* (The Hague and Rotterdam, A. & R. Leers, 1690).

Gray, Thomas, *Correspondence of Thomas Gray: 1734-1755*, ed. Paget Toynbee *et al.*, 3 vols (Oxford, 1935).

Grimm, Melchior, *Correspondance littéraire*, crit. edn Ulla Kölving with Jean de Booy and Christoph Frank; preface Roland Mortier (Ferney-Voltaire, 2006-2013).

Guyot, Edmé-Gilles, *Dictionnaire des Postes, Contenant le nom de toutes les Villes, Bourgs, Paroisses, Abbayes et Principaux Châteaux du Royaume de France & du Duché de Lorraine, les Provinces où ils sont situés et la distinction pour celles pour lesquelles il faut affranchir* (Paris, Chez la Veuve Delatour, rue de La Harpe, aux trois tours, 1754).

Hobbes, Thomas, *Leviathan*, ed. Noel Malcolm (Oxford, 2012).

Horace (Quintus Aurelius Flaccus), *Horace's letters (epistles)*, Society for Ancient Languages, Univ. Alabama, Huntsville, AL http://www.uah.edu/student_life/organizations/SAL/texts/latin/classical/horace/epistulae101.html (last accessed 12 August 2015).

Hume, David, *The Letters of David Hume*, ed. J. Y. T. Greig (Oxford, 1932).

–, *A Concise and genuine account of the dispute between Mr Hume and Mr Rousseau with the letters that passed between them* (London, T. Becket & P.A. De Hondt, 1766).

La Croix, Jean-Luc de, and Luc-Vincent Thierry, *Almanach du voyageur à Paris, et dans les lieux les plus remarquables du royaume* (Paris, Robert-André Hardouin, 1783).

La Mare, Nicolas de, *Continuation du Traité de la police, contenant l'histoire de son établissement, les fonctions, les prérogatives de ses magistrats; toutes les loix, les réglemens qui la concernent... Tome quatriéme. De la voirie, de tout ce qui en dépend ou qui y a quelque rapport* (Paris, Michel Brunet and J.-F. Hérissant, 1738).

Lettres patentes... concernant les nouvelles conditions du bail de la ferme générale et des postes et messageries de France... Registrées en la Chambre des Comptes [17 octobre 1759] (Paris, Imprimerie Royale, 1759).

Locke, John, *Locke's travels in France 1675-1679: as related in his journals, correspondence and other papers*, ed. and introd. John Lough (Cambridge, 1953).

[M. D. B. G. D. S. D. F.] *La Liberté du peuple, lettres de cachet, espionage abolis, et sûreté des lettres de la poste* (Paris, Imprimerie de la Grangé, 1789).

Mazarin, Jules, *Bréviaire des politiciens* (Paris, 1996).

Mercier, Louis-Sébastien, *Le Tableau de Paris* (Paris, 1994), 2 vols.

Milton, John, *The Portable Milton*, ed. and intro. Douglas Bush (New York, 1977).

Montaigne, Michel de, *Œuvres complètes* (Paris, 1962).

[M.T.] *Almanach du voyageur à Paris, contenant une description intéressante de tous les monuments, chefs-d'œuvre des Arts et objets de curiosité que renferme cette capitale; ouvrage utile aux citoyens, et indispensable pour l'étranger. Par M. T**** (Paris and Versailles, 1783), http://www.1789-1815.com/paris_pet_poste.htm (last accessed 4 August 2015).

Le Nouveau secrétaire de la cour, ou Lettres familières sur toutes sortes de sujets, avec des réponses, une instruction pour se former dans le style épistolaire, le Cérémonial des lettres; et les règles de bienséance qu'il faut observer quand on écrit (Paris, Théodore le Gras, 1732)

Le Nouveau secrétaire de la cour, ou Lettres familières sur toutes sortes de sujets; avec des réponses (Nancy, L'Honoré et Chatelain, 1761).

Ordonnance concernant le service que les maîtres des postes seront obligéz de faire sur les ordres qui leur seront [etc.] (Paris, Imprimerie Royale, 1734).

Ordonnance de son Eminence Monseigneur le cardinal de Fleury grand maître et surintendant général des Courriers, postes et relais de France portant règlement pour la diligence et la seureté des malles ordinaires de la route de Lyon à Grenoble (Paris, Louis-Denis Delatour, 2 February 1728).

Ordonnance du Roy qui fixe le prix qui sera payé pour les chevaux de poste servant aux chaises à deux personnes, aux chaises à une personne seule, aux berlines, aux courriers allant en guide, et aux courriers de cabinet (Paris, Louis-Denis Delatour, 17 June 1725).

Ordonnance du Roy portant deffenses à tous courriers de faire conduire des chaises et des berlines par d'autres postillons que ceux des postes [etc.] (Paris, Chez Louis-Denis Delatour, Imprimeur de la Cour des Aydes en la maison de feuë la veuve Muguet, rue de la Harpe, aux trois Rois, 1 October 1726).

Ordonnance [...] *qui fixe à 30 sols par cheval pour chaque poste simple, les doubles postes et postes et demie à proportion, et les postes royales sur le pied de 3 l. par cheval, non compris les guides des postillons, à commencer du 1er juillet 1723 jusqu'au dernier juin 1724* [...] (Paris, Louis-Denis Delatour and Pierre Simon, 24 June 1723).

Ordonnance [...], *qui à commencer du 1*[er] *janvier 1757, fixe à 25 sols par poste le prix de tous les chevaux de poste* [...], (Paris, L'Imprimerie Royale, 28 November 1756).

Perrault, Charles, *Contes*, textes établis et présentés par Marc Soriano (Paris, 1989).

Pétition à l'Assemblée Nationale par les maîtres des postes à chevaux, des routes de Paris à Marseille, et à Montpellier (Paris, Didot le jeune, 1792).

Rabutin-Chantal, Marie de, marquise de Sévigné. *Correspondance* (Paris, 1972).

Richelieu, Armand Jacques du Plessis, duc de, *Testament politique*, ed. Louis André (Paris, 1947).

Rousseau, Jean-Jacques, *Correspondance complète de Jean-Jacques Rousseau*, ed. R. A. Leigh, 52 vols (Geneva; Madison, WI; Banbury, Oxford, 1965-1998).

–, *Julie, or, The new Heloise: letters of two lovers who live in a small town at the foot of the Alps*, translated by Philip Stewart and Jean Vaché (Hanover, MD, 1997).

–, *Œuvres complètes* (Paris, 1959-).

Sade, Donatien-Alphonse-François, marquis de, *Histoire de Juliette, ou Les Prospérités du vice* (Paris, 1987).

Saint-Simon, Louis de Rouvroy, duc de, *Mémoires* (Paris, 1985).

Sanson d'Abbéville, Nicolas, *Carte géographique des postes qui traversent la France* (Paris, Melchior Tavernier, 1632).

Spanheim, Ezéchiel, *Relation de la Cour de France en 1690* (Paris, 1882).

Stendhal, *Mémoires d'un touriste* (Paris, 1891).

Traité de la civilité, nouvellement dressé d'une manière exacte et méthodique et suivant les règles de l'usage vivant (Lyon, Jean Certé, 1681).

Véri, Joseph-Alphonse de, *Journal de l'abbé de Véri*, introd. and notes Le Bon Jehan de Witte (Paris, 1928).

Voltaire, *The Complete works of Voltaire* [*Œuvres complètes de Voltaire*] (*OCV*), ed. Theodore Besterman, *et al.*, (Oxford, 1968-).

–, *Correspondence and related documents*, ed. Th. Besterman, in *Œuvres complètes de Voltaire* (Oxford, 1968-1977).

–, *Questions sur l'Encyclopédie, par des amateurs*, ed. Nicholas Cronk and Christiane Mervaux, in *Œuvres complètes de Voltaire*, vol.42B (Oxford, 2012).

–, *Œuvres complètes*, ed. Louis Moland, 52 vols (Paris, 1877-1885).

–, *Œuvres de Voltaire, avec préfaces, avertissements, notes, etc. par M. Beuchot* (Paris, 1833).

Voyer de Paulmy, René Louis de, marquis d'Argenson, *Journal et mémoires du marquis d'Argenson, publiés pour la première fois d'après les manuscrits autographes de la Bibliothèque du Louvre* (Paris, 1866).

Secondary sources

Altman, Janet, *Epistolarity: approaches to a form* (Columbus, OH, 1982).

–, 'La politique de l'art épistolaire au XVIIIe siècle', in *Art de la lettre, Art de la conversation à l'époque classique en France* (Paris, 1995), p.131-44.

–, '"The triple register": introduction to temporal complexity in the letter novel',

L'Esprit créateur 1:4 (Winter 1977), p.302-10.

Arbelot, Guy, *Autour des routes de poste: les premières cartes routières de la France XVIIe-XIXe siècle* (Paris, 1992).

Bacheri, Roberto, 'Il corno di posta: da mezzo di segnalizazione a strumento sinfonico', *Quaderni di storia postale* 12 (March 1989) [exhibition catalogue].

Bakhtin, Mikhaïl, *The Dialogic imagination* (Austin, TX, 1981).

Bannet, Eve Tavor, *Empire of letters: letter manuals and transatlantic correspondence, 1688-1820* (Cambridge, 2005).

Barthes, Roland, *Essais critiques* (Paris, 1964).

–, *Writing degree zero and Elements of semiology* (Boston, MA, 1970).

Beale, Philip, *History of the post in England from the Romans to the Stuarts* (Aldershot, 1998).

Beaurepaire, Pierre-Yves, *La Plume et la toile: pouvoirs et réseaux de correspondance dans l'Europe des Lumières: études réunies par Pierre-Yves Beaurepaire* (Artois, 2002).

Beebe, Thomas O., *Epistolary fiction in Europe: 1500-1800* (Cambridge, 1999).

Behringer, Wolfgang, *Thurn und Taxis: die Geschichte ihrer Post und ihrer Unternehmen* (Munich and Zurich, 1990).

–, *Im Zeichen des Merkur: Reichspost und Kommunikationsrevolution in der Frühen Neuzeit* (Göttingen, 2003).

–, 'Communications revolutions: a historiographical concept', *German history* 24:3 (2006), p.333-74.

Belloc, Alexis, *Les Postes françaises: recherches historiques sur leur origine, leur développement, leur législation* (Paris, 1886).

Bély, Lucien, *Espions et ambassadeurs au temps de Louis XIV* (Paris, 1990).

–, *Les Secrets de Louis XIV: mystères d'état et pouvoir absolu* (Paris, 2015 [1st edn 2013]).

Bennington, Geoffrey, *Legislations: the politics of deconstruction* (London and New York, 1994).

Biard, Martine, *Postes et messageries en Languedoc de Louis XIV à la Révolution: communiquer dans l'Ancien régime, essai* (Paris, 2011).

Boislisle, Arthur de, 'Le secret de la poste sous le règne de Louis XIV', *Annuaire-bulletin de la Société de l'histoire de France* (1890), p.229-45.

Boog, Jason, 'Thomas Pynchon's Trystero spreads around the world', *Galley cat* (15 June 2012) http://www.mediabistro.com/galleycat/thomas-pynchon-trystero_b53106 (last accessed 10 August 2015).

Bourdieu, Pierre, 'The forms of capital' in *Handbook of theory and research for the sociology of education*, ed. John G. Richardson (New York, 1986), p.241-58.

Brant, Clare, *Eighteenth-century letters and British culture* (London, 2006).

Braudel, Fernand, *Civilisation matérielle, économie et capitalisme, XVe-XVIIIe* (Paris, 1967-1979), 3 vols, translated by Siân Reynolds, *Civilization and capitalism, 15th-18th century* (New York, 1981-1984).

–, vol.1: *The Structures of everyday life* (New York, 1981).

–, vol.3: *The Perspective of the world* (New York, 1984).

Bretagnolle, Anne, and Nicolas Verdier, 'Images d'un réseau en évolution: les routes de poste dans la France préindustrielle', *M@ppemonde* 79:3 (2005), http://mappemonde.mgm.fr/num7/articles/art05301.html (last accessed 29 September 2015).

Brockhaus' Conversations-Lexicon, 13th edn (Leipzig, 1882-1887).

de Broglie, Albert, *Le Secret du Roi: correspondance secrète de Louis XV avec ses agents diplomatiques, 1752-1774* (Paris, 1879).

Cammagre, Geneviève, *Roman et histoire de soi: la notion de sujet dans la Correspondance de Diderot* (Paris, 2000).

Caplan, Jay, *In the king's wake* (Chicago, IL, and London, 1999).

–, Review of James How, *Epistolary spaces*, http://www.cla.csulb.edu/ebro/epistolary-spaces-english-letter-writing-from-the-foundation-of-the-post-office-to-richardsons-clarissa (last accessed 25 October 2015).

Cattani, Adriano, *Storia dei servizi postali nella Repubblica di Venezia et catalogo dei timbri postali* (Venice, 1969).

Cavallo, Gugliemo, and Roger Chartier (eds), *A History of reading in the West* (Amherst, MA, 1999).

Charbon, Paul, *Quelle belle invention que la poste!* (Paris, 1991).

Chartier, Roger, (ed.), *Histoires de la lecture: un bilan des recherches* (Paris, 1995).

–, (*et al.*), *La Correspondance: les usages de la lettre au XIX*[e] *siècle* (Paris, 1991).

Chaum, David L., 'Untraceable electronic mail, return addresses, and digital pseudonyms', *Communications of the ACM* 24:2 (1981), p.84-90.

Chauvet, Michèle, *Introduction à l'histoire postale des origines à 1849* (Paris, 2000).

Chouillet, Anne-Marie, and Pierre Crépel, 'Un voyage en Italie manqué ou trois encyclopédistes réunis (D'Alembert et Condorcet chez Voltaire)', *Recherches sur Diderot et l'Encyclopédie* 17 (1994), p.9-53.

Cornille, Jean-Louis, *La Lettre française: de Crébillon fils à Rousseau, Laclos, Sade* (Paris, 2001).

Craveri, Benedetta, *The Age of conversation* (New York, 2006 [orig. pubd Milan, 2001 as *La Civiltà della conversazione*]), trans. Teresa Waugh.

Dallmeier, Martin, *Quellen zur Geschichte des Europäischen Postwesens 1501-1806* (Kallmünz, 1977).

–, and Martha Schad, *Das fürstliche Haus Thurn und Taxis: 300 Jahre Geschichte in Bildern* (Regensburg, 1996).

Damrosch, Leo(pold), *Jean-Jacques Rousseau: restless genius* (Boston, MA, 2005).

Darnton, Robert, *The Great cat massacre and other episodes in French cultural history* (New York, 1984).

Dauphin, Cécile, Pierrette Lebrun-Pezerat, Danièle Poublan and Michel Demonet, 'L'enquête postale de 1847', in Roger Chartier, *et al.*, *La Correspondance: les usages de la lettre aux XIX*[e] *siècle* (Paris, 1991).

DeJean, Joan, *How Paris became Paris: the invention of the modern city* (New York, 2014).

De Leeuw, Karl, 'The Black Chamber in the Dutch Republic during the War of the Spanish Succession and its aftermath, 1707-1715', *The Historical journal* 42:1 (March 1999), p.133-56.

Deleuze, Gilles, and Félix Guattari, *Kafka: pour une littérature mineure* (Paris, 1975).

Delon, Michel (ed.), *Dictionnaire européen des Lumières* (Paris, 1997).

de Man, Paul, *Allegories of reading: figural language in Rousseau, Nietzsche, Rilke and Proust* (New Haven, CT, 1979).

Denis, Vincent, 'Les Parisiens, la police et les numérotages des maisons, du XVIIIe siècle à l'Empire', *French historical studies* 38:1 (February 2015), p.83-103.

Derrida, Jacques, *La Carte postale: de Socrate à Freud et au-delà* (Paris, 1980), translated as *The Post card: from Socrates to Freud and beyond*, by Alan Bass (Chicago, IL, and London, 1987).

–, *Marges de la philosophie* (Paris, 1972).

Dohrn-van Rossum, Gerhard, *The History of the hour: clocks and modern temporal orders* (Chicago, IL, and London, 1996; original publication *Die Geschichte der Stunde: Uhren und moderne Zeitordnungen* Munich and Vienna, 1992).

Duchêne, Rémi, 'Le secret de la correspondance', in *Correspondances: mélanges offerts à Roger Duchêne* (Tübingen and Aix-en-Provence, 1992), p.267-75.

Duchêne, Roger, *Comme une lettre à la poste: les progrès de l'écriture personnelle sous Louis XIV* (Paris, 2006).

Dumont, Simone, *Un Astronome des Lumières: Jérôme Lalande* (Paris, 2007).

Eco, Umberto, *A Theory of semiotics* (Bloomington, IN, 1975).

Edmonds, David, and John Eidinow, 'Enlightened enemies', *The Guardian*, Friday 28 April 2006, http://www.theguardian.com/books/2006/apr/29/philosophy (last accessed 8 August 2015).

–, *Rousseau's dog: two great thinkers at war in the Age of Enlightenment* (London, 2001).

Elias, Norbert, *Court society* (Oxford, 1983).

–, *The Civilizing process*, trans. Edmund Jephcott (New York, 1978).

Ellis, Kenneth, *The Post Office in the eighteenth century: a study in administrative history* (London, New York and Toronto, 1958).

–, 'The administrative connections between Britain and Hanover', in *Journal of the Society of Archivists* 3 (1969), p.546-65.

Emmison, Michael, and John Frow, 'Information technology as cultural capital', in *Australian universities review* 1 (1998), p.41-45.

Encyclopedia Britannica online, http://www.britannica.com (last accessed 22 September 2014).

Engle, Karen, 'The post of the Post', *Journal of political and social thought* 1:4 (2003), http://www.yorku.ca/jspot/4/engle.htm#RETURN3 (last accessed 10 August 2015).

Farvacque-Vitkovic, Catherine, and Lucien Godin, Hugues Leroux, Florence Verdet, Roberto Chavez, *Adressage et gestion des villes* (World Bank, Washington, DC, 2005), http://www.groupehuit.com/sites/default/files/mediatheque/documents/Adressage%20et%20gestion%20des%20villes.pdf (last accessed 4 August 2015).

Fauque, Danielle, 'Mesure (systèmes et instruments de)' in Michel Delon (ed.), *Dictionnaire européen des Lumières* (Paris, 1997).

Febvre, Lucien, *Studi su Riforma e Rinascimento e altri scritti su problemi di metodo e di geografia storica*, Preface D. Canimori, trad. Di C. Vitanti (Turin, 1966) [original edn Paris, 1957].

Fedele, *Le Antiche poste: Nascita e crescita di un servizio (secoli SIV-XVIII)*, in Clemente Fedele, M. Gallenga, *'Per servizio di Nostro Signore': strade, corrieri e poste dei Pai dal Medioevo al 1870*, preface by G. Andreotto (Prato, 1988).

Flyvbjerg, Bent, 'Habermas and Foucault: thinkers for civil society?', *British journal of sociology* 49:2 (June 1998), p.208-33.

Fontenay, Elisabeth de, *Diderot ou Le Matérialisme enchanté* (Paris, 1984).

Franklin, Alfred, *Dictionnaire historique des arts, métiers et professions exercés dans Paris depuis le treizième siècle* (New York, 1968 [orig. edn Paris and Leipzig, 1906]).

Funck-Brentano, Frantz, *Liselotte, duchesse d'Orléans, mère du Régent* (Paris, 1936).

Goger, Jean-Marcel, 'Transport', in *Dictionnaire européen des Lumières* (Paris, 1997).

Goodman, Dena, *The Republic of letters: a cultural history of the French Enlightenment* (Ithaca, NY, and London, 1994).

–, 'The Hume-Rousseau affair: from private *querelle* to public *procès*', *Eighteenth-century studies* 25:2 (Winter 1991-1992), p.171-201.

–, 'Epistolary property: Michel de Servan and the plight of letters on the eve of the French Revolution', in *Early modern conceptions of property*, ed. John Brewer and Susan Staves (London and New York, 1995), p.339-64.

–, *Becoming a woman in the Age of Letters* (Ithaca, NY, and London, 2009).

Goulemot, Jean, André Magnan, and Didier Masseau (eds), *Inventaire Voltaire* (Paris, 1995).

Grand-Carteret, John, *Vieux papiers, vieilles images; cartons d'un collectionneur* (Paris, Levasseur, 1896).

–, *Papeterie et papetiers* (Paris, 1913).

Grant, J. Kerry, *A Companion to The Crying of lot 49* (Athens, GA, and London, 2008).

Graziani, Antoine, *La Grande Aventure de la poste* (Paris, 1965).

Grillmeyer, Siegfried, *Habsburgs Diener in Post und Politik: das 'Haus' Thurn und Taxis zwischen 1745 and 1867* (Mainz, 2005).

Habermas, Jürgen, *The Structural transformation of the public sphere: an inquiry into a category of bourgeois society* (Cambridge, 1991).

Haroche-Bouzinac, Geneviève, *L'Epistolaire* (Paris, 1995).

–, 'Les lettres qu'on ne brûle pas', *Revue d'histoire littéraire de la France* 103:2 (2003), p.301-308.

Henkin, David M., *The Postal age: the emergence of modern communications in nineteenth-century America* (Chicago, IL, and London, 2006).

Hill, Greg, *Rousseau's theory of human communication: transparent and opaque societies* (New York, 2006).

Hillairet, Jacques, *Dictionnaire historique des rues de Paris*, vol.2 (Paris, 1963).

Hiller, Albert, *Das große Buch vom Posthorn* (Wilhelmshaven, 1985).

How, James, *Epistolary spaces: English letter writing from the foundation of the Post Office to Richardson's Clarissa* (Aldershot, 2003).

Ingram, David, 'Foucault and Habermas on the subject of reason', in *The Cambridge companion to Foucault*, ed. Gary Gutting (Cambridge, 1994), p.215-61.

Innis, Harold, *Empire and communications* (Toronto, 1951).

Jakobson, Roman, *Selected writings*, vol.II (The Hague, 1971).

'Joanna', Review of Sune Christian Pedersen, *Brudte Segl: Spionage og censur i enevældens Danmark*, http://thehandwrittenletter.blogspot.com/2009/02/broken-seals.html (last accessed 17 August 2015).

Johannessen, Finn Ehrard, Review of Sune Christian Pedersen, *Brudte Segl: Spionage og censur i enevældens Danmark* [Broken seals: espionage and censorship in absolutist Denmark] (Copenhagen, 2008), *Scandinavian journal of history* 34:4 (December 2009), p.459-61.

Kafka, Franz, *Briefe an Milena* (New York, 1952).

Kahn, David, *The Codebreakers: the story of secret writing* (New York, 1967).

Kalmus, Ludwig, *Weltgeschichte der Post* (Vienna, 1937).

Kauffman, Linda S., *Special delivery* (Chicago, IL, 1992).

Kaufmann, Vincent, *L'Equivoque littéraire* (Paris, 1990).

Kavanagh, Thomas M., *Writing the*

truth: authority and desire in Rousseau (Berkeley, CA, 1987).

Kelly, Michael (ed.), *Critique and power: recasting the Foucault/Habermas debate* (Cambridge, MA, 1994).

Kermode, Frank, *The Art of telling: essays on fiction* (Cambridge, MA, 1983).

Kieblowicz, Richard, *News in the mail: the press, post office, and public information 1700-1860* (New York, 1989).

Kipper, Jean, 'La lettre et son acheminement postal', in Jean Lerat (ed.), *La Lettre dans tous ses états* (Barcelona, 1991), p.165-78.

Klüber, Johann Ludwig, *Patriotische Wünsche das Postwesen in Teutschland betreffend* (Weimar, 1814).

König, Emil, *Schwarze Cabinette: eine Geschichte des Briefgeheimniss-Entheiligungen, Perlustrationen und Brieflogen, des postalischen Secretdienstes, des 'kleinen Cabinets', der 'Briefrevisionbureaus' und sonstiger Briefgeheimnisverletzungen* (Berlin and Leipzig, 1899).

Koselleck, Reinhart, *Critique and crisis: Enlightenment and the pathogenesis of modern society* (Cambridge, MA, 1988).

Kramer, Richard, *Distant cycles: Schubert and the conceiving of song* (Chicago, IL, 1994).

Kraut, Robert, Michael Patterson, Vicki Lundmark, Sara Kiesler, Tridas Mukophadhyay and William Scherlis, 'Internet paradox: a social technology that reduces social involvement and psychological well-being?', *American psychologist* 53:9 (1998), p.1017-1031.

Lacan, Jacques, *Ecrits* (Paris, 1966).

–, *Speech and language in psychoanalysis* (Baltimore, MD, 1981).

Lefebvre, Henri, *The Production of space* (Oxford, 1991 [1st French edn, 1974]).

Le Goff, Jacques, 'Merchant's time and church's time in the Middle Ages', in *Time, work and culture in the Middle Ages*, trans. Arthur Goldhammer (Chicago, IL, 1980), p.29-42.

Lenain, Louis, *La Poste de l'ancienne France: La Poste dans la Drôme et l'Ardèche des origines à 1920* (Arles, 1972).

Lilti, Antoine, *Figures publiques: l'invention de la célébrité 1750-1850* (Paris, 2014).

Livet, Georges. 'La route royale et la civilisation française de la fin du XVe au milieu du XVIIIe siècle', in Louis Trénard *et al.*, *Les Routes de France depuis les origines jusqu'à nos jours* (Paris, 1959), p.110-13.

Luiten van Zanden, Jan, *Wages and the cost of living in southern England (London) 1450-1700*, http://www.iisg.nl/hpw/dover.php (last accessed 4 August 2015).

McKenna, Anthony, 'La correspondance de Pierre Bayle', in *Les Grands intermédiaires culturels de la République des Lettres: études de correspondances du XVIe au XVIIIe siècle*, ed. Christiane Berkvens-Stevelinck, Hans Bots and Jens Häseler (Paris, 2005).

Mandrou, Robert, *L'Europe absolutiste: raison et raison d'état (1649-1775)* (Paris, 1977).

'Mapping the Republic of Letters', https://republicofletters.stanford.edu/ (last accessed 30 July 2015).

Marchand, Patrick, *Le Maître de poste et le messager: une histoire du transport public en France au temps du cheval 1700-1850* (Paris, 2006).

Marshall, Alan, *Intelligence and espionage in the reign of Charles II, 1680-1685* (Cambridge, 1994).

Maurel, André, *La Marquise Du Châtelet: amie de Voltaire* (Paris, 1930).

Melançon, Benoît, *Diderot épistolier* (Montreal, 1996).

–, *Sévigné@internet: remarques sur le courrier électronique et la lettre* (Montreal, 1996).

Mély, Benoît, *Jean-Jacques Rousseau: un intellectuel en rupture* (Paris, 1985).

Meunzberg, Werner, *500 Jahre Post: Thurn und Taxis* (Regensburg, 1990).

Mience, Yvette, *Histoire des postes du Rhône* (Lyon, 1997).

Morazé, Charles. *La Politique routière en France de 1716 à 1815* (Paris, 1988).

Mousnier, Roland, *La Vénalité des offices sous Henri IV et Louis XIII* (Paris, 1970).

Murray, Evelyn, *The Post Office* (London, 1927).

National Archives, *Currency converter*, http://www.nationalarchives.gov.uk/currency/ (last accessed 29 September 2015).

Nodé-Langlois, Christian, 'La poste internationale de 1669-1815' (Doctoral dissertation, Paris, Faculté de droit et de sciences économiques, 1960).

North, Gottfried, *Die Post: Ihre Geschichte in Wort und Bild* (Heidelberg, [2nd edn] 1995).

Nougaret, Pierre, *Bibliographie critique de l'histoire postale française* (Montpellier, 1970).

Oakley, Stephen P., 'The interception of posts in Celle, 1694-1710', in *William III and Louis XIV: essays 1680-1720, by and for Mark A. Thomson*, ed. Ragnhild Hatton and J. S. Bromley, (Liverpool, 1968), p.95-116.

Perrault, Gilles, *Le Secret du Roi* (Paris, 1993).

Perrot, Michèle, 'Le secret de la correspondance au XIXe siècle', in *L'Epistolarité à travers les siècles* (Stuttgart, 1990), p.184-88.

Peter, Bernhard, 'Wappen der Grafen und Fürsten von Thurn und Taxis', at http://www.dr-bernhard-peter.de/Heraldik/thurntaxis.htm (last accessed 29 September 2015).

Picard, Liza, *Restoration London* (London, 1997).

Plebani, Tiziana, 'La correspondenza nell'antico regime: lettere di donne negli archivi di famiglia', in Gabriella Zarri (ed.), *Per lettera: la scrittura epistolare femminile tra archiivio e tipografia, secoli XV-XVIII* (Rome, 1999), p.43-78.

Pomeau, René, *et.al.*, *Ecraser l'infâme* (Oxford, 1994).

Poussou, Jean-Pierre, 'Transports', in Michel Figeac (ed.), *L'Ancienne France au quotidien: vie et choses de la vie sous l'Ancien Régime* (Paris, 2007), p.1061-65.

Pynchon, Thomas, *The Crying of lot 49* (New York, 1986; orig. pub. 1966).

'Pynchon Wiki', http://cl49.pynchonwiki.com/wiki/index.php?title=Main_Page (last accessed 10 August 2015).

Racevskis, Roland, *Time and ways of knowing under Louis XIV: Molière, Sévigné, Lafayette* (Lewisburg, PA, and London, 2003).

Rey-Debove, Josette, and Alain Rey (ed.), *Le Petit Robert de la langue française 2010* (Paris, 2010).

Robinson, Howard, *The British Post Office: a history* (Princeton, NJ, 1948).

–, *Carrying British mail overseas* (London, 1964).

Roche, Daniel, *Les Républicains des lettres: gens de culture et Lumières au XVIIIe siècle* (Paris, 1988).

–, 'Avant-propos' to Pierre-Yves Beaurepaire (ed.), *La Plume et la toile: pouvoirs et réseaux de correspondance dans l'Europe des Lumières* (Artois, 2002).

Rose-Redwood, Reuben S., 'Governmentality, geography, and

the geo-coded world', in *Progress in human geography* 30:4 (2006), p.469-86.

Rosen, Charles, *The Romantic generation* (Cambridge, MA, 1995).

Rübßam, Joseph, 'Zur Geschichte des internationalen Postwesens im 16. und 17. Jahrhunderte nebst einem Rückblick auf die neuerere historisch-postalische Literatur', *Historisches Jahrbuch* 13 (1892), p.15-79.

Saada, Anne, and Jean Sgard, 'Tremblements dans la presse', in Theodore E. D. Braun and John B. Radner (eds), *The Lisbon earthquake of 1755: representations and reactions*, *SVEC* 2005:02, p.208-24.

Saunders, Frances Stonor, 'Stuck on the flypaper', *London review of books* 37:7 (9 April 2015), p.8.

Schafer, R. Murray, *The Soundscape: our sonic environment and the tuning of the world* (Rochester, VT, 1977).

Schnaitl, Brigitte, *La Poste française: ihre Entwicklung und Erbreiterung sowie die Aufbau des französichen Wegenetzes im 18. Jahrhundert im Konnex politischer und gesellschaftlicher Ereignisse* (Salzburg, 1995).

Sherman, Stuart, *Telling time: clocks, diaries and English diurnal form, 1600-1785* (Chicago, IL, 1985).

Siegert, Bernhard, *Relays: literature as an epoch of the postal system*, translated by Kevin Repp (Stanford, CA, 1999).

Sombart, Werner, *Der moderne Kapitalismus. Historisch-systematische Darstellung des gesamteuropäischen Wirtschaftslebens von seinen Anfängen bis zur Gegenwart*, 3 vols (Munich and Leipzig, 1916-1927; new edn Munich, 1987), vol.II:1.

Soper, Horace N., *The Mails: history, organization and methods of payment* (London, 1946).

Stix, Franz, 'Geschichte der Wiener Geheimen Ziffernkanzlei von ihrend Anfängen bis zum Jahre 1848', *Mitteilungen* 51 (Institut für Geschichtsforschung, Vienna) (1937), p.131-60.

Starobinski, Jean, *La Transparence et l'obstacle* (Paris, 1957).

Steinhausen, Georg, *Geschichte des Deutschen Briefes* (Zurich, 1968).

Studeny, Christophe, *L'Invention de la vitesse: XVIII*[e]*-XX*[e] *siècles* (Paris, 1995).

–, 'L'éveil de la vitesse: la France au galop de la malle-poste', *Revue de la Bibliothèque nationale* 40 (Summer 1991), p.44-55.

Tantner, Anton, 'Addressing the houses: the introduction of house numbering in Europe', *Histoire et mesure* [online] 24:2 (2009), http://histoiremesure.revues.org/3942 (last accessed 29 September 2015).

Thieme, Karl, 'Zur Geschichte des Posthorns', in *Posthornschule und Posthorn-Taschenliederbuch* (Leipzig, 1908).

Thompson, Edward P., 'Time, work-discipline and industrial capitalism', *Past and present* 38 (1967), p.56-97.

Thurn und Taxis family website: http://www.thurnundtaxis.de/en/family/in-regensburg-for-250-years/history.html (last accessed 29 September 2015).

Todorov, Tzvetan, *Mikhaïl Bakhtine: le principe dialogique* (Paris, 1981).

Touchard-Lafosse, Georges, *Chronique de l'œil-de-bœuf, des petits appartements de la cour et des salons de Paris, sous Louis XIV, la Régence, Louis XV et Louis XVI* (Paris, 1860 [1st edn 1800]).

Trinquier, Alain, *Tarifs postaux 1644* http://atrinquier.pagesperso-orange.fr/tarifs/bureau/t1644.html (last accessed 17 August 2015).

Turkle, Sherry, *Alone together: why we expect more from technology and less from each other* (New York, 2011).

Urban dictionary http://urbandictionary.com (last accessed 10 August 2015).

Vaillé, Eugène, *Le Cabinet noir* (Paris, 1950).

–, 'Le conditionnement de la lettre et les marques postales jusqu'à la Révolution', *Bulletin d'informations, de documentation et de statistique de la P.T.T.* 12 (1938), p.17-29.

–, *Histoire générale des postes françaises* (Paris, 1947-1953).

–, *Histoire des postes jusqu'à la Révolution* (Paris, 1946).

–, 'La poste et la presse sous l'ancien régime', *Bulletin d'information, de documentation et de statistique du Ministère des P.T.T.* 9 (1936), p.33-68.

Vaillot, René, *Avec Mme Du Châtelet*, in René Pomeau (ed.), *Voltaire en son temps* (Oxford, 1988), vol.2.

Vickery, Amanda, 'Do not scribble', *London review of books* 32:21 (4 November 2010), p.34-36.

Vincent, David, *The Culture of secrecy: Britain, 1832-1998* (Oxford and New York, 1998).

Vincent-Buffault, Anne, *L'Exercice de l'amitié: pour une histoire des pratiques amicales aux XVIII*[e] *et XIX*[e] *siècles* (Paris, 1995).

Wacjman, Judy, *Pressed for time: the acceleration of life in digital capitalism* (Chicago, IL, 2014).

Wallerstein, Immanuel, *The Modern world system: capitalist agriculture and the origins of the European world economy in the sixteenth century* (New York, 1974).

Waquet, Françoise, 'L'espace de la République des Lettres', *Commercium Litterarium: la communication dans la République des Lettres* (Amsterdam and Maarssen, 1994), p.175-89.

Webster's New World dictionary of American English, 3rd college edn (New York, 1988).

Whyman, Susan, *The Pen and the people: English letter writers 1660-1800* (Oxford and New York, 2009).

Wilson, Anthony C., 'A thousand years of postal and telecommunications services in Russia', *New Zealand Slavonic journal* (1989-1990), p.135-66.

Zaretsky, Robert, and John T. Scott, *The Philosophers' quarrel: Rousseau, Hume and the limits of human understanding* (New Haven, CT, 2009).

Zilliacus, Laurin, *From pillar to post: the troubled history of the post* (London, 1956).

Index

address, 58, 61-62, 68, 89-94, 102-103, 106, 135-36, 154, 160-66
Alembert, Jean Le Rond d', 6, 60, 97, 130, 132
Argental, Charles-Augustin de Ferriol, comte d', 71, 131, 136, 137

Bannet, Eve Tavor, 2n6, 23n1, 34n59-63, 61n37, 64n42, 65n50, 102, 156n40, 171, 180n63
Bayle, Pierre, 70, 70n73, 79, 82
Behringer, Wolfgang,
  'Communications Revolutions', 1, 6n16, 27n20, 30n35, 30n39, 83, 87n129, 171, 173n20, 173n22, 175n37, 176n39, 177n46, 178n50-51, 179n55, 179n57-58, 180n60-61, 180n63-64, 181n68-69, 183n79
  Im Zeichen des Merkur, 1n3, 6n16, 29n34, 32n48, 168n4, 171, 175n33, 176n39, 180n63
  Thurn und Taxis, 1n2, 10, 23n1, 23n3-4, 27n20, 27n22-23, 28n24, 25, 28n28, 29n34, 30n40, 31n41, 31n43, 32n48-49, 48n119, 55n11
Bély, Lucien, 96n8, 104n39, 105n43-44, 106n47-49, 107n53
billet, 59-62, 73
Black Cabinets, 4, 9, 13, 28n27, 40, 49, 58, 81, 95-123, 125, 132-38
Brant, Clare, 1n2, 54n4, 66n52, 70, 164n62, 176n38, 188n99
British post, 32-34, 108-11

censorship, 130, 132, 139, 160
Chauvet, Michèle, 2n7, 35n67, 35n69, 36n71, 36n71, 36n74, 42n99, 42n100, 50n126, 56n11, 72n85, 75n92, 75n94, 79n97, 81n102, 86n123-24, 86n127, 91n141
collection, 72-75, 90, 188
communication, 1, 4
  postal, 4, 16-21, 23, 192-93
  tele-, 10, 20
consolation, 8, 11-15
conversation, 11-12, 14-16, 164-66, 175-76
conveyance, 75-85
countersignature (*contreseing*), 64, 71, 135
cryptology, 106-109, 162, 164-65
'cultural capital', 167, 171

Damilaville, Étienne Noël, 68, 71, 130, 135
Deffand, Marie de Vichy-Chamrond, marquise du, 15, 134
definitions, 5-7
delivery, 85-94, 179-80, 184-86, 190-93
Derrida, Jacques, 5n15, 11, 16n55, 19-21, 25n16, 107n52
Diderot, Denis, 6, 14, 53, 56-57, 60, 68, 97, 149, 183n80
diligence, 79, 84-86
directeur des postes, 37, 43, 90, 128
Dohrn-van Rossum, Gerhard, 1n1, 30n37, 31n41, 31n47, 87, 173n21, 178n48-49, 178n51, 178n54
Duchêne, Roger, 182, 183n80, 183n82, 184n83, 184n85-87, 186n96
Du Peyrou, Pierre-Alexandre, 145, 146n15, 162-65

envelopes, 55, 57-58
epistolary distance, 146-47, 152, 154, 157, 162-66, 180-89, 192-93
epistolary space, 7, 126, 174-76
espionage, 104-108, 118-22

Ferme générale des Postes, 39-41, 43, 46, 52, 60, 79, 130-31
folding, 54-55, 59-61
franking privilege (*franchise*), 71, 130, 137
French post, 1-2
  history, 35-43

Goethe, Johann Wolfgang von, 10, 180
Goodman, Dena,
- *Becoming a Woman in the Age of Letters*, 56, 175
- 'Epistolary Property', 97n9-10, 104n37, 173
- 'The Hume-Rousseau Affair', 141n3
- *The Republic of Letters*, 3n8, 29n32, 96n8

Great Britain, 32-34, 108-11

Habsburg territories, 25-32, 118-21, 167-70
Hobbes, Thomas, 98-99, 100n24, 101
horse post (*poste aux chevaux*), 36-37
Houdetot, Elisabeth Françoise Sophie La Live de Bellegarde, comtesse d', 149, 151, 154n34, 157, 158
house numbering, 91-92
How, James, 2n6, 3, 7n20-21, 34n58, 49n123, 108n57, 126n7, 164, 174, 182n76, *see also* epistolary space
Hume, David, 85, 141, 146, 162, 163

impatience, 185-89
infrastructure, 13, 84-85, 171, 174
ink, 53, 56-57, 63, 191
interests,
- economic, 8, 24-25, 44, 48, 52, 188-89
- political, 8, 23, 25, 48-52
- psychological, 9-15, 187-88
- social, 9-12

'international' post, 3-4, 31, 43-52

Kafka, Franz, 15-19, 89, 166, 189, 191
Kalmus, Ludwig, 3, 7n22, 24n9, 25n11, 26n17, 26n19, 27n23, 43n103-104, 48n120, 96n4, 96n6, 119n90, 119n92, 168n4
'king's secret', the, 99-100
König, Emil Bruno, 95n4, 98n14, 105n45, 107n51
Kosseleck, Reinhart, 98-99, 100n24, 101

Lacan, Jacques, 16n54, 18, 20n66
letter format, 54-55, 58
letter post, 36, 43, 79
lettre de cachet, 97, 108, 126
Louis XIV, 38, 41, 81, 83, 105, 111, 115, 175
Louis XV, 116, 118
Louvois, François Michel Le Tellier, marquis de, 36, 39-41, 50, 111-13, 182-83

mail boxes, 42, 72, 73, 91, 182
maître des courriers (letter post master), 37-38, 43, 90, *see also directeur des postes*
maître des postes (horse post master), 36-39, 79
malle-poste (mail coach), 84-86, Fig.7
Marchand, Patrick, 3, 9n27, 24n5, 37n76-77, 40n90-91, 72, 75n93, 79n96, 81n101, 84n113, 86n124, 89n134, 91n140-41, 91n143, 170n12, 171n13
materiality, 53-54, 102-103, 150, 175
Mercier, Louis-Sébastien, 42n100, 73, 84, 116-18, 182n73, 187n93
message services, 5-6, 24, 44, 52, 72, 81, 125-26, 148-49, 151, 152, 188

news, 10, 30, 180-81, 188
newspapers, 40, 180

Palatine Princess, Elisabeth Charlotte von der Pfalz, *known as*, 105, 112-13
paper, 54-56
paquet, 66-69, 131, 139, 156
Penny Post, 33-34, 42, 71
pens, 56-57
petite poste, 42, 65, 68, 71-75, 117-18, 126, 179, Figs 1, 3, 4, 8
politesse, 61-62
postage, 4, 44, 64-72, 127-29, 142-46, 158-60
postage stamps, 65
postal promise, 192-93
postal superintendents, 41
post cards, 20
post horn, 32, 167-71, 189-90, 192
postilion, 36, 75, 79
postmodern, 1, 5, 19-21, 189-93
post office, 3, 7, 21, 72, 73, 75, 89-90, 126, 184, Fig.2
post road, 75-79, 179

pragmatics, 2-4, 53-94
privacy, 57, 64, 95-123, 147, 173-75, 185, *see also* secrecy
publicity, 54, 95-123, 173-75
Pynchon, Thomas, 4-5, 29n34, 35, 81, 95, 176, 187, 189-93

raison d'État, 96-104, 114
reading aloud, 64
relays ('posts'), 4-5, 20, 23-25, 30, 35-36, 67, 84
Republic of Letters, 10-11, 13, 16, 70, 125, 174
Rey, Marc-Michel, 142, 149, 154n34, 156-59, 161, 162n55
rhetoric, 61-63
Robinson, Howard, 32n50-51, 33n52, 32n56, 34n57, 34n64, 51n131-33, 58n25, 86n126, 87n128, 108n55-56, 110n64, 110n68-69, 168n5, 171n14, 178, 179n56
Rousseau, Jean-Jacques, 2n5, 4, 9n29, 16, 61n36, 66, 70, 81n103, 85, 92, 111, 136, 141-66, 189
  Confessions, 159, 162
  Contrat social, le, 142
  Deuxième Discours, 147
  Émile, 186-87
  Julie, ou la Nouvelle Héloïse, 70, 142, 146-48, 149, 150, 156, 157, 159, 161
  Lettre à d'Alembert, 148, 156
  Lettre à M. de Beaumont, 156
  Lettres de la montagne, 162n55
  Lettres écrites de la montagne, 138
  Premier Discours, 147
  Profession de foi d'un vicaire savoyard, 159
  Rêveries du promeneur solitaire, 152, 163

Saint-Simon, Louis de Rouvroy, duc de, 114-17
Schnaitl, Brigitte, 6n18, 85n118, 86n125, 87n130, 89n134
Schubert, Franz, 169-70
seals, 60-61, 63, 96-97, 102-105, 132, 136-37, 157, 162
secrecy, 57-58, *see also* privacy *and* Black Cabinets
Sévigné, Marie de Rabutin-Chantal, marquise de, 7n22, 82, 101, 111-12, 141, 180, 182-89
Siegert, Bernhard, 8, 28n29, 29n33, 54, 98, 101, 103n36
space, 171, 173-76
speed, 32, 75, 84-89, 177-80, 184-85
Studeny, Christophe, 79n95, 81n104, 84n117, 87n131, 93n153
surveillance, 160-63, *see also* Black Cabinets
Sweden, 79, 99, 105, 126

Thurn and Taxis,
  palace, 10, 180
  post, 4, 25-32, 34, 43, 46-48, 52, 119-21, 167-68, 176, 179, 189, 191
time, 178, 181-89
Turgot, Anne Robert Jacques, 79, 116, Fig.6

Vaillé, Eugène,
  Cabinet noir, Le, 29n30, 96n4, 96n7, 97n13, 98n14, 104n40, 105n42, 107n51, 111n71, 112n72-73, 113n76-77, 114n79-81, 115n83, 116n85, 117n86, 118n89
  Histoire des postes jusqu'à la Révolution, 7n22, 35n65-66, 40n89, 40n92, 58n
  Histoire générale des postes françaises, 7n22, 28n29, 29n33, 37n78, 37n79, 40n89, 41n93-95, 44n110, 48n117, 50n127, 50n129-30, 51n134-35, 52n136, 64n44, 65n46, 66n55, 96n7
  'La poste et la presse sous l'ancien régime', 180n63
Venice, Republic of, 8, 24-25, 47
Villayer, Jean-Jacques Renouard, comte de, 42, 71, 91, 179
Volland, Louise-Henriette (Sophie), 53, 56-57, 68
Voltaire, François-Marie Arouet, *known as*, 4, 10-16, 63, 68-72, 81n103, 90, 94, 125-40, 141, 144, 159, 160, 164, 189
  Candide, 15
  correspondence, 2n5, 4, 8n23, 12-

15, 68n63, 84, 92, 104, 108n54, 126n5-6, 127
Dictionnaire philosophique, 8, 11-12, 14, 125, 134, 139
Essai sur les mœurs, 12
Lettres philosophiques, 126
Pucelle d'Orléans, La, 125
Questions sur l'Encyclopédie, 8, 11-12, 14, 49n122, 107-108, 126-27, 138, 183n78
Siècle de Louis XIV, 14n48,
Trois Manières, Les, 14

Warens, Françoise Louise Eléonore de la Tour, baronne de, 153, 154n33, 156
Whyman, Susan, 2n7, 3, 23n1, 33n53, 33n55, 66n52, 70, 71n77, 72, 81n99, 83n112, 86n122, 87n128, 93n151, 95n3, 97, 108n58, 109n61, 109n63, 173n23, 175n34, 176, 178n54, 180n65, 181n66, 183n81, 187

'zero sign', 157